Therapeutic Interventions
for Forensic Mental Health Nurses

Forensic Focus

This series, now edited by Gwen Adshead, takes the currently crystallising field of Forensic Psychotherapy as its focal point, offering a forum for the presentation of theoretical and clinical issues. It will also embrace such influential neighbouring disciplines as language, law, literature, criminology, ethics and philosophy, as well as psychiatry and psychology, its established progenitors.

Forensic Focus 19

Therapeutic Interventions for Forensic Mental Health Nurses

*Edited by Alyson M. Kettles,
Phil Woods and Mick Collins*

Foreword by Malcolm Rae

Jessica Kingsley Publishers
London and Philadelphia

First published in the United Kingdom in 2002 by
Jessica Kingsley Publishers Ltd,
116 Pentonville Road, London
N1 9JB, England
and
325 Chestnut Street,
Philadelphia PA 19106, USA.

www.jkp.com

© Copyright 2002 Jessica Kingsley Publishers

Library of Congress Cataloging in Publication Data
A CIP catalog record for this book is available from the Library of Congress

British Library Cataloguing in Publication Data
A CIP catalogue record for this book is available from the British Library

ISBN 1 85302 949 1

Printed and Bound in Great Britain by
Athenaeum Press, Gateshead, Tyne and Wear

For all forensic nurses who are striving towards evidence-based care and to develop the recognition they deserve.

Contents

Acknowledgements

Our thanks must go to Dr Adam Coldwells, Development and Research Manager at Grampian Primary Care NHS Trust, for his help and support.

Alyson Kettles would like to thank her parents, Mrs Margaret Kettles and Mr Alan Kettles, for all their support and critical questioning over the years.

Foreword

Those concerned with mentally disordered offenders travel on a continually evolving path towards understanding, knowledge and the development of effective models of care and treatment. There have been welcome developments in the last decade in the literature on this topic area although there remains a paucity of information and knowledge, with a limited body of research to draw upon. Consequently practitioners have often depended on opinions or experience-based practice, which has often proven to be a barrier to effective treatment and care.

The contributors to this exemplary book all have a track record of positive developments and are respected in their own particular field. Collectively they bring a distinctive and optimistic approach to this complex and challenging speciality. Practitioners, teachers and those who manage and lead services now have available a valuable resource that provides both a foundation and a range of new ideas, which will enable them to tackle with confidence the challenges presented by individual forensic patients and the expectations of society.

This book is timely, as it comfortably fits with the contemporary national mental health and forensic policy priorities and the expectations of the mental health National Service Framework and National Plan and the increasing expectation for evidence-based practice. The aim of the text is to provide examples of skills and interventions developed around patients' criminal and antisocial behaviour, applied in a range of settings. The key theme running through each chapter is the integration of forensic care with other parts of the mental health and social care system, and it is particularly helpful for non-specialist practitioners. The allied themes of reshaping practice in line with the best evidence and education are regarded as an integral part of practice, rather than an entity on their own.

The book imaginatively provides a unique focus on dilemmas that constantly challenge forensic nurses. These, along with a focus on interventions, are not usually spotlighted, but nevertheless, are important in providing holistic and effective care. For example, a creative approach to the complex concept of rule breaking and the extraordinary difficulties often encountered, which can undermine relationships, is imaginatively tackled.

The future direction for forensic nursing is set out, signalling how best forensic nurses can contribute effectively in a variety of roles. This expands the current scope of what is regarded as forensic nursing in the UK to include work with victims and their families, domestic violence in the community, and work with educational and health programmes, such as anti-violence and emotional health in schools.

This book confirms the growing maturity of forensic nursing. It will help to inform and remove uncertainty, whilst assisting professional development in line with clinical governance expectations. It will help to foster and sustain new ideas and transform policy into evidence-based practice. Readers will be provided with an impetus for further study and practice development. Hopefully texts such as this will mean that forensic nurses can continue to overcome some of their frustrations. Even more significantly, mentally disordered offenders will be more likely to receive the treatment and interventions they are entitled to.

Malcolm Rae
Nursing Officer, Mental Health
Department of Health

CHAPTER 1

Introduction

Alyson M. Kettles, Phil Woods and Mick Collins

INTRODUCTION

Forensic nursing is becoming more recognised as a speciality of mental health nursing, and has a specific group of skills and interventions developing around patient offending and antisocial behaviour in a range of settings from high security to community care. Change in this field in the last two decades has been rapid and is set to continue. While there are some perceptions of forensic nursing being pre-dominantly custodial, this is largely historical, with forensic nursing embracing change just as readily, if not more so, than other professional groups. Change has been a result of a combination of nursing history, politics and the influence of the media. Forensic nursing has a history and politics which are well documented elsewhere (Chiswick 1993; McComish and Paterson 1996; Topping-Morris 1992). High security has borne considerable media attention in the last decade (Berlin and Malin 1991; Department of Health 2000a), although medium and low security, and indeed community health care, have received similar attention with reference to forensic issues (Department of Health 1993a; Ritchie, Donald and Lingham 1994). Forensic nursing has had to be reactive to reports and inquiries (Kettles and Robinson 2000a), which may have been one catalyst in the continua-tion of the discipline striving towards refining and maintaining the balance between custody and caring.

IMPACTS OF MENTAL HEALTH POLICY ON FORENSIC NURSING

There is a strategic direction towards the integration of forensic high and medium secure services within the overall mental health care system. This is owing to the responsibility for commissioning of high security services being redirected from the High Security Psychiatric Service Commissioning Board to district health authorities. Services must operate within a whole-systems approach, ensuring sufficient facilities are provided for patients to identify care pathways that facilitate the smooth progression of care through appropriate levels of security.

There are proposals in place to provide extra secure places. In particular, there is regional development of long-term medium and low secure beds, the lack of which is acknowledged to be causing system pressures within current medium secure provision. Furthermore, there are people with mental health problems inappropriately placed within prisons as a result of this pressure.

Prioritising forensic mental health

The government has made forensic mental health a strategic priority within some key documents relating to mental health service provision over the next five to ten years (e.g. Department of Health 1998a, 1999a, 2000b).

Modernising Mental Health Services (Department of Health 1998a) and the National Service Framework for Mental Health (Department of Health 1999a) include priorities addressing gaps in services for people with severe and enduring mental illness who require secure accommodation, closer integration of services and strengthening assessment criteria and outcome measures. The NHS Plan (Department of Health 2000b) further emphasises these points, particularly in regard to inappropriate levels of detention and long-term provision. It makes financial commitment to provide extra resources and staffing, specifically in relation to high security services and severe personality disorder.

The context of forensic nursing

The context of forensic nursing must necessarily encompass security and the maintenance of a safe environment for both patients and staff. The *Report of the Review of Security at the High Security Hospitals* (Department of Health 2000a) was commissioned to conduct an independent review of all aspects of physical and relational security at the English high security hospitals. This review concluded with 86 recommendations for improving security and clinical practice. Such recommendations have received mixed views from both patients and clinicians and will undoubtedly have an impact on future forensic nursing interventions.

It is generally acknowledged that any mental health care setting cares for people who have high levels of disadvantage, social exclusion and homelessness. However, it must be recognised that forensic environments generally cater for those with more complex needs. Those with the most complex of needs are likely to be in high security hospitals for many years, with the average length of stay being seven or eight years (Department of Health 2000a).

AIM AND PURPOSE OF THIS TEXT

The aim of this text is to provide examples of the many interventions that are currently in use by forensic nurses; however, it is not exhaustive. Some of these interventions have developed as specialised interventions from general mental health and have developed to fit the specific client group in secure settings (Schafer 1997). Other interventions have developed quite differently, as they were originally intended for other purposes (such as diversional therapy or occupational therapy). However, these are now emerging as having a place as a forensic nursing therapy in their own right. These therapies are used nowadays to stimulate cognitive functioning and to alter mood, rather than the more traditional use, which was often to occupy the patients' time. More rarely, a few interventions have developed specifically in response to the nature of the forensic population, usually in high, regional or medium secure settings. An example of this is cognitive-analytic therapy for learning disability and firesetting (Clayton 2000).

There is an emerging body of evidence in the literature for the use of forensic nursing interventions. However, much of this at present is anecdotal. Further, the United Kingdom Central Council for Nursing, Midwifery and Health Visiting and University of Central Lancashire (1999) clearly state after an extensive literature search that nursing research appears to depend on opinion- or experience-based practice, and that it is difficult to say at what stage opinion-based practice becomes evidence-based.

Within this text we have sought to present the available evidence for both current and emerging practice. We have tried to draw together evidence for conventional or traditional interventions such as those conducted with violent offenders. Emerging interventions are presented, and for some their effectiveness is currently being studied. Others already have some level of evidence to support their use.

Necessarily, client groups must be discussed, along with the nature of the index offence, the length of time they are likely to be in the care situation and the complexities of that care. The context of care is as important as the care itself. For example, two thirds of the high security hospital population in England and Wales have committed serious crimes: 26 per cent homicide and 37 per cent wounding (Department of Health 2000a). Furthermore, 9 per cent have committed sexual offences of various kinds. This sort of offending behaviour has a major impact on the interventions which forensic nurses are required to provide. Two thirds of this group are classified as suffering from a primary Mental Health Act (England and Wales) or (Scotland) classification of mental illness; nearly 30 per cent psychopathic disorder. Additionally 15 per cent of these are women (Department of Health 2000a). Coid *et al.* (1999) retrospectively recorded, from a representative sample, all admissions to secure forensic psychiatry services over a seven-year period. They found that 16 per cent of admissions were from personality disordered patients and 84 per cent from mentally ill patients; and proportionally more personality disordered patients were admitted to high security than to medium security care (28 per cent and 14 per cent respectively).

With the advent of clinical governance (Department of Health 1998b) evidence-based practice is pre-eminent, and clinical care must be based on both the best available assessment and the best available evidence. Not only that, but professional competence becomes a serious and complementary issue that assumes much greater importance than previously. Clinical governance assists the change process further in that it aims to enable staff to conduct audit, research, quality and effectiveness project work that is directly relevant to their clinical practice. Clinical governance is the lynchpin to pull all this work together so that overlap is minimised and clinicians can work in ways which benefit patient care. The term 'seamless' has been an aim of care for some time now, but clinical governance and associated government policy will aim to bring it closer to reality.

Nursing competence has been addressed within several studies conducted on behalf of the various professional bodies (McAleer and Hamill 1997; National Board for Nursing, Midwifery and Health Visiting for Scotland 1998; Runciman 1990). The results of these studies have been incorporated into basic nurse education. Competence is an issue that is now receiving the attention it deserves within the field of forensic nursing with advanced competencies beginning to be identified (Watson 1999; Watson and Kirby 2000) and competency framework development (United Kingdom Central Council for Nursing, Midwifery and Health Visiting and University of Central Lancashire 1999). What is encouraging is that forensic nursing competence is being taken seriously at the level of the professional bodies for the first time.

Not only is individual professional competence a major issue, but so too is multidisciplinary working, as clinical practice can often overlap professional boundaries. Clinicians need to work in ways that benefit both the patient and the service being provided. For example, clinical risk assessment and management is fundamental to the likelihood of any therapeutic intervention being successful yet the process is relatively haphazard.

Neilson et al. (1996) highlight several issues in relation to risk assessment. For example, outcomes in terms of two risk behaviours during admission (self-harm and violence) were not related to recording risk assessment and supervision levels. Patients admitted compulsorily to hospital were more likely to have a supervision level recorded but were also more likely to abscond. They conclude that issues of risk are not adequately addressed in care planning.

The MacLean Report (MacLean 2000) states that 'assessment of risk is important in reaching many decisions about the sentencing and management of offenders, but is often done in an unstructured manner' (p.1). If structured within appropriate theoretical boundaries such assessments have the potential to provide the basis for individualised care regimes focusing on positive health outcomes and interventions based on individual need. The ultimate outcome should be not only that of successful rehabilitation but also to assist care teams in their decision-making and duty of care. This would, on the one hand, provide a level of structure that is no greater than necessary for a client and, on the other, protect the public interest. This text has not focused on clinical risk assessment, as there is a wealth of literature covering the subject, but seeks at this point to raise the readers' awareness that clinical risk assessment will often be the precursor to effective forensic nursing interventions.

Fortunately the developments in care and the changes in roles that forensic nurses are now experiencing may help this situation. Forensic nurses have been busy for some time now filling the gaps in both the criminal justice system and the health care system. Roles in court diversion schemes, accident and emergency departments, police stations, community rehabilitation, sex offender therapy programmes, care of women and other specialist populations in high security care, nurse lawyers and nurses working in prisons are just some of the ways in which forensic nurses have developed from their historical past. In the future we may see forensic nursing roles developing with the victims and their families, with educational and health programmes such as anti-violence and emotional health in schools and other educational establishments, with domestic violence in the community and with the client who is awaiting trial.

The full range of clinical conditions which forensic nurses encounter in the course of their practice all require careful management based on good clinical assessment. In Western countries the move is towards an integrated educational and therapeutic programme based on specific models of care, such as the Duluth Model for Domestic Violence, which is an educational programme for men who batter (Pence and Paymar 1993), or approaches such as psychosocial interventions. The aim is to give educational information and to teach altered or alternative ways of coping and functioning. This enables the patient to recognise precursors to certain behaviours and to retain more control over their own behaviour in the situation. Educational developments mean that we know so much more about what triggers some reactions and the ways in which people learn, at an early age, about coping mechanisms and strategies for dealing with certain situations. Therefore, rehabilitative education can go hand-in-hand with therapeutic activities, and nursing management in the clinical situation ensures that this can happen.

Now it is time to expand further into the realms of evidence for our practice and of outcomes of care. This is what will be presented in the subsequent chapters. There is no doubt that individual practice can be of an excellent standard, but there is an urgent need to improve the co-ordination of care for each mentally disordered offender to ensure quality risk management, improved outcome and easier transition through differing levels of security.

THE CONTENT OF THE TEXT

Chapter 2 addresses the implications of clinical governance for forensic mental health nursing. John Gibbon and Alyson Kettles discuss quality in the NHS; clinical governance; a framework for clinical governance in forensic care; quality drive; quality assurance mechanisms; the challenges for forensic nurses; the change process and the need for new ways of working with health professionals who are increasingly tired of change and the associated implications; the National Institute for Clinical Excellence and the Clinical Standards Board for Scotland; identifying standards; and the need to monitor performance and the issue of self-regulation.

Chapter 3 explores the interface of competence and clinical effectiveness. Carol Watson discusses the development of a framework of competencies for forensic mental health nurses. The emphasis from governments on Clinical Governance and clinical effectiveness, has given fresh impetus to the search for a framework of mental health competencies in general and forensic mental health nursing competencies in particular. Identified competencies are discussed for forensic nursing, in the context of education, supervision, personal values and quality of care.

Chapter 4 addresses nursing interventions and future directions with patients who are said to break rules and test boundaries constantly. Penny Schafer discusses the broad concepts of 'rule breaking' in relation to various groups of forensic patients such as the personality disordered patient. Unspoken and unmet expectations, discrepancies, guidelines, limit setting, boundaries, splitting, distortions and violations are all addressed in relation to forensic patients considered to be difficult to care for and untrustworthy.

Chapter 5 addresses psychoeducational interventions for practitioners in forensic health and social care. Dennis Cross and Stephan Kirby discuss the concept of psychoeducation and its application within forensic nursing. Teaching and learning are not new ideas within forensic care but the specific application of education as an intervention in itself is. However, here these ideas are not discussed in isolation, but rather as a part of an integrated framework of psychological approaches to caring for the mentally disordered offender.

Chapter 6 addresses nursing interventions and future directions with the severely mentally ill. Paula Ewers and Paul Ikin explore the development of psychosocial interventions (PSI) for the severely mentally ill and their current application to forensic care.

Chapter 7 addresses nursing interventions and future directions with severely assaultive patients. Mark Chandley discusses the particular features of this difficult group. He concentrates on both staff and environmental qualities as essential pre-cursors to providing effective interventions.

Chapter 8 addresses nursing interventions and future directions with exercise therapy. Lesley Adams provides a historical overview of the current literature of the use of exercise in psychiatry, forensic services and the criminal justice system. Dis-cussion focuses on why psychiatric patients are considered less physically fit than the general population. Included are: national and local health priorities and the mentally ill offender; health promotion and mental health; ethical issues; and spe-cialised roles already in place.

Chapter 9 addresses nursing interventions and future directions with women in secure services. Anne Aiyegbusi discusses the challenges faced by forensic nurses in providing care to female mentally disordered offenders, whose complex presen-tations are well known to forensic clinicians, though they do not fit neatly into any formal diagnostic group. She describes this particular population, their distinct needs, and a clinical nursing paradigm for working therapeutically with the women patients in question.

Chapter 10 addresses nurse therapists and future directions. Paul Rogers and Kevin Gournay provide a historical account of nurse therapy in the context of the-oretical frameworks; the emerging research; the move of nurse therapists into forensic care; and what nurse therapy can offer.

Chapter 11 addresses nursing interventions and future directions with sex offenders. Mary Addo explores the purpose and the nature of current treatment ini-tiatives for sex offenders and the way forward considering the following: the present state of affairs and the scale of the problem; the philosophy of treatment programmes and their strengths and weaknesses; assessing risk factors and related management; preparing to work with sex offenders in the new millennium; the need for multi-agency, multi-professional shared learning; the need to stretch knowledge and skills of intervention providers; and the need for change and a rethink of service delivery in the new millennium.

Chapter 12 addresses nursing interventions and future directions with in-patient therapy. Stephan Kirby and Dennis Cross discuss how nurses (and other health professionals) must be committed to the development of individual and col-laborative alliances with users of mental health services within in-patient settings to prepare them to self-manage their problems, achieve and maintain optimum independent functioning and reintegrate into a wider social life. They provide a very lucid clinical vignette in support of this approach.

Chapter 13 addresses spiritual nursing interventions and future directions for care. John Swinton discusses how nursing care and intervention needs to be grounded in the spirituality of the person being cared for. He describes an urgent need for spiritual competence in the health care professions and how spirituality is fundamental to all the other areas of care.

Chapter 14 addresses nursing interventions and future directions in community care for mentally disordered offenders. Helen Edment outlines the role of the forensic nurse and the use of various interventions in community forensic outreach care.

Chapter 15 addresses forensic nursing interventions and future directions for forensic mental health practice in the 21st century. Phil Woods, Mick Collins and Alyson Kettles in this final chapter draw together all the previous chapters and synthesise the themes that are seen to emerge. Discussion focuses on the possibilities for the future of forensic nursing.

CONCLUSION

A positive role for the future

Recently, the question has been asked whether forensic nursing will exist in the future (Mason 2000a). Its terminology has been compared to the names of some diseases of the 19th century that no longer exist in our vocabulary. The use of the term 'forensic nursing' has only existed for about 30 years, despite the client group having been nursed in secure environments for considerably longer (Mason 2000b). Nursing itself was slow to develop, despite some very forward-thinking pioneers (Robinson and Kettles 1998), and since the birth of the forensic nurse its development has been rapid by comparison. It is this rapid development with international interest, professional representation and new lines of forensic nursing research enquiry that, for the foreseeable future at least, will ensure forensic nursing is not just a nine-day wonder.

Such rapid development is positive, as it not only enables forensic nurses to continue to develop their skills, interventions and care, but it also encourages the research, audit and development skills that are now being demanded of nurses. We not only need to build up our competencies in the aspects of practice that have been neglected so far, but we also need to continue to develop existing practice with a sound research basis.

This chapter has set the scene and subsequent chapters will give examples of current or emerging interventions. The future directions related to their particular intervention or approach to care will be outlined and discussed. The fact that each author can see the ways in which the intervention is going and the directions in which it needs to go is positive in itself.

CHAPTER 2

The Implications of Clinical Governance for Forensic Nursing

John Gibbon and Alyson M. Kettles

INTRODUCTION

This book may seem an unusual place in which to place a chapter around the subject of clinical governance. Yet if we acknowledge it as a major foil for the development of the discipline, and specifically the role of the forensic nurse, then this is surely the vehicle to use.

The Department of Health (2000c) published a consultation document entitled *A Health Service of All the Talents: Developing the NHS Workforce*. Within the report the focus is upon the need to review both the current workforce, the ability to sustain and increase the numbers of staff available, and make the best use of the skills they have. There were a series of stated goals outlined below:

o team working across professional and organisational boundaries

o flexible working to make best use of the skills that staff have

o streamlined workforce planning that stems from the needs of patients

o maximising the contribution of all staff by removing professional barriers

o modernising education and training, based upon required skills

o developing new and more flexible careers for staff

o expanding the work force to meet expected needs.

These goals will clearly have an impact on the quality of current services and future expectations of care delivery. Yet those involved in delivering forensic health care will see within these goals some contentious issues with which they are working all the time, as well as a range of targets that they are struggling to address.

Mentally disordered offenders are 'individuals with mental health problems who have come into contact with the criminal justice system' (McCann 1999). This description, however, simplifies the complications of caring for this particular client group. Forensic nursing is a sub-branch of psychiatric nursing currently developing its own particular knowledge base, although many of the issues faced are mirrored within general psychiatry (Reynolds and Cormack 1990; Whyte 1985). Those receiving care within forensic settings are a diverse group; many present with complex needs and support is often provided through a multi-agency approach, requiring a co-ordinated and collaborative approach amongst the professionals involved.

It is often the case with individuals arriving into care environments through the legal system that a level of local or national media interest follows. The perceived level of dangerousness, or notoriety of the offence associated with the individual, often generates this interest. The care package provided to cope with such circumstances is therefore more prone to scrutiny and places a pressure on services to make 'correct' decisions. What becomes obvious with patients involved in such arenas is that the risk of recidivism is a major part of the assessment required to decide on future therapeutic interactions and placement. Providing both a well-motivated and capable multi-agency workforce is then paramount if effectively delivered and monitored services are to respond to the demands laid down by such expectations.

The position of quality within the current NHS has to be seen to be in line with the contexts set by both the NHS National Plan for England (Department of Health 2000b) and the Scottish NHS Health Plan (Scottish Executive 2000). These have been noted as a radical rethink of the service that is currently provided and that is notably still based upon the principles that were set out by Bevan over 50 years ago. There is a requirement to embrace a model that requires the professions to recognise, measure and be accountable for all components of patient care.

So why the interest in quality? In the White Paper *The New NHS: Modern, Dependable* (Department of Health 1997, p.17), the then recently elected Labour government stated that 'the New NHS will have quality at its heart'. This statement marks the start of a ten-year development and implementation of a national quality improvement programme aimed at meeting shortfalls in the National Health Service. It aims to 'guarantee fair access and high standards to patients wherever they live'. This action was initiated by a range of pressures that were seen as both undermining and destabilising health care delivery within the NHS. Most notably included were the claims of inequalities in access in the delivery of care (postcode prescribing) and the damaging revelations regarding quality care processes. These breakdowns in accepted standards culminated in the cervical cancer screening failures at the Kent and Canterbury Hospital (National Health Service Executive 1997) and similarly in breast screening services at Exeter. In these cases many people had been wrongly diagnosed and treated owing to ineffectual methods in checking test results. Further revelations regarding the conduct of health care professionals in abusing their positions have placed a requirement upon professionals to justify and evidence their practice.

Clinical governance and its supporting structures are, then, there for a reason. It has far-reaching implications for health care professionals, their self-regulation, practice and education. All to result in evidenced improved care for patients.

WHAT IS CLINICAL GOVERNANCE?

Clinical governance is 'a Framework through which NHS organisations are accountable for continuously improving the quality of their services and safeguarding high standards of care by creating an environment in which excellence in clinical care will flourish' (Department of Health 1998b, p.33). The expected outcome being to ensure clear national standards for service supported by a consistent and evidence-based guidance to raise quality standards within the NHS. The Department of Health (1998b) also sets out the four main components of clinical governance for NHS Trusts:

o clear lines of responsibility and accountability for the overall quality of clinical care

o a comprehensive programme of quality improvement activities

o clear policies aimed at managing risks

o procedures for all professional groups to identify and remedy poor performance.

Although the term clinical governance is quite new, not just to the NHS but also internationally, the concepts within draw on established fields of work. Initially it is recognisable that the ideas owe much to the movement for good corporate governance from industry. Power (1997), as well as others, has observed an increased culture of measurement, accountability and evaluation being developed; this has been reflected in changes to the way that private and public sector organisations are both managed and held to account (Cadbury 1992; Department of Health 1994; Nolan Committee 1995).

At a corporate level, clinical governance means that chief executives will be accountable on behalf of NHS trust boards for assuring the quality of NHS trust services and will provide boards with regular reports on quality, in the same way they do finance. This is a significant development for the health service as, until now, the chief executive has been accountable only for the financial position of the trust.

There is little doubt that previous NHS reforms encouraged the ethos where the business of boards was dominated, almost exclusively, by financial issues. It was rare for clinical considerations to be central to discussions or decisions of boards, and indeed only two of the statutory 11 board members were required to have a clinical background. It has been argued that 'this created a gulf between NHS managers and the clinicians responsible for delivering the care to patients' (Oyebode, Brown and Parry 1999, p.8). Managers were perceived as having to implement constant and relentless cuts in resources without regard to the implications for clinical practice, whether or not this was actually the case. Clinicians often saw themselves as struggling to maintain the semblance of an adequate clinical service.

Although it is the chief executive who has to account to the secretary of state (England) or the minister for health and social care (Scotland) for clinical standards, the implication and principles of clinical governance apply to all those who provide and manage care in the NHS. *A First Class Service* (Department of Health 1998b) makes it clear that 'quality is everybody's business'.

THE CHALLENGE OF CLINICAL GOVERNANCE

The term clinical governance hides a radical change in concept, for the way in which quality can be re-identified and placed within a framework, not as a stand-alone entity. While doubt persists about how clinical governance will be developed and supported there are few that can argue with the principles of putting quality improvement at the top of the health care agenda.

The principles of clinical governance provide a framework to pull together disparate quality assurance mechanisms into a systematic form. As a transparent activity it also affords the recipients of health care the chance to interrogate the health system and its response to need. A point worthy of note is that clinical governance will provide a guide to those involved in the dispensation of health care, whilst being just as relevant to those same people when they receive treatment themselves.

Change is a word that those working in health care have come to love or fear. In fact, there would be some justification in proposing that both the NHS and private health care providers are suffering 'change' fatigue. The need for new ways of working with health professionals, who are increasingly tired of change and the associated time implications, could in itself be one of the larger hurdles we are now facing. The agenda is a complex one, yet clinical governance presents quality as being just as important as finance. If, however, this particular Pandora's box is to be opened, one area that will provide some of the potentially more challenging statistics will be that of forensic psychiatry. Psychiatry is often accused of being an inexact science. Within forensic psychiatry and most notably within high security environments the further dynamic exists of public perception and political expediency regarding the need to 'treat' patients who are seen as a high risk and dangerous.

The problem then of identifying the standards, which are linked to the care of those in these areas, becomes twofold. First, how are distinct treatment/methodology protocols devised? And second, can politics be removed from the equation of the expected outcomes for this group of patients? This problem is probably best illustrated by the debate currently surrounding the care of people designated as having a 'dangerous and severe personality disorder' (Home Office and Department of Health 1999). The issues for this group of patients may not always be ones of treatment, but of quality of life within the confines of maintaining public safety.

If grasped and driven, the concepts to be addressed by clinical governance provide a fulcrum for change, which has long been needed. There is a growing understanding that we should have input regarding the health care we wish to have. Health care cannot afford continually to expand the range of treatments and care options available to an increasingly aware public in an *ad hoc* and uncontrolled manner. Clinical governance if used correctly allows those involved in providing that health care to be instrumental in providing the input to a balanced and evidence-based future. One that may not provide all the options, but at least those available will be on an equitable basis.

MAKING SENSE OF THE CLINICAL GOVERNANCE JIGSAW

So the challenge to develop quality services has been well and truly laid down. Is there, however, any need to pick it up? It should be noted here that there are now, in effect, two National Health Services running approximately in parallel, but which are not exactly the same. The NHS for England and Wales is not the same as the NHS for Scotland any more. To ensure the process of clinical governance runs smoothly, statutory bodies standing outside the NHS but closely associated with it have been created. These are the Clinical Standards Board for Scotland (CSBS), the National Institute for Clinical Excellence (NICE), the Commission for Health Improvement (England) and the Scottish Health Technology Board.

Both NICE and the CSBS will be responsible for identifying, providing and disseminating national evidence-based guidelines for local adaptation, clinical audit methodologies and information on good practice. The jurisdiction of NICE is over the English and Welsh NHS. The jurisdiction of CSBS is over the Scottish NHS and (for forensic clinical issues) over patients from Northern Ireland in secure environments in Scotland. The functioning of NICE and CSBS has superseded the functions previously taken up by a range of organisations supported by the Department of Health in England and Wales, and its equivalent in Scotland, such as the National Centre for Clinical Audit and Effectiveness Bulletins.

One of the key functions expected of NICE and the CSBS is systematically to review and appraise interventions, including current and new drugs and technologies, and their effect on the NHS. They have emphasised that these guidelines, and therefore related clinical practice, will be based upon evidence of cost-effectiveness. So the challenge to clinicians will be to maximise population health gains avoiding accusations of 'care by postcode' that have been prevalent. Practice is intended to be standardised and to use the established best methodologies.

Dissemination of guidance produced will be achieved by working nationally with the Departments of Health, the various Royal Colleges, academic units and health care industries. At a local level NHS organisations, e.g. trust and health authorities or health boards, will be the channels used. The CSBS and NICE are two different bodies with slightly different remits and the evidence or standards produced by one do not have to be taken up by the other. Once information has been disseminated down to the local levels, individual organisations will move to implement recommendations. This will occur via the clinical leads for the organisation and then through local clinical governance structures.

The role of the other new statutory bodies, the Commission for Health Improvement and the Scottish Health Technology Board, is to provide national leadership in developing and monitoring high-quality clinical practice in clinical governance to assure patients that effective systems for delivering high-quality care services are in place (or will be introduced as soon as possible, where they are lacking). They will be responsible for leading the development and dissemination of clinical governance principles, and monitoring and reviewing implementation of NICE and CSBS guidance. They will also be responsible for providing independent scrutiny of clinical governance arrangements, and overseeing and assisting with investigations or inquiries into serious service failures, as appropriate. They will commend what is good and disseminate that back through its structures enabling national use of good practice. Regular reviews of clinical governance will encompass:

o patients' experiences – how they were treated, the outcome of their care

o clinical teams – what they do, and whether their approach is aimed at providing high-quality care

o corporate strategy – whether policies and strategies promote excellence and not just 'business as usual'.

The inclusion of the special health authorities for the first time within an NHS quality framework has obvious implications for forensic services. Initially there will be problems in defining and developing standards and expectations for the treatment of those cared for within this group. However for the first time there will be an impetus behind the assessment and care pathways designed to address 'seamless' care from conditions of high security to local community forensic services. Although there will be local initiatives and flexibility in the design and delivery of forensic initiatives, they will all need to reflect both the clinical governance process and incorporate identified good practice or defined standards.

QUALITY ASSURANCE MECHANISMS

Having been defined in many different ways, approaches to measuring and improving the quality of health care have become confusing, leading to misunderstanding and hindering efforts to improve care. Past approaches can be described under the headings of quality assessment, quality assurance, clinical audit, and quality improvement, including continuous quality improvement. And there has been little consensus on how they should be defined or used.

Quality assessment compares the performance of expectations, standards or goals (Shaw 1986), and is often assumed to be the responsibility of professionals. The use of quality validations do not in themselves facilitate any more than aiming to identify defects or deficiencies that are inherent in any system (Morris and Bell 1995). The result is that using quality measures allows the recognition of opportunities to improve the area being addressed (i.e. services can be validated or rejected based on the quality standards set). Yet the identification of such factors does not give solutions, or any declared intentions by those undertaking the quality assessment that they will take corrective action.

Limitations within quality assessments can often be related to the challenge of measurement. Within forensic psychiatry this is a subject that has facilitated much debate in the area of clinical risk assessment (CRA). Although CRA is not a therapeutic intervention in itself, it is the foundation for conducting any intervention with patients in secure environments. As a system of measurement of risk, it is used on an individual basis; but recent evidence has shown that there is much work to be done to utilise it to best advantage for both patients and staff.

EVIDENCE IN THE LITERATURE FOR CLINICAL RISK ASSESSMENT

Risk assessment has become one of the major issues facing nurses and other forensic health care staff (Hollin 1997; Monahan 1997). There are differing viewpoints. For example, Rose (1998) argues that the language of risk is more about control than about care, whereas Woods, Reed and Robinson (1999) describe a therapeutic approach to risk, which is designed specifically to care throughout the patient's stay in hospital and through the move into the community.

The concept of risk is broad and well defined in the literature (Monahan 1981, 1988; Vinestock 1996). Robinson and Collins (1999) state that '[g]uidelines on what constitutes a good risk assessment are profuse' (p.11).

There is, however, some consensus from the literature about which items should be included in a risk assessment and what combinations of risk are likely to constitute dangerousness. One of the most common types of risk that forensic psychiatric nurses are concerned with is the risk assessment of serious violence and sexual violence, and the prediction of such violence (Allen 1997; Hart 1998). This is for the safety of the general public, but it is also because of the not inconsiderable risk to the staff working in forensic care. Given that this risk of violence and aggression, with its associated stress response in staff, including traumatic stress, is becoming well documented, it is appropriate to ask what might impinge upon the risk assessments that are currently in use.

Risk management is about using good assessment techniques and criteria that are appropriate to the client group. Numerous individual risk assessment tools have been identified and many examples are to be found in the literature, such as the HCR–20 violence risk assessment scheme (Webster et al. 1997). Crighton (2000) states that 'there has, until recently, been a lack of structure in the approaches taken to both risk assessments and risk management in prisons and other forensic contexts' (p.23). In a study setting out to review the way in which forensic clinical risk was monitored, Kettles, Robinson and Moody (2000) aimed to identify the nature and extent of current risk assessments in use within forensic psychiatric settings. To get a feel for the type and nature of risk assessments in use, this study set out to answer a number of questions:

o How many risk assessments are there in current use?

o To what extent are these multidisciplinary?

o What areas of risk do they cover?

o What is the research base for these?

DISCUSSION OF THE STUDY

The most striking aspect revealed by the study was the variety of instruments in use. Although every unit that responded was attempting to use some form of CRA, there was little uniformity. Many units have or are developing their own form of risk assessment, which may have some basis in research evidence. Others are using some form of tool or instrument that does have a research background but may not have good reliability or validity. What this implies is that there is not enough communication between units and between professionals.

The lack of consistency of items for inclusion in the types of risk assessment reviewed may be of more concern, as it would appear that no single tool covers every aspect of CRA. The numbers of respondents who stated that other CRAs were needed, especially related to sex offending and self-harm, shows the concern over these areas and the lack of consistency across the UK. Clinical governance is there to help by creating a system that is integrated, where people work together and where patients can trust the staff. Clinical risk assessment is fundamental to any work done with patients in forensic settings. There is some national guidance on risk management, and risk assessment for violence by psychiatric patients is available (NHSME 1994a; 1994b).

The tools may have to be used in the future in different ways. For example, the pathology-based tools may be of more use in establishing mental status at the initial admission and then at identified points during the progress of the patient or client through the system. Normative CRAs may be used to show the progress of the patient or client as they improve and as the main assessment throughout progress towards full rehabilitation. There is an urgent need for some level of standardisation, a strengthening of reliability and validity, and a stronger basis in research evidence for the tools that are currently in use.

To enable a seamless approach to transition to and from differing levels of security, we need to have some reliable risk assessment instruments that professionals can use in a co-ordinated way to the benefit of the patient. One role for NHS Trusts in the future will be the bringing together of forensic staff to enable a coherent CRA strategy as the patient moves through the system.

One of the most influential formulations of work around quality assessment is arguably Donabedian's application of a systems-based framework – that of structure, process and outcome. Donabedian (1988) stated that the relations between these components of care must be known before any particular one can be used to assess quality.

Within a UK setting, by far the largest area of what has been categorised by Lynch (1993) as part of forensic nursing activity, namely 'correctional/institutional nursing', occurs within the four high security hospitals of Rampton, Ashworth, Broadmoor and the State Hospital Carstairs, and a system of regional and medium secure units. These types of care environments do not easily support measurable patient criteria, which have been used in monitoring 'mainstream' health activity. There is little benefit in reviewing waiting list and discharge criteria. Even if members of the multi-professional team can see patients within set time periods or deal with the assessment process on time, this may still have little bearing on the ability of forensic institutions to provide access to their services. Equally, the rate at which patients who are seen as needing forensic care are treated also provides challenging issues to those wishing to establish activity-based outcomes.

So what are the forensic implications for clinical governance? The framework can be seen as an attempt to group the previous professional quality approaches, those of quality assessment and clinical audit, bridging these to the more managerial approaches of quality assurance and quality improvement. The consultation document *A First Class Service: Quality in the New NHS* (Department of Health 1998b), describes a systematic model that 'marries clinical judgement with clear national standards'. In the field of mental health and, therefore, by default forensic nursing, this is most clearly illustrated through the Mental Health National Service Framework (Department of Health 1999a). A range of national initiatives has been identified and targets set. Key requirements of clinical governance include:

- a comprehensive strategy to be developed by each organisation, including a range of quality improvement methods, which should be linked closely to staff personal development programmes
- a clearer focus on the processes of care, including clinical decision-making and the concepts of appropriateness and evidence-based care.

In his review of the educational aspects of forensic nursing, Whyte (2000) concludes: 'the challenge I throw down to nurses wishing to be perceived as "forensic" in speciality is to provide me and your peers with good case study material and empirical research evidence to support your assertions' (p.25). Clinical governance may not in itself be a research model, but does give a framework in which some of the challenges stated above can begin to be answered.

CLINICAL GOVERNANCE AND FORENSIC NURSING PRACTICE

So far this chapter has given an overview of how clinical governance has come to be, the parameters it works within and some of the challenges that this presents to practitioners. This policy development has, however, to be reflected within forensic nursing practice. Many of the reasons for patients being present within what is loosely defined as the forensic nursing client group arise from their actual or perceived risk, to themselves or others. What follows is a discussion of how a clinical governance framework can help to develop forensic nursing practice.

Initially it is more likely that the term *framework* is the important concept. Clinical governance in itself is not attempting to readdress practice; it does however provide a systematic approach to the justification and application of the practice nurses adopt with clients. A case in point may be best illustrated by a conceptual example.

The difficulties in risk management of forensic patients have been discussed. One of the most frequently documented areas is the potential for violence or its actual occurrence. It is known that violence can result from a wide range of precursors. Some of these reasons will link directly to the individual and the way in which they perpetrate behaviour. Others will be linked to external stressors that affect the person. In an effort to address these facts, particularly in relation to the management of violent incidents and the ways in which practitioners can reduce the potential for their occurrence, the Royal College of Psychiatrists (1998) produced practice guidelines. These clearly identify the factors that can precipitate violent incidents.

As a nurse on a ward this might be an area of practice that is of real concern to you and your colleagues. Not just because of the effects upon patients but also the issues of staff support and ability to cope with the pressures placed on the team. You are therefore faced with a problem, which, if it can be more effectively managed, will result in a series of positive outcomes for patient care and staff development. As stated above the need here is to use a framework to address the outcome.

What's your evidence?

The ability to use evidence-based practice is central to nursing care. Evidence-based practice has been defined as 'the process of systematically finding, appraising and using contemporaneous research findings as a basis for clinical decisions' (Long and Harrison, 1996, p.6). By setting evidence in the context of researched data and 'clinical expertise', there is the potential for a far more readily available source of evidence to be ignored. That area is the patient's own notes and records, along with the current knowledge of the staff caring for the patient.

This is a valuable starting point in establishing the reality of staff perceptions of a patient's problem. Do the records support the perceived concept of the patient being a violent individual, if so is it a regular occurrence, or a recent behaviour with no previous episodes? A review of more than one patient, using these parameters, will give a current picture of violence as a care issue on the ward. This can be further refined and a local audit carried out. A clinical audit team or the ward multidisciplinary team may undertake such audits. There is also going to be a range of recording mechanisms used by any health care provider to enable monitoring of corporate issues. One of these will be incident reporting procedures. A spate of problems or internal investigations may have occurred that provide relevant data or action plans, which can be included within a review of violence and its prevalence in the area being studied.

Quality improvement

Once the reality and extent of the problem has been addressed and contextualised, practice can be challenged and designed towards agreed outcomes. It is important at this stage that the new practice developed now starts to incorporate the implementation of relevant research findings, providing an evidence-based care programme. There may be several ways of tackling this process. Resources available will include library facilities, professional journals and other members of the multidisciplinary team. There are also many websites now dedicated to health care information, providing access to the most current thinking and practice. Clinical nurse specialists may be available within your area, who will be able to support practice initiatives, and the continuing growth of the nurse consultant role should again provide avenues for ensuring best practice is included.

It is important to note that all the above initiatives require effective channels of communication. This has been an area of practice which has constantly come under criticism within forensic services. Documenting of care given and initiatives undertaken is also vital. The initial phase of this framework will reveal how successful, or not, staff documentation is in enabling care to be based on evidence or perception. It should also reveal just how effective current communication practices are. The aim of all these interventions is to justify and deliver quality improvement in patient care.

Managing the change

The first two steps detailed above demonstrate that clinical governance provides a tool for challenging current practice and implementing best practice solutions. The initial focus for this process was in dealing with violence as an issue for staff. What has resulted from this exploration is a range of initiatives to help achieve a better management of violence.

Implementing changes in practice is now the issue, and it is in focusing on the delivery of change that the functioning of clinical governance is best portrayed. There is an enormous amount of literature in many professional publications arguing that the theory/practice gap is widening (Basset 1993; McSherry 1997; May, Alexander and Mulhall 1998). Health care providers are now expected to ensure that there are robust infrastructures being established to develop, maintain and monitor the standards of the quality of care offered both by the organisation and by individual practitioners.

Thus, the issue of developing strategies to address violence and its management will go far beyond the ward. If the problems perceived by the initial evidence prove to be a clinical risk for the provider, then it will be necessary to review current practice and the policies, procedures and training undertaken by the staff. In effect, dealing with a single clinical issue could result in a corporate change of practice.

DEVELOPING A FRAMEWORK

The discussion around clinical governance frameworks has predominantly focused on the corporate approach. Whilst this is inevitable as the chief executive is directly responsible for delivery, there are many parallels between the organisational requirements and those of the ward or individual practitioner.

The range of clinical issues which will identify the forensic environment varies from other environments owing to the clinical risks attached. It is, therefore, important that those operating within such remits can meet clinical governance requirements. The three key components are:

o Practice and professional development

o Clinical risk and audit

o Research and development

Key area 1: Practice and professional development

Corporate rationale

This is to ensure that the organisation and those practising under the Chief Executive's jurisdiction have the correct knowledge, skills and competencies to meet the requirements of their roles.

Practitioner involvement

Lifelong learning is one of the main supports for practitioners in this key area. Achieving the skills and competencies needed to fulfil any role will need assessment of the current expectation placed on the nurse, both in grading and patient expectation. It will also involve developing new skills as the scope of an individual's practice changes. Improving practice means managing ineffective practice both in nursing and other clinical staff.

Skills to use would therefore include Individual Development and Professional Reviews, use of post-registration updating requirements (Wallace 1999), clinical supervision, reflection on practice, attending further training or updates on relevant practice areas, and writing for local and national publications. Communication is key to development; if services are developing or new practice is being evaluated in an area, do not assume that colleagues are aware, or understand. Presentations and leaflets, along with similar information for patients and carers, will go a long way towards an inclusive culture.

Key area 2: Clinical risk and audit

Corporate rationale

The objective is to enable the development of good practice, establishing efficient and effective standards of care, whilst reducing the occurrence of harmful or adverse events.

Practitioner involvement

The aim should be to enable you to justify and focus on improving nursing practice. Staff should be involved in the evaluation of effectiveness and quality of treatments. Within forensic nursing practice there is a wide range of potential for this particular aspect of practice. With many care strategies being practitioner-led and the role of nurses increasing, there is a need for nurses to set the standards and adopt new practices, whilst integrating them with competent risk-assessment criteria. Guidelines and procedures can further impact on consistent good practice being reproduced across a service. This key area again provides a learning forum for practitioners in involving patients. The complaints mechanism provides both a direct link for patient involvement in addressing their concerns, and an opportunity for them to be associated with creating satisfactory changes in practice.

Skills to be utilised here include quality improvement processes, such as clinical audit, patient satisfaction surveys, user focus groups, clinical risk reduction programmes and learning from adverse events. Incorporation of standards into practice will allow the easier monitoring of practice and enable practitioners to address national agendas, e.g. the Mental Health National Service Framework (Department of Health 1999a), within their routine systems. Poor clinical performance can then be addressed or challenged in line with identified procedures or accepted standards. As data collection grows within forensic services, it will need staff to become far more adept at critical analysis of statistics and clinical indicators of practice. Conversely the use of effectively collected information will enable far more credible platforms for the formation of patient care pathways.

Key area 3: Research and development

Corporate rationale

The objective is to focus on and develop a system for meeting research needs for the patient population, whilst providing research opportunities for staff, disseminating findings and providing sound clinical practices based upon the best scientific evidence.

Practitioner involvement

As identified above the potential range of information that nurses will be faced with will only increase. Clinical information is often complex and in some cases can require specialist skills and sophisticated packages to analyse. Such situations have been blamed for the reluctance of nursing staff to implement research findings. Within the field of forensic nursing, the research infrastructure is still relatively underdeveloped, although this situation again provides ample opportunity for nurse involvement.

The research that a particular health care provider will undertake will depend on the resources available to them. Becoming involved is not generally difficult, allowing for differing levels of engagement. Interestingly, the inclusion of patients and service users has increased markedly in the recent past, the political imperative being one of the main reasons behind this. Nurses should also become aware of those fields of practice which will receive the most prominence. Recent national focus has been on the confidential inquiry into suicides (Appleby, Shaw and Amos 1997); the present treatment issues surrounding the treatment of the dangerous and severe personality disordered offender (Home Office and Department of Health 1999) will also result in resources becoming available for research in such fields.

Skills to develop include an understanding of basic research principles. This is now addressed through the process of nurse education. Information systems used by the area in which you work, such as risk or incident reports, can be analysed and may provide good initial research data.

Following on from this there is a series of key questions and tasks that need to be considered:

1. What facilities exist within your particular trust to enable you to become either actively involved or aware of what is happening?

2. Is there access to current reports and data either through a library or remote access points such as the internet?

3. Learn how to put a research proposal together, and review professional journals for opportunities to apply for funds or travel scholarships.

4. Visit other forensic teams or work in another area of your trust to view systems and how they have incorporated research into practice.

5. Become active in finding out what the clinical governance agenda is within your trust and how this impacts on your practice.

The aim of this section is to provide nurses with a framework in which to embed their practice alongside the key areas of clinical governance.

CONCLUSION

Clinical governance is concerned with the responsibility of the organisation to develop effective care reflected through a series of structures and processes. Achieving the desired outcome requires a programme that drives quality but is far larger than a pure quality initiative, being composed of a complex matrix of support mechanisms. These activities need to be owned and led in the main by clinicians both individually and collectively. Clinical governance is not the method by which this will occur. Rather it is the means by which processes are formed into a structured framework, linking the corporate agenda and able to both support and challenge clinical practice.

Within a forensic environment the issues raised are unique in the focus they take. Frequently they will require a balancing act between patients' rights and protection of the patient, the public and staff, effective risk management, and rehabilitation. The recent inclusion of the European human rights legislation into UK law has further complicated the issue. Nursing practice needs to involve itself heavily within the clinical governance framework. This will provide a range of opportunities not just to address improvements in the quality of care witnessed by patients, but also to facilitate major changes in the role of nursing and its evidence base in leading treatment strategies outside the medical model as the 21st century progresses. Clinical governance can be seen as a reflection of the changing expectations of society. Emphasis is being placed upon individual practitioners to understand their own practice better, committing to a continuing model of development.

CHAPTER 3

Exploring the Interface of Competence and Clinical Effectiveness

Carol Watson

INTRODUCTION

The development of a framework of competencies for forensic mental health nurses is not a new concept: literature on the subject can be found from the late 1970s (see Niskala 1986). But the emphasis from government health departments, in all four countries of UK, on clinical governance and clinical effectiveness, has given fresh impetus to the search for a framework of mental health competencies in general, and forensic mental health nursing competencies in particular (see for example Department of Heath 1999b; Scottish Office 1998a). Tarbuck (1994a) identified competencies for forensic services, and work at the State Hospital Carstairs (Watson and Kirby (1999) in Robinson and Kettles (1999)) and by the United Kingdom Central Council for Nursing, Midwifery and Health Visiting (UKCC) and University of Central Lancashire (1999) are only two examples of the ongoing quest for a practicable, applicable and credible set of competencies that describe what forensic nurses do.

The nature of competence, and how it is recognised or measured by the individual practitioner and the organisation, has been the subject of much academic argument, both in pre-registration and post-registration education over many years. Beattie (1987), for example, argued that nursing was a complex integrated multidimensional construct rather than a collection of tasks, skills and processes. However, current policies for all professionals in the fields of health and social care insist that they be able to demonstrate their competence and that organisations ensure their staff are competent to deliver on complex agendas. The UKCC has moved from outcomes-based programmes to competency-based programmes for pre-registration nurses, and many post-registration specialties are also developing competency frameworks to enable practitioners to articulate what it is they do to meet the specific health or social care needs of their patients or clients.

However, the development of a competency framework *per se*, may not guarantee improvements in the quality of care delivered to patients and clients. Merely enabling practitioners to develop competencies does not in itself enable the practitioner to practise effectively within their care environment. This chapter aims to draw together some of the strategies that can be employed to assist organisations, managers, educationists and practitioners themselves to address this issue, and to clarify the elements needed to ensure effective safe practice.

HOW DOES COMPETENCE IMPACT ON PRACTICE?

Many claims have been made about the role of post-registration education and its impact on care and service delivery (see for example Haber, Fagan-Pryor and Allen 1997; Morrison 1990), whilst other studies point to the limitations of education, especially education which is not grounded within the clinical arena (see for example Ash 1996; Cioffi 1997; Lynn 1995; Mason and Chandley 1990; Montgomery 1997). Yet no particular staff characteristic, either demographic or experiential, has been consistently related to in-patient outcomes across studies independent of treatment programmes (Paul and Menditto 1992). Nevertheless, government departments of health and professional bodies alike recommend competency models of continuing professional development (CPD) as one means to ensure quality of services that meet patient and client needs. To achieve this, a competency framework must aim to engage practitioners, their managers, service providers and education and training organisations within the wider context of clinical effectiveness.

Individual practitioners must be:

o enabled to identify which competencies they have and which they lack to carry out their roles effectively

o empowered and motivated to access training and education to enhance existing, or develop additional, competencies

o supported and supervised within the practice environment until they gain the practical experience to become fully competent

o engaged in self-appraisal, clinical supervision, peer review and management appraisal to ensure that their competence is maintained.

Managers and service providers need to:

o develop an organisational strategy which links the clinical needs of patients and clients with the roles and functions of clinical staff

○ determine the competency sets for each role

○ determine the clinical outcome measures that competency-based training should aim to achieve

○ develop an infrastructure to support competency-based learning, including induction, clinical supervision, secondments and exchanges

○ provide teaching and learning resources in relation to their specialism

○ develop and deliver a competency-based appraisal system

○ engage with accredited experts in the field, such as advanced practitioners, and academics to establish the nature and scope of training and education required

○ commission education and training.

Educationists need to:

○ collaborate closely with service organisations to identify the education and training needs for both pre- and post-qualifying practitioners

○ continue to develop flexible modes of learning that are evidence-based (where possible)

○ respond positively to the need for practitioners to gain accreditation for practice-based competencies within an academic framework.

SO WHAT IS COMPETENCE?

The UKCC Commission for Nursing Midwifery Education *Fitness for Practice* (UKCC 1999) defines competence as 'the skills and ability to practise safely and effectively without the need for direct supervision'. However, certain principles underpin this statement, not least that upon registration nurses must be able to apply 'knowledge, understanding and skills to perform to the standards required in employment, and assume the responsibilities and accountabilities necessary for the protection of the public' (p.35). The National Board for Nursing, Midwifery and Health Visiting for Scotland (NBS 1999b) defines competency within the context of post-registration CPD as '*knowledge, skills and attitudes,* within a matrix of developmental practice education research and management' (p.3) in a range of specialist domains, such as infection control, critical care nursing, and nursing people suffering from severe and enduring mental illness.

Each competency is the result of the development of knowledge, skills and attitudes gained through the processes of formal education and informal practice-based experience. This may seem relatively straightforward, until one considers the sheer volume of a single competency. Table 3.1 outlines the range of knowledge and skills required to participate effectively in psychiatric observation, as well as the attitudes (and values) that need to be explored; and this is a basic building block competency for all newly qualified mental health nurses! Additional knowledge and skill is needed to enhance this competence within the particular constraints of a therapeutic alliance in a secure setting.

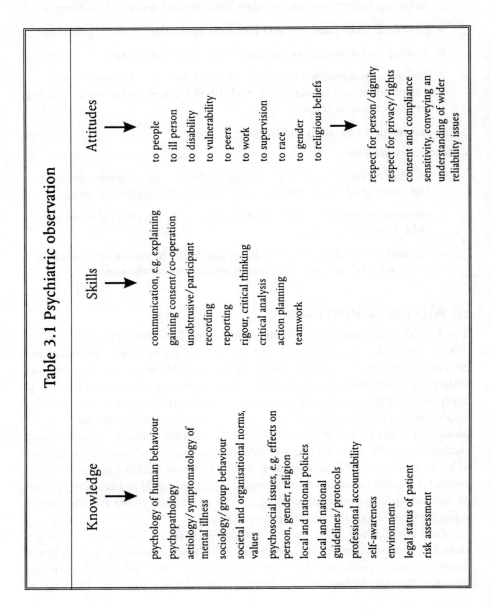

Table 3.1 Psychiatric observation

Knowledge	Skills	Attitudes
psychology of human behaviour	communication, e.g. explaining	to people
psychopathology	gaining consent/co-operation	to ill person
aetiology/symptomatology of mental illness	unobtrusive/participant	to disability
sociology/group behaviour	recording	to vulnerability
societal and organisational norms, values	reporting	to peers
psychosocial issues, e.g. effects on person, gender, religion	rigour, critical thinking	to work
local and national policies	critical analysis	to supervision
local and national guidelines/protocols	action planning	to race
professional accountability	teamwork	to gender
self-awareness		to religious beliefs
environment		
legal status of patient		respect for person/dignity
risk assessment		respect for privacy/rights
		consent and compliance
		sensitivity, conveying an understanding of wider reliability issues

This process of individual competency analysis must be undertaken to ensure that staff are aware of all aspects of the competency and that appropriate training can be designed and delivered. This analysis also helps to clarify the different levels of knowledge and skill required by qualified practitioners and health care assistants. Generally the attitude aspects are the same for all grades and all professions.

The issues around competence and competence appraisal are many and varied. How can individuals demonstrate that they are competent to deliver care or treatment beyond the level of their basic qualification? It is not enough to say 'I've been doing this for years, therefore I am competent!' How is competence maintained within the context of a developing knowledge base? How long does it take to become competent? Does competence in one area, for example delivering substance abuse counselling or psychoeducation packages to people with severe and enduring mental illness in a psychiatric intensive care unit, transfer to another care setting, such as a medium or high secure unit? How does a manager, who does not have advanced clinical competencies, assess the performance of a practitioner who has? And how can an organisation be sure that competence is up to date and evidence-based, or in line with best practice?

In addition, which competencies will contribute most to the care and treatment of mentally disordered offenders, and which staff should have them? Patients present with complex needs, some of which are offence-specific, some offence-related, and all within the range of mental health problems. Developing packages of care for this patient group involves more than just buying off-the-shelf sex offender treatment programmes or moral reasoning packages and providing staff with the training to deliver them. Staff at all levels require induction to the patient group and the setting, basic secure environment competencies and a range of core care competencies in order to support the therapeutic milieu (Watson and Kirby 2000).

Individual practitioners must address some of these issues, and others must be addressed by the managers responsible for the strategic direction of the service. It is of course relatively straightforward where there is a post-registration qualification, like a postgraduate diploma in cognitive behaviour therapy. But how can the practitioner be sure that they are competent to run a psychoeducation group, or a social skills group with a particular group of patients, and based on current best practice?

Reflection on practice and assessment of one's own competence are professional requirements, and there are professional and commercial packages designed to assist in this (see NBS 1999a; Professional and Practice Development Nurses Forum 1999). In essence they enable practitioners to ask the questions for themselves, source the answers and provide a portfolio of evidence benchmarked against guidelines or best practice statements, using a combination of self-assessment and peer review. The practitioner must demonstrate both that they understand the underpinning knowledge and that they have the skills and attitudinal aspects of the competency, and they generally must provide up-to-date reference material on the subject. It is important to have a mentor or supervisor for this activity, which can be incorporated into existing clinical supervision, or can provide a useful basis for developing regular supervision.

Where a deficit in any aspect of the competency is identified, the mentor and practitioner can formulate an action plan to address it. Learning activities range from a period of supervised practice or a visit to another unit, to a secondment, distance learning modules or a literature review. It may be that the organisation will help with support in the form of resources or time, especially where the competency is crucial to the clinical agenda. This evidence of competence can also be used to gain accreditation against academic modules; many organisations now develop in-house education and training, then have them accredited by higher education institutions or as NVQ/SQA awards.

Competencies are organised in domains, and at a foundation level describe direct patient care. Table 3.2 is based on the Fitness for Practice Domains (UKCC 1999) and domains identified by Tarbuck (1994a) and the NBS (1999b). The knowledge required and the skills performed become more complex with the level of competence and the expected role outcomes. The competency domains may be generic but the competencies must be relevant to the specialism and be directed towards and focused upon practitioners.

Table 3.2 Practice competency domains

Competence = Knowledge + Skills + Attitudes in a range of domains, such as:

- professional/ethical practice
- care/treatment delivery (includes interpersonal)
- enabling patient/client centredness
- problem framing and solving
- care management
- risk assessment and risk management
- teamwork and collaboration
- personal/professional development
- reflective and evidence-based practice

CORE COMPETENCIES

While the core competencies must be inclusive of the key elements of knowledge, skills and attitudes, they must also be underpinned by the professional values and attitudes perceived to be intrinsic to forensic mental health care. These include respect for persons and individual human rights and a commitment to the prevention of discrimination, alienation, scapegoating and institutionalisation. They should reflect the current focus on multi-professional and multi-agency working as well as personal and professional self-awareness in terms of CPD. It is also important to acknowledge the societal bias in terms of mentally disordered offenders, and provide support and guidance on the public health and education role which must be undertaken by forensic mental health nurses.

In addition, core competencies need to be reflected in organisational policies. In order to empower staff to achieve competence and generate models of best practice, whether that is in searching or delivering psychoeducation-based group therapy, guidance on how these competencies are to be applied must be explicit in policies and protocols. This then enables practitioners to demonstrate competence by implementing the policies. Embedding competence within practice in this formal way enables practitioners to identify their learning, or CPD needs, and understand what they need to do to achieve competence. It is also more likely that the infrastructure will be there to support them.

Registered practitioners are equipped with the competencies they were required to demonstrate at the point of registration – for example, an understanding of mental illness and its effect on behaviour. In addition, through experience and personal and professional development activities, they will have enhanced those fundamental competencies. Specialist competencies must also grow from these. In Scotland recently, forensic practitioners identified three domains of practice that required enhanced or advanced competencies (NBS 2000):

o risk assessment and management

o professional and legal aspects of care

o interpersonal competencies, particularly around professional boundaries.

These were in addition to core safety and security competencies described for high security care (Watson and Kirby 2000), which should be incorporated into the induction process. Table 3.3 on p.54 gives examples of some of the competencies in these domains.

All registered mental health nurses are required to demonstrate a knowledge of the relevant Mental Health Act when they qualify. There is, however, additional underpinning knowledge and skills required to be able to apply their understanding of the Act to mentally disordered offenders in the context of secure care (for example accessing the Mental Welfare Commission; the impact of criminal procedures legislation on care and treatment; the nature of the therapeutic alliance in secure settings; how to support an individual during court proceedings, etc.).

Unqualified staff, such as health care assistants, also require induction, training and supervision; clarity is needed in relation to their specific roles and duties in the team, and competencies described to support those roles. A careless remark or action born of lack of knowledge or understanding can seriously undermine the therapeutic processes involved, for example, in anger management. Experienced staff will be able to demonstrate many of these competencies at an expert level through higher levels of cognitive skills such as critical thinking, reflection, analysis and judgement. Their experience is essential in the support and supervision of less experienced colleagues.

However, there is also a need to define the forensic therapeutic repertoire more clearly, and to articulate the unique therapeutic attributes of forensic nursing, which distinguish it from the stereotypical gatekeeper role. Forensic nursing is not only about managing dangerousness and assessing and managing risk. Nurses cannot be deemed to be specialist forensic nurses solely because they care for this patient group. Treatment-specific competencies related to specialist psychological interventions and delivered by advanced practitioners such as nurse specialists, occupational therapists, psychologists and others, are essential to support the broad spectrum of treatment approaches delivered by multi-professional teams. For example:

o cognitive behaviour therapy

o psychosocial interventions

o psychodynamic psychotherapy

o anger management

o dialectical behaviour therapy

o offence-specific approaches

o treatment to address substance abuse.

Competency frameworks should include mechanisms that enable both professional development and succession planning. This will also ensure that education and practice development can be planned, managed and evaluated. Such a framework allows practitioners to build on their existing expertise and further develop it. Many accredited courses already exist for some specialist interventions, but the selection of appropriate staff to access these programmes is subject to a wide range of variables. A competency ladder enables practitioners to identify their particular strengths and areas of interest and thus take more control of their career planning and professional development. Likewise, managers can identify potential in specific areas and more closely match development opportunities with appropriate staff.

CLINICAL GOVERNANCE AND THE ROLE OF THE ORGANISATION

Clinical Governance is about accountability and about structures and processes. It will achieve the desired outcomes of improved quality and public reassurance about standards of care only if it is underpinned by a wide range of activities, most of which require to be owned and led by clinicians individually and collectively. Clinical Governance is not the sum of all these activities; rather it is the means by which they are brought together into a structured framework and linked to the corporate agenda. (Scottish Office 1998b, p.2)

Recent government policy has placed the emphasis on clinical governance as a way of ensuring that patients receive care and treatment of the highest quality delivered by clinicians who have the competencies to meet their patients' or clients' needs. This political drive, coupled with some well-publicised cases of medical negligence, has certainly assisted the competence agenda to develop in all specialties within the NHS. The UKCC scoping study on nursing in secure environments (UKCC and University of Central Lancashire 1999) also emphasised the need for appropriate induction, supervision and training to ensure that care and treatment are delivered to a high standard, and that the safety of the public, staff and patients is not compromised. However, quality care and treatment is more than having enough competent clinicians. Rapid changes have taken place in the nature, systems and processes of health care, resulting in a complex redeployment and subsequent re-skilling of staff.

Clinical governance puts the patient at the centre of care and service planning and delivery. From this perspective, the competencies required of staff are derived from the identified health and social care needs of the patient group (NBS 1999b; see Figure 3.1). Within forensic mental health this includes considerable knowledge of the criminal justice system as well as the health and social care systems, and many competencies are appropriate to the full range of professionals within the care team. Examples of these core care competencies are as described in Table 3.3 on p.54 (NBS 2000).

Clinical effectiveness, however, does not only rest on the competence of staff to deliver effective care and treatment. A complex infrastructure is required, consisting of audit of practice, research and development, clinical practice evaluation, clinical support and supervision. Appropriate specialist interventions or approaches must be identified and levels of competence differentiated for the whole range of staff who work in secure environments or with mentally disordered offenders in the community. For example, to ensure that patients receive appropriate treatment for a specific problem, say lack of anger control or inappropriate sexual behaviour, groups of staff would require to be competent at different levels

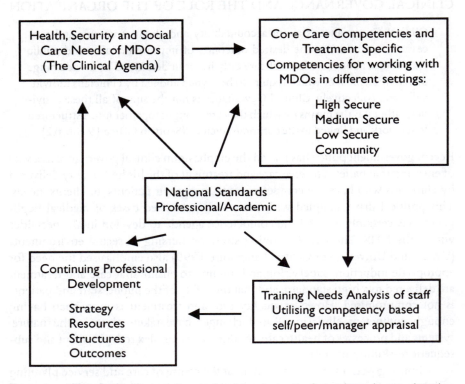

Figure 3.1 The relationship between client need and Continuing Professional Development (CPD)

to deliver an integrated approach and achieve appropriate clinical outcomes. There would be a need for:

- o psychologists and nurse specialists to deliver Level 3 one-to-one therapy, using an accredited treatment model

- o other professionals including nurses, doctors, occupational therapists and social workers to deliver Level 2 group work that had a psychoeducational approach and was linked to the Level 3 work

- o ward-based staff, including health care assistants who understood the nature of anger and how it is manifested in mentally ill people, as well as having a basic understanding of the treatment regimen, to support the therapeutic milieu (i.e. at Level 1).

Sufficient numbers of each level would be required to deliver the treatment, and provide the clinical supervision to those less experienced. Those with Level 3 skills and knowledge, which would usually include a formal cognitive behaviour therapy qualification, might also be involved in training, assessing and supporting other staff in the group work or in the basic training of health care assistants. An evaluation infrastructure, such as research or clinical audit, would also be required. In addition, therapeutic space is needed in the patient's day to enable these treatments to be delivered, and substantial logistical issues must also be addressed: where will the therapy take place, how will the patients access them, how will the referral system work, what are the staffing implications? Without this infrastructure it would be difficult to ensure that competent practice actually developed, and that treatment was clinically effective.

To train staff to use a particular technique does not make them competent. Supervised clinical practice enables them to develop their competence, and clinical assessment and appraisal are required to ensure that practice meets professional standards and the needs of patients. This means a considerable investment in time, anything from three months to two years. Service providers must ensure that staff already have or are able to develop these competencies, and a training needs analysis can be used to map the current competency level and skill mix of staff against that required to meet patient/client need. This in turn will inform the CPD strategy for all clinical staff.

The strategy must incorporate the competency framework into the appraisal system, which will help to generate an education and training strategy for all care staff from health care assistants through qualified practitioners, and up to the levels of specialist practitioner qualification and consultant nurse. The development of such a competency ladder is an essential component in the development of integrated, high-quality forensic care, and would provide the basis for an integrated approach to CPD in forensic services, enabling organisations to recruit, retain and support staff within a framework of national standards. In addition, nurses themselves must take responsibility to identify their learning needs based on the needs of their patients, and thus play a proactive and positive role in their own CPD.

Links need to be developed with education providers to commission modules or to gain assistance in the development of in-house education programmes. A forum for discussions around professional regulation and national standards might also be considered in order to link closely to the national clinical governance agenda. Employers have a need to understand the standard that practitioners achieve in order to establish fitness for purpose, and to ensure that competency levels are transferable across services. There is a danger with in-house ward-based training that the practitioner will only be recognised as competent in that specific organisation. The competency framework should provide a starting point in establishing a national standard for units and modules related to forensic care. Where there is a network of forensic services this work can and should be shared, in order to work towards a seamless approach to care and treatment throughout the whole of the patient journey, from high security to community. As previously outlined, policies to support practice must also be developed or reviewed.

Resources must be allocated, and the necessary structures put in place to facilitate CPD in respect of processing applications, monitoring and supervising learning, preparation of supervisors and assessors, as well as systems to evaluate learning experiences for individuals and the organisation. By developing a range of competencies with detailed outcomes linked to care standards, performance appraisal and development needs can be progressed in an integrated structured way.

COMPETENCY ACQUISITION: THE PRACTITIONER'S ROLE

The acquisition of competencies can be a lengthy process and not only involves this complex infrastructure within the organisation, but also requires a motivated workforce. To establish the appropriate competencies for ensuring that staff can deliver a service that meets patient/client need at a local level, it is important to establish and acknowledge those existing competencies, built up over years of experience, that remain appropriate. As stated earlier, there are published processes that prepare practitioners to evidence their existing competencies or work towards enhanced competence. But developing a practitioner to become more competent, or with a broader range of competencies targeted to the specific needs of the patient group, is in itself a complex task for individual practitioners and for educationists. Aside from the organisational and professional issues in relation to changing practice and enhancing services, there is evidence that what practitioners learn, where they learn and how they learn will influence their ability to put that learning into practice (Knowles 1984). The practice environment has to be a supportive learning environment with opportunities for personal and professional growth, in the context of continual audit and review and in a culture of mutuality and collaborative working.

As multidisciplinary and multi-agency working has become recognised as an essential component of organisational success, so competencies around these areas have become more explicit. However, there is a perception amongst forensic mental health nurses that within the multidisciplinary team they have the least professional credibility to utilise enhanced competencies and less influence in developing services which meet patients' needs (Kettles and Robinson 2000b). Yet the practitioner's responsibility for actively contributing to the care and treatment milieu, as well as for their personal and professional development, is undoubtedly core to their professional role. In relation to maintaining their registration, practitioners must develop a portfolio of evidence that clearly demonstrates how they have applied their learning to practice (NBS 1999a; see Figure 3.2). In respect of a portfolio to demonstrate an advanced level of competence, the purpose is similar; it should enable them to:

- o identify current competencies related to their roles; this requires reflection on prior learning and experience, developing a CV

- o gather evidence of acquired knowledge and skills; this can be time consuming and may involve preparing a literature review, or a paper on guidelines or best practice, developing a teaching pack or a paper for publication, carrying out clinical audit activity, statements of support from colleagues and supervisors, undertaking a period of supervised practice, conducting a patient satisfaction survey

- o identify current and future learning needs and opportunities: What learning is required? Is it a formal course, a period of supervised practice, an exchange or secondment, or a mixture of several of these? Are there options?

- o develop an action plan that identifies the resource implications and the support they will need, which can then be discussed with a line manager during an appraisal or performance review: How much will it cost (including replacement/travel/subsistence costs if appropriate)? Who will provide supervision, and how will it be assessed? What support do you need from your organisation, what commitment will you give? What are the expected outcomes in relation to practice?

- o prepare a *verifiable* record of learning that will enable the practitioner to gain credit against formal programmes of education and training and is recognised by their employer.

LEADERSHIP AND CLINICAL SUPERVISION

The purpose of supervision in this context is to enable staff to benefit from a relationship involving reflection on practice under the guidance of a skilled and experienced supervisor and to help them to develop portfolios of evidence that will reflect their contribution to the organisation's clinical agenda. The supervisor is responsible for assessing competence and must be a credible and appropriately qualified practitioner. It is essential that the attitudinal aspects of competencies are monitored and appraised with the same rigour as the knowledge and skill. This requires well-developed leadership skills, not just in supervisors but also in senior ward/unit staff and managers. In addition, good supervision will promote professional self-confidence as well as competence. Treatment-specific competencies provide an ideal opportunity for interprofessional education and supervision, with the added benefits of closer collaboration and better teamworking (Barr 1999).

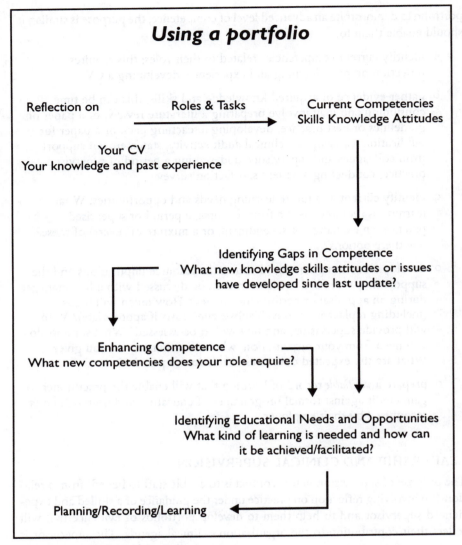

Figure 3.2 (Adapted from NBS 1999a)

PROFESSIONAL ISSUES

The UKCC (1992a) Code of Conduct indicates that nurses, midwives and health visitors must act to:

- o safeguard and promote the interests of individual patients and clients
- o serve the interests of society

○ justify public trust and confidence

○ uphold and enhance the good standing and reputation of the professions.

On a day-to-day basis, forensic practitioners have to make judgements around all of these standards. Nurses in particular need to be aware of their professional accountability and the legal implications of expanding their roles. The UKCC (1996a) guidance on expanding the scope of professional practice underpins much of the regulation in relation to enhancing and developing competence. In addition, practitioners need to adhere closely to policies and protocols, and ensure that they have ongoing clinical supervision. Those working as nurse specialists in medium and high security services often access external supervision, as they may be the only competent practitioner in their field in the organisation. This supervision is often linked to their accreditation criteria, but it is a benchmark of good practice that enables clinicians to benefit from an external perspective, so important in secure care where both patients and the organisation itself can present significant challenges to one's professional practice.

Attitudes and values are the context in which we care, and within any competency framework these need to be explicit. We need to be clear about the human rights of our patients, then build in the necessary strategies to maintain their safety, the safety of those around them and the safety of the public. In addition, the language used within the competency framework should reflect the philosophy of care and treatment rather than the traditional language of custody (e.g. parole). However, this should not be misinterpreted as detracting from the legitimacy of some of the core competencies, especially those related to maintaining patient and public safety, for example by the development of euphemisms such as *care* and *responsibility for control and restraint*.

Values aren't just about statements and charters, they are demonstrated in the working practices of staff. Values must be made explicit in the policies and guidelines used by staff, and in the structures and processes available to them to support their practice and to ensure quality and effectiveness.

FUTURE DIRECTIONS

To address the needs of forensic mental health nurses in the future we must begin with the issues around pre-registration education, and more broadly for education and service collaboration. There is more to nursing than competencies. While competencies encapsulate attitudes and values, the ethical principles on which we build our profession must be taught effectively and applied at both pre- and post-registration levels. Students should be exposed to the full range of mental health services, including forensic services within pre-registration programmes, so that they can critically appraise those ethical principles from a forensic practitioner perspective.

Those training to be mental health professionals are not exposed to the same experiences as their more experienced colleagues were in the past. Much of the practice placement experience is in the community; there are few complex institutions which care for individuals who require long-term residential or in-patient support. Subsequently (and thankfully), there are far fewer people suffering from the once endemic problems generated by long-term institutional care. However, unless students gain experience in in-patient care, they are ill prepared to develop the additional range of competencies required to work in secure care settings.

In addition, interprofessional education at both pre- and post-registration might support better interprofessional working (Barr 1999), enabling each of the professions to concentrate on putting the patient at the centre of their philosophies, and recognising their own and each other's worth in the complex matrix of forensic care. All professions share an ethical framework and much could be gained from multiprofessional and interprofessional educational approaches to this essential and sometimes neglected area of professional life. Closer collaboration between faculties of health, nursing and medicine would facilitate interprofessional education at post-qualifying levels too, and enable education to respond to the real-life, real-practice, multidisciplinary team issues that competency-based education is designed to address.

Service providers also need advice and assistance to design in-house packages that can be accredited. Such competency-based training modules need to demonstrate around 150 hours of learning for a 15-credit module at Level 2 or 3. Collaboration on the design and implementation of these modules, without the sometimes stifling bureaucracy inherent in education and training institutions, would encourage more of these skills-based modules to be generated. Accreditation for practice-based learning at the same level as for theoretical learning needs to be developed in order that all aspects of caring are recognised as having professional and academic value.

Clinical leadership too is an essential element in developing competent practitioners and in succession planning; this requires yet another set of competencies. Organisations must have experienced and motivated clinical leaders and managers who can enable staff to participate actively in their own professional development. Assessment, appraisal and facilitation skills, as well as the motivation to ensure appropriate levels of support and supervision, are of fundamental importance in clinical leaders. Further investment is still needed in the development of competencies for interprofessional clinical leadership within mental health generally and forensic mental health specifically.

The most important outcome of competency-based education is the clinical benefit to the patient. Accreditation of treatment approaches and achievement of service standards are essential benchmarks and signposts in relation to the appropriateness of the competency base for both the organisation and individual practitioners. Guidance from professional bodies as well as from those government bodies responsible for service standards (such as the Clinical Standards Board for Scotland or the National Institute for Clinical Excellence) is crucial, and they should be involved in the development of the competency frameworks to the same degree as the service providers and academic institutions.

The development of competency frameworks at a national level, (certainly in Scotland) is already well under way. But their implementation within the services will be the real test of their efficacy. The previous example of providing competency training in specific specialist interventions, such as anger management or inappropriate sexual behaviour, and then ensuring that the organisation develops and maintains an infrastructure to support the delivery of the intervention is a useful model to consider. It is, however, dependent on the commitment, collaboration and expertise of senior managers and clinicians to co-ordinate and champion the developments, and to ensure that logistical challenges are overcome.

SUMMARY

The successful implementation of any framework is dependent on collaborative working at all levels. Within organisations, staff and managers must work in partnership to have a common understanding of the competencies and adapt them to meet local needs. They must generate and adapt the necessary policies, protocols and systems to support the CPD of staff at all levels. In addition, within units and teams, experienced practitioners in all of the professions must work to develop the support structures and education and training packages for direct care staff to enhance and extend their current competencies.

At a strategic level, organisations must work with each other and with education providers to develop short courses, modules and practice-based packages, including induction packages. Competency frameworks can provide a vehicle for career progression and an integrated approach to CPD. They will support the clinical governance agenda if they are operationalised as part of an integrated infrastructure embedded in the culture of a learning organisation.

Table 3.3 Examples of core care competencies

Professional, legal and ethical aspects of care:

- Apply knowledge and understanding of theoretical factors which underpin professional, legal and ethical aspects of care.
- Undertake nursing practice, taking account of legislation and national strategies which impact upon forensic care.
- Engage in ethical nursing practice in accordance with professional standards and the specific characteristics and needs of forensic mental health service provisions.

Interpersonal competencies:

- Actively engage with service users, professional colleagues and other disciplines in discharging professional role and responsibilities.
- Demonstrate knowledge and understanding of theoretical factors which underpin interpersonal competencies.

Risk assessment (Level 1):

- Undertake assessment and analysis of risk to and/or from client groups within forensic mental health settings and other environments.
- Apply knowledge and demonstrate understanding of issues and factors which underpin risk assessment.
- Demonstrate knowledge and understanding of theoretical factors which underpin risk management.
- Contribute to risk management measures in terms of minimising risk and facilitating care delivery of individual patients/clients.

Risk assessment (Levels 2/3):

- Undertake assessment and analysis of risk to and/or from client groups within forensic mental health settings and other environments.
- Identify key risk factors, in terms of client groups, behavioural patterns and care settings.
- Utilise a risk assessment framework which is evidence/experience-based and accessible to other disciplines and agencies.
- Utilise the stages of identification and assessment to inform the care-delivery process.

- Take into account key factors which relate to level of risk/harmful outcomes.

- Contribute to the collection of data and information which underpin assessment and risk analysis.

- Engage in liaison with other disciplines, carers and family to maximise the effectiveness of risk assessment processes.

- Recognise the predominant linkage between substance abuse and increased levels of risk.

- Collaborate with other disciplines in the assessment process.

- Demonstrate evidence of a developing knowledge base, in relation to 'concepts of risk and risk taking' within care delivery.

- Ensure that risk assessment output is disseminated to and understood by individual clients, family/carers and other disciplines.

- Apply knowledge and demonstrate understanding of issues and factors which underpin risk assessment.

- Critically appraise the interface between risk and the provision of forensic mental health services.

- Undertake a review of forensic nursing roles as they apply in your setting.

- Examine models of risk assessment and risk factors.

- Work in accordance with organisational policies/standards in contributing to risk assessment output.

- Identify core criteria which underpin risk assessment frameworks.

- Access and disseminate research which relates to risk assessment.

- Apply knowledge of legislation and national strategies within your workplace.

- Demonstrate an awareness of other contextual (social environment) factors which may constitute risk/harmful outcomes.

Courtesy of National Board for Nursing, Midwifery and Health Visiting for Scotland (NBS 2000)

CHAPTER 4

Nursing Interventions and Future Directions with Patients Who Constantly Break Rules and Test Boundaries

Penny E. Schafer

INTRODUCTION

This chapter explores the relationship between the unmet expectations of nurses and the tendency to describe groups of patients as 'constantly breaking rules and testing boundaries'. The potential problems of the therapeutic relationship and typical challenges that interdisciplinary treatment teams face are also illustrated. The discrepancy between views of patients as constantly breaking rules and testing boundaries and conceptualisations of the therapeutic relationship are discussed. This discrepancy is potentiated when guidelines of boundary maintenance and limit setting are recommended as nursing interventions outside of the context of the therapeutic relationship. The inadequacy of the concept of boundaries to guide nurses in establishing therapeutic relationships is also examined and an alternative conceptualisation of therapeutic boundaries suggested. Decreasing treatment resistance and enhancing motivation are suggested as nursing interventions consistent with this proposed conceptualisation.

Who are the patients described as constantly breaking rules and testing boundaries? How many times does a patient have to break rules and test boundaries before being described as *constantly* breaking them? The answer to these questions is dependent upon knowing the expectations of the patient held by those describing the behaviour. Clearly, there is more than one group of forensic patients who may repeatedly break rules and test boundaries. Forensic patients experiencing foetal alcohol syndrome or effects (Boland *et al.* 1998), with acquired brain injury (Jackson and Martin 2000), or with traits of personality disorders (Melia, Mercer and Mason 1999) may experience impulsivity and failure to learn from experience. While any one of these groups of patients may be described by some as constantly breaking rules and testing boundaries, patients who display traits of personality disorders frequently provoke the strongest reactions among mental health professionals.

PERSONALITY DISORDERS

Antisocial personality disorder is probably the most prevalent DSM-IV Axis II diagnostic category (American Psychiatric Association 1994) found among forensic patients. A survey of a sample representative of the general population in Canadian penitentiaries (Motiuk and Porporino 1991) discovered a lifetime prevalence rate of antisocial personality disorder of 74.9 per cent when severity and exclusion criteria were ignored. When severity and exclusion criteria were applied, the lifetime prevalence rate dropped to 56.9 per cent. There is also a high percentage of borderline personality disorder and narcissistic personality disorder among those who commit violent crimes (Bernard 2000). Paranoid personality disorder also appears in the literature as a disorder common to the forensic population (Preston 2000).

Melia et al. (1999) described personality disordered forensic patients as being intensely concerned and preoccupied with the protection of self, while showing little concern for others. Additionally, they described these patients as having an exaggerated moral outrage when their own personal rights were violated, even though they blatantly disregarded the rights of others. This description of personality disordered forensic patients is not unlike other descriptions (Hufft and Fawkes 1994; Norton 1996; Peternelj-Taylor and Johnson 1995), where exploitation and manipulation of others are prominent behaviours. However, as Preston (2000) has observed, the nature of these disorders predisposes patients to be resistant to treatment, and affects their ability to trust. Clearly, patients who are characterised as personality disordered present a clinical challenge that may result in their being described as constantly breaking rules and testing boundaries when expectations of compliance with treatment are not realised.

WHAT ARE THE UNSPOKEN EXPECTATIONS?

Typically, expectations regarding attendance at group and individual sessions and compliance with institutional rules are clearly communicated to patients. However, nurses may hold a number of expectations of their patients that operate outside of their awareness and influence their relationships with patients (Peplau 1952). Nurses may not expect personality disordered patients to benefit from treatment.

Such an attitude promotes disengagement and conceptualisation of the patient in terms of management rather than treatment. Nurses may also expect patients to validate the nurses' own views of themselves as caring, helping professionals, and behave in a manner that promotes feelings of comfort for the nurse.

As helping professionals, nurses are likely to expect that patients will demonstrate progress in relation to the nursing care provided, or at least acknowledge the nurses' expertise, recognise their good intentions, and express gratitude for the care they receive. In the forensic environment, where the potential for chaos exists and where threats to personal safety may take the form of physical intimidation and verbal abuse, maintaining a sense of comfort may be a priority for the nurse. Nurses are more likely to have positive perceptions of those patients who meet their expectations (Kelly and May 1982) and who contribute to feelings of comfort by accepting treatment and the therapeutic relationship as presented by the nurse.

WHEN EXPECTATIONS ARE NOT REALISED

Patients who break rules and test boundaries are not likely to meet the unexpressed expectations of the nurse. While awareness of the expectations held of patients guards against the needs of nurses becoming uppermost in therapeutic relationships, the greatest potential for problematic relationships exists when nurses are unaware of the expectations they hold of patients (Peplau 1952). Power struggles and withdrawal, rather than collaboration and engagement, may dominate the relationships between nurses and patients. Genuine caring may be replaced with a covertly negotiated distorted form of caring (Norton 1996). Lastly, strained relationships between treatment team members also may have an adverse effect on the treatment environment.

Power struggles and withdrawal

The power inequality in the therapeutic relationship has been widely recognised, and attempting to achieve more equitable relationships has been the focus of many theoretical approaches to the therapeutic relationship and treatment. However, the nursing literature rarely describes the forensic personality disordered patient as vulnerable. Instead, these patients are often described as manipulative, while forensic nurses are described as needing to guard against being exploited (Melia *et al.* 1999). Still, in a recent study, forensic patients perceived nurses as possessing 'a lot of power' over their futures and expressed that they did indeed feel vulnerable (Schafer 2000). It is also well recognised that forensic patients may feel coerced to participate in treatment (Group for the Advancement of Psychiatry 1994). While patients may engage in power struggles to avoid feeling vulnerable or to retain a sense of control over their treatment, nurses may engage in power struggles to guard against exploitation or to assert their authority and expert status.

When nurses expect that patients will recognise and value their expertise and accept the treatment plan they formulate, they may engage in power struggles when they perceive their expert power to be threatened, as Hardin *et al.* (1985) found in a study of nurse therapists with limited experience. However, asserting the status of expert by directing patients is more likely to decrease patients' sense of control, increase their vulnerability and mobilise their defences (Miller and Rollnick 1991). Patients' defences may take the form of breaking rules and testing boundaries, which may in turn increase nurses' efforts to assert expert power and authority. The therapeutic interests of patients may be distorted to justify this rigid approach, and confirm a growing perception of patients as manipulative. Consequently, a vicious cycle is created. Nurses, becoming increasingly exasperated, may consider patients as unmotivated or, worse yet, hopeless; while the difficulties of patients in trusting others and their efforts to overpower others may be potentiated. Nurses who believe patients are unmotivated or hopeless may ultimately withdraw from them.

Distorted forms of caring

The distorted forms of caring that forensic patients characterised as personality disordered have experienced (Norton 1996) may emerge in the nurse–patient relationship (Schafer 1999). Patients may be suspicious of any form of genuine caring on the part of the mental health professional, thereby making it difficult for mental health professionals to establish therapeutic relationships. For example, forensic patients will not use aggression, violence, or threats of violence as long as the nurse is not overly challenging and provides favourable reports. Although this may provide the illusion of a comfortable working relationship for both the nurse and the patient, the relationship established is not therapeutic; rather it replicates destructive patterns and demonstrates the nurse's failure to establish therapeutic boundaries. In this situation, the nurse's need to feel comfortable is satisfied through the therapeutic relationship. At the same time the patient's need to avoid being challenged, and to confirm existing views (Melia *et al.* 1999) is gratified.

Comfort within the therapeutic relationship is a genuine need of the nurse. It is not this need that is problematic, rather the satisfaction of this need through distortion of the therapeutic relationship. Ultimately, the nurse's comfort should stem from knowledge, clinical competence, and collegial relationships, and not from the distortion of the therapeutic relationship.

Splitting

Personality disordered patients typically have histories coloured by abuse, exploitation, and rejection (Melia *et al.* 1999; Norton 1996). They have learned to use
rejection of others as a method to defend their egos. Patient behaviours that repeatedly demonstrate rejection of the nurse may be in direct conflict with the nurse's
expectation that the patient will accept and appreciate the help offered. Repeated
rejection by the patient may magnify the seductive pull of 'keeping secrets' for the
nurse, may perpetuate boundary violations, and may split the treatment team.

Splitting is a commonly used defence mechanism (Gallop 1985, 1992; Melia
et al. 1999). Patients may use one or both forms of splitting – splitting either by
coercion, or by the more seductive form of keeping secrets (Melia *et al.* 1999;
Shimmin and Storey 2000). Melia *et al.* (1999) described the coercive form of
splitting as the pressure that the patient exerts on those staff attempting to be consistent. Patients will present themselves as victims of uncaring rigid staff members
who will not disregard rules, as others have, to help them.

Patients using seductive secrets as a method of splitting staff often paint a
picture of the staff member as a hero rather than a villain. Patients may describe
how a particular staff member is 'special', or as 'the only one who has ever
listened', or as 'the only one that they ever talked to about this'. Once the relationship is established as 'special', the patient may invite the staff member to keep a
'secret', which solidifies the relationship as special and perpetuates conflict among
team members (Peternelj-Taylor 1998).

Clearly, splitting is destructive for both the patient and the treatment team.
Comfort needs, unrecognised expectations, conflict between treatment team
members, and a knowledge deficit or inability to identify splitting as a pattern are
among the probable explanations as to why nurses may participate in the patient's
efforts to split treatment team members.

Forensic mental health nurses are often employed in institutions where social
control is at least a secondary if not the primary function. Because of their hours of
work, nurses, more so than those in other professional disciplines, are likely to
spend more time in the institution when security functions and custodial care
dominate the institutional activities. Consequently, the nurse's conceptualisation
of the patient's testing behaviour as manipulative and exploitative may reflect the
custodial and security functions of the nurse's role. Treatment team members who
primarily fulfil roles associated with therapeutic interventions may conceptualise
the patient's testing behaviour within the context of treatment as an expected
defensive response. The way nurses conceptualise the patient's testing behaviour is
a reflection of the scope and depth of their knowledge, their abilities, and the roles
they fulfil. Differing conceptualisations of the patient's testing behaviour may
amplify the patient's effort to split treatment team members. However, more often,

differing conceptualisations of the case among treatment team members results in splitting of treatment team members in the absence of any significant efforts on the part of the patient to use splitting, as the following clinical vignette illustrates.

Paul entered treatment with a history of frequently being verbally aggressive with institutional staff, a pattern of behaviour that he repeated in his current treatment programme. He identified his behaviour as inappropriate and expressed a desire to change. However, his aggressive behaviour resulted in reluctance among some treatment team members to approach him and discuss his inappropriate behaviour. Instead, these treatment team members carefully monitored his behaviour and cited incidences of his aggressive behaviour as the reason for a strict treatment agreement or his discharge from the treatment programme. Generally, this group of treatment team members viewed Paul as difficult, unmotivated, and a threat to the safety of the unit. Other treatment team members considered the aggressive behaviour a treatment target and assisted Paul to intervene.

Paul began to respond selectively to treatment team members who assisted him to examine his aggressive behaviour and to try new ways of interacting, while he avoided those he perceived as not interested in helping him, or as he sometimes described as 'wanting to see him fail'. Paul viewed treatment team members' refusal either to rehearse mentally or to accompany him in situations he identified as high risk for him to use aggression as evidence of their desire to see him fail.

Divergent views of Paul dominated treatment team discussions. However, despite this, reports of Paul's use of aggression decreased as treatment progressed. Treatment team members who conceptualised Paul's aggression as a treatment target viewed this as progress. Treatment team members who conceptualised Paul's case in terms of management felt that Paul was being selective in his responses to staff. However, Paul never asked treatment team members (he perceived as willing to help him) to break a rule, nor did he claim to have special relationships with these team members. The only difference that Paul noted among treatment team members was their willingness and ability to help him. As Paul continued to decrease his aggressive behaviour and use assertiveness, views of Paul among treatment team members became less divergent. However, themes of power and control continued to dominate the interactions between a select number of treatment team members and Paul. For example, some nurses failed to assist Paul in accessing medical attention for migraine headaches. In their view he was not overly distressed, a view that these nurses substantiated with their unconfirmed interpretation of his pacing behaviour. Furthermore, they were particularly distressed and voiced disagreement when other treatment team members assisted Paul to access medical attention, resulting in prescription of an antiemetic medication.

THE DISCREPANCY

Whether patients described as constantly disregarding rules or testing boundaries have a diagnosis of a personality disorder or an acquired brain injury, the behaviour is clearly related to the patient's pathology. While this group of patients may present us with our greatest challenge, to label this group of patients as 'too difficult to manage' (Melia *et al.* 1999), constantly breaking rules and testing boundaries, or unmotivated is not consistent with the conceptualisation of the therapeutic relationship in nursing.

If the therapeutic relationship is a partnership central to promoting change and growth in the patient (Peplau 1952), then motivation and engagement in treatment are functions of the relationship and not exclusively characteristics of the patient (Miller and Rollnick 1991; Preston 2000). Testing behaviour stems from the patient's pathology, which determines the therapeutic interests of the patient and, as such, should remain central to the therapeutic relationship. Considering the patient's pathology as a threat to the integrity of the relationship displaces the patient's needs from their central position in the therapeutic relationship.

Although boundary violations may result from under-involvement with the patient (Smith, Taylor *et al.* 1997), forensic mental health nursing has focused primarily on boundary violations resulting from over-involvement. When over-involvement occurs, descriptions of patients as exploitative and manipulative promotes views of the patient as bad or evil (Mercer, Mason, and Richman 1999), while the nurses are portrayed as victim of boundary violations (Gallop 1993). Boundary maintenance guidelines governing self-disclosure, length and location of interviews, and physical contact may assist the nurse to guard against over-involvement. However, boundary guidelines alone are not adequate to guard against under-involvement and to guide the nurse in establishing and maintaining therapeutic relationships. The therapeutic interests of the patient can be distorted to meet the needs or expectations of the nurse, such as seeing the patient punished for testing behaviour while following boundary maintenance guidelines.

Therapeutic boundary maintenance provides the foundation necessary for a therapeutic alliance, by fostering both a sense of safety and also the belief that nurses will always act in the patient's best interest (Smith and Fitzpatrick 1995). In essence, therapeutic boundaries create a space for the patient that is free of the interpersonal obligations that have dominated earlier relationships. In this space, the patient is safe to self-reflect and explore new behaviours. Therapeutic boundaries function to protect the psychotherapeutic process, the patient, and the mental health professional (Smith and Fitzpatrick 1995). Clearly, establishing and maintaining therapeutic boundaries is central to the therapeutic process.

Viewing patients' pathologies as a threat to therapeutic integrity may allow nurses to maintain views of themselves as caring competent professionals while also victims of boundary violations (Gallop 1993), and to avoid the awareness of inadequate personal and professional resources necessary to intervene effectively. However, this view also renders nurses helpless to intervene effectively, since nurses do not determine the pathologies that their patients present. Nurses, as victims, may view themselves as powerless and not responsible for boundary violations that occur in the nurse–patient relationship. Accordingly, if nurses do not see themselves as responsible for the problem, they probably will not perceive themselves as responsible for, or capable of, finding a solution. Viewing a patient's pathology as a threat to therapeutic integrity leads to the formulation of interventions focused on 'managing' the patient and on reducing personal risk, such as setting limits and following rules or guidelines for boundary maintenance.

Setting limits and following boundary maintenance guidelines is an attractive solution in the face of the overwhelming complexity of intervening effectively with patients described as constantly breaking rules and testing boundaries. However, emphasising setting limits and boundary guidelines in isolation from the therapeutic process may leave the therapist or nurse unprepared and confused about techniques to handle these issues (Bridges 1995). Ultimately, over-simplistic interventions may potentiate testing behaviour and power struggles within the therapeutic relationship, and may amplify the discrepancy between conceptualisations of the therapeutic relationship and nursing interventions. Nurses lacking adequate resources to intervene effectively have two options: to recognise their limitations, or to attribute the ineffectiveness of nursing interventions to the patient's pathology. While recognising limitations is the more difficult option, the potential for professional development, and ultimately for effectively responding to the clinical challenge, is greatest when limitations are recognised.

NURSING INTERVENTIONS

While setting limits and following boundary guidelines may seem like logical ways to intervene with testing behaviour, these interventions do not adequately address the complexity of the challenge. Clearly, the forensic environment, coupled with the difficulties with trust and treatment resistance that characterises personality disorders, contributes to the complexity of intervening effectively. The personal and professional resources, or competencies of the nurse, are the third factor in this equation. It is essential that nursing interventions consistent with conceptualisations of the therapeutic relationship take into account the significant contextual factors of the forensic environment and the resources of the nurse, and are responsive to the patient. It is also essential that conceptualisations of therapeutic boundaries guide nursing practice and reflect the complexity of establishing therapeutic relationships.

If a boundary marks a limit or margin (Pillette, Berck and Achber 1995), 'crossing the line' is a boundary violation (Smith, Taylor *et al.* 1997). Yet nurses are described as crossing boundaries out of necessity to help patients (Melia *et al.* 1999). Perhaps, as Owen (1995) suggests, the concept of boundaries is not adequate to guide therapeutic relationships. Drawing on what emerged from a study of therapeutic relationships and therapeutic boundary maintenance in a forensic setting (Schafer 2000), therapeutic boundaries might be conceptualised as 'the walls' that house the therapeutic process. However, the walls are not merely a margin or limit. Instead they are compiled of the resources of the nurse, significant contextual factors of the forensic environment, and treatment-relevant characteristics of the patient (such as motivation, treatment resistance, and ability to trust).

Therapeutic boundary maintenance is a dynamic process that requires nurses to possess the resources necessary to intervene effectively in a manner responsive to the patient's treatment-relevant characteristics and to be aware of the influence of the context of treatment. When the nurse's resources are limited, the ways in which the contextual factors may manifest in the relationship are not recognised, and the patient experiences treatment resistance and difficulty trusting, the space the walls create is insufficient for the psychotherapeutic process. Conversely, when the nurse's resources are adequate, manifestations of the significant contextual factors are recognised, and the patient is motivated, the walls are larger and a space sufficient for the psychotherapeutic process is created. Ultimately, interventions to address testing behaviour aim to create a sufficient space for the psychotherapeutic process.

Resources of the nurse

Nursing education and continuing education specific to forensic mental health nursing is one method of increasing the resources of the nurse in the way of theoretical knowledge. While knowledge in the absence of clinical supervision may not develop into abilities and clinical competence, knowledge of personality disorders provides the foundation for understanding the patient's testing behaviour and for formulating realistic expectations of the patients. Knowing that patients who demonstrate characteristics of personality disorder are likely to experience difficulty trusting, and that personality disorder predisposes the patient to treatment resistance (Preston 2000), the nurse can realistically expect that:

- o *they will be tested.* Patients with traits of personality disorders are likely to test nurses before trusting them. They are likely to test to determine if the nurse will give them choices or will use power to force them, as well as testing to determine nurses' willingness and ability to help before trusting them.

o *there will be ruptures in the therapeutic relationship.* Patients' histories of disruptive relationships may manifest in the therapeutic relationship.

o *boundary issues will be an aspect of treatment.* While it is a characteristic of antisocial personality disorder that the personal boundaries of others may not be respected, borderline personality disorder is often characterised by an inability to discern personal boundaries and by a sensitivity to changes in relationship boundaries.

o *patients may develop sexual expectations.* For the incarcerated forensic male patient the opportunity to interact on a social level with female nurses may be a seductive force when facing a lengthy incarceration, with limited opportunities to develop romantic relationships (Schafer 2000). (The author could find no equivalent study for female patients.)

o *progress will not be steadily progressive.* Rather it will be marked by periods of lapse (Prochaska, Norcross, and DiClemente 1994).

Fortunately, forensic mental health nurses do not work in isolation. Treatment teams are valuable resources to the nurse facing the challenges of working with patients who repeatedly break rules and test boundaries. Team meetings and case conferences present opportunities for the nurse to express reactions to patients' behaviours and to receive the support necessary to identify realistic expectations rather than to personalise the patients' behaviours.

Melia *et al.* (1999) developed a triumvirate model of delivering nursing care to patients with personality disorders. Basic to the model is a team of three nurses who work together to deliver nursing care. Two nurses interview the patient and then debrief with the third. No nurse fulfils the role of interviewer or debriefer continuously. Instead, they rotate through the positions. Although many treatment teams may not have the resources required to implement the triumvirate model of nursing, clinical supervision remains a necessity. While interpersonal skills or techniques can be demonstrated outside the context of the relationship, interpersonal competence can only be evaluated within the context of the relationship (Peplau 1989).

Understanding significant contextual factors

In addition to knowledge of personality disorders, an understanding of the significant contextual factors of the treatment environment is necessary to establish therapeutic boundaries and create a safe space sufficient for the psychotherapeutic process. The nurse unaware of the significant contextual factors may unknowingly violate boundaries.

Power, time, gender relations, regulations, learning, and the multiple roles of the nurse emerged as significant contextual factors in a study conducted in one forensic setting (Schafer 2000). Associated with each of these contextual factors are a host of potential boundary violations. Nurses need to be aware of how the contextual factors are being manifested in the therapeutic relationship, and what the patient experiences as a boundary violation. Such awareness is not easily achieved. Nurses may discover the walls that house the therapeutic process only after metaphorically making contact with them. Boundary maintenance requires that nurses recognise when they have made contact with a wall, repair any damage, and acquire sensitivity to the location of the walls in each therapeutic relationship.

Nurses may abuse power to fulfil personal needs (Gallop 1998). While clinical supervision guards against nurses abusing power, understanding both the patient's pathology as well as the significance of contextual factors, and having the ability to use that understanding to promote the patient's therapeutic interests facilitates the establishment and maintenance of therapeutic boundaries. The ability to apply the knowledge in the event of a clinical challenge, as in the clinical vignette below, is particularly important.

> When asked during an initial interview how he was adjusting to the treatment environment, a patient responded: 'I would rather hit people than look at them.' Which led to feelings of fear in the nurse. However, knowing that relationships characterised by inequitable power distribution might lead to feelings of vulnerability in the patient whereby the patient might attempt to re-create dynamics of previous relationships, the nurse decided to discuss the patient's comment openly. When asked if his comment applied to the nurse, the patient responded 'yes'. The patient agreed that he was considerably larger than the nurse and that the nurse did not pose a physical threat to him. When asked to explain how he was threatened by the nurse, he identified the inequitable power distribution in the relationship and the potential that what the nurse reported about their interactions could have a negative impact on his future. Together they negotiated that the nurse would share the progress notes recorded after each interview with the patient at the beginning of their next session. After their third session, the patient stated that he no longer felt the need to review the progress notes.

The nurse in this vignette created a safe place for the patient to explore his reaction to the nurse by demonstrating a willingness and ability to help. The actions taken by the nurse promoted the patient's identification with the nurse based on her ability to help, rather than on the need to overpower and avoid feelings of vulnerability.

Working with resistance

The patient's testing behaviour is most likely to escalate during times of vulnerability, such as when the patient feels coerced to participate in treatment programmes or to comply with regulations imposed by others in authority. However, as the Group for the Advancement of Psychiatry (1994) asserted, coercion and motivation are not mutually exclusive. Instead, the relationship between coercion and motivation is dynamic and a patient may feel varying degrees of both with dramatic shifts occurring. This view is consistent with contemporary conceptualisations of motivation as a dynamic relationship factor rather than solely a characteristic of the patient (Kennedy 2000; Miller and Rollnick 1991). Motivation as a relationship factor is indirectly influenced by the characteristics of the nurse, and is amenable to interventions.

Motivational interviewing (Miller and Rollnick 1991), collaborative relationships, feedback and immediacy are interventions consistent with conceptualisations of the therapeutic relationship aimed at decreasing treatment resistance and increasing trust and motivation.

Motivational interviewing

Motivational interviewing is a counselling approach for initiating behavioural change by helping clients to resolve ambivalence about change (Miller and Rollnick 1991). Miller and Rollnick (1991) emphasised the avoidance of confrontation that increases the patient's vulnerability, leads to power struggles, and increases the patient's resistance. Instead, they recommended strategies such as promoting patient choices, and the use of caring confrontation to reveal and develop discrepancies between the patient's desired behaviour or goals and current behaviour.

Preston and Murphy (1997) suggested that engagement of treatment-resistant patients was promoted by giving the patients a choice, and by supporting their efforts towards self-efficacy. Schafer (2000) found that movement – from feeling coerced to feeling motivated – was facilitated by 'being given a choice to "take it or leave it"; being assisted to consider the options or being asked "what do you have to lose?"; and gaining a sense of self-efficacy and having "control over feelings and thoughts".' (p.155). This finding provides further support for these recommended approaches.

Collaborative treatment plans

Testing behaviour is escalated when patients feel vulnerable, such as when they are being confronted and pressured to accept the view of experts. Logically, involving the patient in the development of treatment plans and contingencies is an approach consistent with the therapeutic interests of the patient and conceptualisations of the therapeutic relationship as a partnership (Peplau 1952). In a patient satisfaction survey, Ford, Sweeney and Farrington (1999) found considerable variation in the amount of involvement patients had in their care plans. While some patients were not aware of their care plans, others had been informed about them, but only two of the 37 participants in their study had copies of their care plans. It is not enough to inform patients of their treatment plans: if the therapeutic relationship is a partnership, then the treatment plan should be the result of a collaborative effort.

A treatment plan that is mutually established with the patient is based on a comprehensive assessment that identifies the patient's treatment needs, and includes the identification of treatment goals and the interventions to achieve these goals. Having clear shared objectives and interventions may enhance the therapeutic relationship by increasing the patient's ability to trust the nurse, decrease feelings of vulnerability associated with the therapeutic relationship, and, as Freeman and Reinecke (1995) and Preston (2000) assert, decrease treatment resistance. A participant in a recent study (Schafer 2000) described not knowing the objectives or direction of the relationship as demeaning and analogous to being a turtle with a hare sitting on its back holding a carrot on a ten-foot pole out in front. While the hare knows what the turtle is aiming for, that information is not shared and the turtle is expected to follow blindly. A treatment plan that is developed collaboratively has the potential to reduce both the feelings of vulnerability experienced by the forensic patient and the associated testing behaviour.

In addition to reducing the vulnerability that the forensic patient experiences in the therapeutic relationship, treatment goals provide direction in the relationship and provide a means for patients to monitor their progress, thereby enhancing a sense of self-efficacy. Furthermore, treatment goals provide the foundation for providing the patient with feedback on their progress, and to examine the effectiveness of the treatment plan.

Feedback and immediacy
Providing the patient with feedback or using immediacy requires that the nurse is open, honest, and direct. Immediacy is sometimes equated with a here-and-now focus. Two other forms of immediacy also warrant mentioning: (1) immediacy related to the nurse's disclosure of personal reactions to the patient's behaviour, and (2) relationship immediacy, whereby the development of the relationship is explored (Egan 1990). The potential effectiveness of immediacy may be lost if the context of the relationship is not considered. Disclosing personal reactions may create the potential to reinforce distorted forms of caring in the therapeutic relationship as in the following clinical vignette.

A patient and two nurses working the same shift rotation had developed what the nurses described as a good relationship. They described the patient as always polite and grateful for any assistance they offered him. The patient typically presented himself as vulnerable and revealed his gratitude in his written work. He acknowledged noting the facial expression of the nurses when he shared his written work with them. Perceiving that the nurses approved and appreciated his written work, he continued to express his gratitude and later expressed affection through his writing. On one occasion the nurses asked the patient to return an unauthorised item he had in his possession. The patient felt outraged and betrayed, and was verbally abusive to the nurses. The nurses were shocked, and questioned the patient's suitability for treatment since he had experienced boundary issues before. They wondered if they should share with him how they had been shocked, hurt and disappointed by his behaviour.

The patient in this situation appeared to be caring for, or meeting the expectations of, the nurses as he perceived them. In return, he expected not to be challenged. To share with the patient that they were shocked by his behaviour and found themselves questioning his suitability for treatment without consideration of the development of the entire relationship may reinforce a distorted form of caring. The patient, being informed that he had violated the covertly established relationship agreement, is likely to feel a need to justify his reaction, feel rejected, and withdraw, knowing all along that he was likely to be misunderstood in the end. Ideally, the potential for a distorted form of caring is identified early. The patient may have been asked to clarify his intentions of repeatedly expressing his gratitude, while the nurses explored their reactions and questioned if they were perpetuating the interaction pattern. In this situation, relationship immediacy is more appropriate than the nurses' disclosure of personal reactions to the patient.

Providing patients with feedback on their progress towards treatment goals keeps them informed, invites them to be partners in the therapeutic process, and reduces treatment-related resistance (Preston 2000). In a study addressing therapeutic relationships in the forensic setting (Schafer 2000), receiving specific feedback was associated with therapist characteristics of being 'direct', 'open', and 'honest', and reflected the nurse's commitment to the participants. However, for participants in the same study, vague or non-specific positive feedback was reason for suspicion. Participants worried that they were not receiving meaningful feedback that would ultimately help them stay out of jail. Providing patients with specific feedback promotes a sense of control in patients that reduces the vulnerability patients may feel, and subsequently reduces the patient's needs for defensive reactions.

The following vignette illustrates how a treatment team incorporated many of the aforementioned interventions to reduce treatment resistance and establish therapeutic relationships with a patient who had previously failed to complete the treatment programme successfully.

It was Dave's second admission to the treatment programme. Although he had completed many of the assignments and stayed for the duration, he was described as not completing the programme. Themes of power and control that had dominated his initial admission had not been addressed. In fact, the treatment team was able to identify a number of ways in which they had potentiated these themes and failed to intervene effectively with Dave.

Upon his second admission, Dave quickly attempted to re-establish patterns of power and control in his interactions both with staff and other patients. The nurse assigned as Dave's primary therapist negotiated a treatment plan with Dave that identified issues of power and control. Dave was initially defensive, as it was not until the end of his first admission that the treatment team had shared with him concern about his controlling behaviour. The treatment team discussed with Dave the course of treatment during his prior admission. Ways in which the treatment team had perpetuated the controlling behaviour (which was later cited as the reason for his not successfully completing the programme) were identified. For example, the treatment team acknowledged that by authorising Dave to manage the unit cleaning supplies and store them in his room they reinforced this controlling behaviour. The treatment team avoided power struggles by providing Dave with choices and following through with consequences. Instead of repeatedly demanding that Dave complete an autobiography within a specific timeframe, as the treatment team had done during his previous admission, the expectation that Dave would complete an autobiography was clearly communicated to Dave. When he did not meet this expectation he was advised that his failure to meet the expectation would be reflected in his final treatment summary. Additionally, Dave was frequently provided with feedback on his behaviour. If he failed to decrease inappropriate behaviour, such as engaging in horseplay with co-patients to relieve his boredom, he was asked to complete a behaviour cycle and present it to his treatment group. If he was unwilling to complete the behavioural cycle behaviours affecting the group were brought to the treatment group.

Two months into the treatment program, Dave maintained that he was not going to change all the inappropriate behaviour that the treatment team identified. However, he was following through with treatment expectations. Acknowledging how the treatment team contributed to patterns of control during his previous admission and avoiding power struggles with Dave appeared to be instrumental in enhancing his engagement in treatment. Despite his verbalisations that he would not be changing the inappropriate behaviour he received feedback on, these behaviours decreased as treatment progressed.

FUTURE DIRECTIONS

It has been argued here that a tendency to view the pathology of patients described as personality disordered as a threat to therapeutic integrity exists in forensic mental health nursing, and that this tendency is not consistent with the conceptualisation of the therapeutic relationship in nursing. Instead, viewing the patient's pathology as a threat is consistent with views of the patient as bad and inspires interventions to manage or punish the patient and maintain institutional order, rather than to promote the therapeutic interests of the patient. Personality disorder, like any mental illness, is a factor that nurses must be responsive to if they are going to intervene effectively. The inadequate preparation of nurses and other mental health professionals to intervene effectively with forensic patients who exhibit traits of personality disorders is currently recognised (Shimmin and Storey 2000). Also recognised is the need for nurses, even in the face of extreme acting out behaviour, to intervene in ways that preserve the therapeutic relationship (Mason 2000c). Emerging in response to these realisations is a renewed effort to establish frameworks of forensic mental health nursing competencies, as described elsewhere in this text. Models of delivering nursing care in the forensic environment (Melia *et al.* 1999), as well as forensic nursing graduate programmes and diploma and undergraduate courses specific to forensic nursing (Forensic Nursing Education 1999) are also emerging.

Clinical supervision is a necessity. The competencies of mental health nurses are largely dependent on the scope and depth of their knowledge and the clinical areas for which clinical supervision has been provided (Peplau 1989). Furthermore, nursing interventions that demonstrate an impact on the patient's behaviour representative of the patient's pathology need to be identified. Clearly, forensic mental health nursing research is required, first to identify effective interventions and subsequently to identify necessary competencies of forensic mental health nursing. Considering the positive relationship between therapeutic alliance (Horvath and Luborsky 1993) and treatment outcome in psychotherapy in general, and specifically in correctional programmes (Nicholaichuk, Templeman and Gu 1998), establishing therapeutic alliance appears to be a necessary competency for forensic mental health nurses, even with patients who constantly break rules and test boundaries. Consequently, nursing interventions must promote the therapeutic relationship. Intervening with those patients who present forensic mental health nurses with one of their greatest challenges requires that forensic mental health nurses possess adequate personal and professional resources. Facing a clinical challenge is stressful and threatening when resources are not adequate to respond to the challenge. However, facing a clinical challenge can be energising for the nurse with the necessary resources to respond.

CHAPTER 5

Using Psychoeducational Interventions Within an Integrated Psychological Approach to Forensic Mental Health and Social Care

Dennis Cross and Stephan D. Kirby

INTRODUCTION

This chapter focuses on the management of educational interventions for users of forensic mental health and social care services and their families. The application of these educational interventions is proposed within a framework of integrated psychological approaches for the treatment of psychosis relating to offending behaviour. The aim of the chapter is to encourage forensic mental health and social care practitioners to utilise the knowledge and skills in teaching and learning that they have normally acquired during their preparatory training and further developed during post-qualification professional development programmes. The focus of these programmes is frequently related to the supervision of students, but related theory and experience can be readily applied to patient and carer education for those with relevant grounding in forensic health and social care. In addition, some writers in the field of psychoeducation argue that practitioners will require further training in psychosocial interventions to implement this approach successfully.

Fadden (1998) points out that the training of practitioners in psychosocial interventions is a very important factor in relation to whether interventions are successful or not. Those studies where practitioners delivering the interventions did not receive specialist training were not successful (McCreadie *et al.* 1991; Vaughan *et al.* 1992) whereas those who received training, and in particular where close supervision monitored adherence to the treatment programme was in place, were highly successful (Brooker *et al*. 1994; McFarlane, Lukens and Link 1995; Randolph, Eth and Glynn 1994). Studies by Brooker *et al*. (1994) and McFarlane *et al*. (1995) demonstrate that mental health practitioners can be trained in family interventions, and that these interventions can be delivered in routine clinical practice settings, but that careful training and supervision are required for success.

Solomon (1996) states that psychoeducational interventions combine educational and therapeutic objectives, offering didactic material about the ill relative's disorder and therapeutic strategies to enhance the family's communication and coping skills with the goal of reducing the patient's rate of relapse. However, the most recent development of family education differs from psychoeducation in that its primary goals are didactic and supportive rather than therapeutic. Interventions are focused upon improving family members' quality of life by reducing stress and burden, and only secondarily on benefiting the ill relative. In the forensic mental health and social care setting, psychoeducational interventions are focused mainly on functioning and attitudes, thereby improving the quality of life for patients. Secondly, there is a need to help relatives and friends to cope with difficult situations and support the patient in their care programmes.

Here, we are attempting to provide an approach that is readily available to the people who are in urgent need of help, but we do have some cautions. The educational interventions are one part of an integrated psychological approach, and we must strongly recommend that they are only carried out within the context of a multidisciplinary team approach to forensic health and social care. Furthermore, as the proposed educational interventions will be very challenging owing to the nature of the client-group, the practitioners will require high-quality clinical supervision throughout their application to practice.

Further problems and barriers to the implementation of psychoeducation, as with other forms of patient education, include the fact that many health and social care practitioners have, in the past, been traditionally ill prepared to teach (Redman 1971; Schoenrich 1976). What they did teach was often poorly understood and no checks or evaluations were built into the patient education programmes (Stanley *et al*. 1984). In recent years, teaching and learning components have been included in nursing, social work and occupational therapy programmes. This has recently provided many practitioners with skills and knowledge in teaching methods and educational theory. However, a further barrier may be that of giving conflicting information because of the lack of standardised materials. Patient education has also not been given a high priority in budgetary terms, even though it could be argued that giving insufficient information increases non-adherence with medical treatment and care resulting in additional pathology (Ley 1988). Keeping patients and their families well informed and increasing self-management of mental health problems can be very cost-effective as well as beneficial to their quality of life in forensic health and social care settings.

WHAT IS THE PURPOSE OF PSYCHOEDUCATION?

Psychoeducation can be seen as very much part of health education and mental health promotion. It addresses those who already have established serious mental health problems and therefore take on the role of 'patient' for a period of time. In forensic mental health and social care this may be temporary but is usually long term with intermittent periods of ill health and wellness. With this client group it is not necessarily the duration of the illness that is the trouble, but the severity of the mental health problems and the resultant impact this has on interpersonal behaviours.

Psychoeducation has been used successfully with families of patients with mental health problems over the last 20 years. Modification of these family-centred models is proposed by the authors for use with mentally disordered offenders to have a positive impact upon the patient's functioning and attitudes. The main differences between other forms of health education and psychoeducation relate to attitudinal and motivational issues. Patients with severe mental health problems in forensic settings are sometimes more vulnerable as a result of their mental health problems, and can be more dependent on and passive towards health and social care practitioners. This does vary and the degree of dependency and passivity often fluctuates throughout patients' experiences of forensic health and social care.

Psychoeducation has been defined by Goldman and Quinn (1988) as the education or training of a person with a psychiatric disorder in subject areas that serve the goal of treatment and rehabilitation. The main purpose of psychoeducation is to combat the shame, guilt and mistrust suffered by people treated in forensic health and social care settings, so that patients and their carers can seek help without the fear of being labelled or feeling a failure. Educating patients and their carers (friends and relatives) about mental illness and the treatment of mental health problems should be used within an integrated psychological approach to care that is underpinned by the creation of a more positive climate where it is acceptable to talk about feelings, emotions and problems. For example, Hogarty *et al.* (1991) consider that educating patients and their carers about medication, its uses and its side-effects may contribute towards improved adherence to prescriptions.

In addition, Hayes and Gnatt (1992) argue that psychoeducation has been described by all its providers as a model that empowers. For families, psychoeducation provides a format that helps them move beyond shame and stigma, to develop the skills and knowledge to meet professionals on an equal footing, and to expect respect and support for their ill family members. It also gives families specific management techniques that might help them to be useful as well as caring to the patient in their midst. For patients, it appears that psychoeducation provides a sense of dignity and self-esteem as practitioners trust them with information and place the tools for self-care in their hands. It asks patients to share in their treatment, instead of being passive recipients or adversaries. The knowledge and skills learned in the psychoeducation programme clarifies for patients the understanding of the parameters of their mental health problems. This awareness empowers patients to become who they are, to be more than a 'mentally disordered offender' or a 'schizophrenic'; to be a person with problems who faces the same life tasks as everyone else.

PSYCHOEDUCATION WITHIN AN INTEGRATED PSYCHOLOGICAL APPROACH TO CARE

Researchers (Goldman and Quinn 1988; Viggiani 1997) are agreed on the need to combine a series of elements, as nuclear components of mental health and social care intervention. These elements relate to the integrated psychological approach, among which are:

o *engagement*: where treatment is tailored to patients' needs and optimal level of independence; collaboration in the process is negotiated and work is focused upon the patients' preferences

o *self-management of the illness*: where patients' abilities are supported to supervise and manage their own disorder and prepare them to take on a central role in the long term

o *rehabilitation*: where reconstruction of patients' functional abilities and mitigation of incapacity is addressed through helping patients to identify resources and increase adaptive behaviours

o *environmental support*: where collaboration with relatives is developed through psychoeducational interventions.

Viggiani (1997) discusses the implementation of family education programmes that were implemented within an integrated psychological approach by Goldman and Quinn (1988) and Harmon and Tratnack (1992). These programmes utilised both structured and experiential approaches. In both programmes, the 'learners' were suffering with serious mental health problems. These psychoeducational programmes were evaluated as successful when the participants and their carers reported a significant increase in knowledge of their 'illness', their mental health problems and the resources available to them. These studies were concerned with improving the overall treatment of mental illness, particularly schizophrenia, and have important implications for forensic mental health and social care practice.

Hill and Shepherd (2000) state that central to the notion of psychoeducation is the belief that the delivery of knowledge can have a positive effect upon behaviour and mental state. They suggest that psychoeducation programmes can be aimed both at carers and at individuals with serious mental health problems. Much of the emphasis with the latter group is centred on the principles of self-management of their mental health care. In forensic health and social care, working with individuals with serious mental health problems will probably involve the structured method of delivery, but the importance of involvement of carers should be acknowledged. A most important issue raised by these authors is that psychoeducational processes need to have the full backing and co-operation of all involved to be successful. Furthermore, they need to be part of and integrated into a long-term management strategy.

However, in spite of the recognition that schizophrenia results from several factors and should therefore be approached in a multidimensional way, Fernandez et al. (1999) argue that integrated treatment models have been very little used. These authors consider that the time is now right to remedy this situation because of a growing consensus on the necessity to combine and integrate the different therapeutic procedures to cover all the needs presented by people with serious mental health problems.

A number of research studies have supported the value of family psychoeducation and argue that the approach has made a significant impact upon people with serious mental health problems and their carers by providing support, information and management strategies (Brooker et al. 1994; McFarlane 1994; Randolph et al. 1994). These psychoeducational programmes have helped people with serious mental health problems and their families to manage their lives without frequent hospitalisations. It is not unreasonable to suggest that psychoeducational interventions could also be helpful within a therapeutic approach to forensic mental health and social care. Users of forensic mental health and social care services present further challenges owing to the legal restrictions that have been placed upon them, their offending behaviour and sometimes low literacy skills. However, if one of the main purposes of psychoeducation is to combat stigma, then these patients are most at risk and will also require educational strategies to manage their lives more positively. These psychoeducational interventions can be helpful not only for those in forensic settings who are preparing for discharge back to the community, but also for others who require long-term care in a secure environment. In both settings, the patients may be helped to take more responsibility for their own care and to live more meaningful lives.

DESIGNING PSYCHOEDUCATIONAL PROGRAMMES

Psychoeducation involves the practitioner working in a collaborative relationship with the person with mental health problems, and sometimes their family. This implies that all parties have an active role to play in the development of new understandings and coping methods. These interventions are characteristically open and honest within the confines of a professional relationship underpinned by a therapeutic alliance. The practitioner needs to be clear about the boundaries of the relationships within this therapeutic alliance, including rules of confidentiality and duty of care.

Engagement within this kind of collaborative therapeutic alliance can be threatening to all parties concerned. People with mental health problems in forensic services have often had little active involvement in their own care. For some patients and their families this will be a welcome and refreshing change, but for others the increased responsibility can be quite daunting and unwelcome. Many patients within forensic mental health and social care settings will feel quite hopeless about the prospect of change, whilst others will be weighed down with low motivation. The patients' and families' abilities to participate in the psychoeducational interventions will need to guide the pace of the process. If individuals who are being treated in forensic health and social care settings are not able to participate in the psychoeducational activities or willing to make decisions about their lives, it will be very difficult to proceed.

MOTIVATING PATIENTS AND THEIR FAMILIES

French (1994) states that 'motivation' is a word that essentially means 'reasons for behaviour'. He goes on to say that the fundamental assumption from this is that every piece of human behaviour is carried out for a particular reason. A study of motivation can help the practitioner to carry out two basic skills that begins with an assessment of the patient's needs and motives. The second skill is to provide reasons for others to do particular things, to incite action. Practitioners in forensic mental health and social care settings must encourage, provide incentives and give reasons for the behaviour expected from the patient. In order to motivate patients in forensic settings practitioners must be able to identify an appropriate type of motivation and then set up the motivational condition that is likely to bring about the required behaviour. When using psychoeducational interventions, the programme itself should be intrinsically motivating in that the person should find it interesting in itself with good learning materials and well thought-out activities. This type of intrinsic motivation gets patients to join in because of enjoyment, or just for the fun of it.

In extrinsic motivation theories (Hull 1943; Skinner 1953) the motivating factor is not part of the action taken, but on completion of the activity something is gained or some desirable goal is achieved. The goal is usually set in the future and in the forensic setting is often set in behavioural terms. When the goal is stated, a model is adopted that envisages the patient or the family moving from an unacceptable state of affairs on a journey of change toward the goal. Some goals for patients and their families in forensic mental health and social care settings are by their nature difficult or impossible to achieve. Therefore, goal-setting should be realistic and attainable, and there may well be the need to set intermediate goals, in a step-by-step approach. Sometimes, the practitioners set goals, but it is more acceptable that they are identified in a therapeutic alliance between practitioner, patient and family. Patients sometimes accept goals that are set by practitioners, but more often they are perceived to be an imposition upon them.

To develop motivation in forensic settings the practitioner, patient and the family should (adapted from French 1994, p.219):

o work together to identify the desired behaviour

o agree realistic and appropriate goals

o agree intermediate goals if necessary

o identify appropriate motivating factors

o select and use social skills that will set up the motivating conditions

o evaluate the effects of motivational action together, and adapt.

Harmon and Tratnack (1992) suggest that, when designing psychoeducational programmes for people with serious mental health problems, a didactic method should be used. The information should be conveyed in a non-threatening, non-confrontational manner. The length of the lecture must be adjusted to the participants. These authors found 30 minutes to be the patient's limit of concentration. However, some educators would argue that this teacher-centred method is not designed to meet individual needs and could be criticised on the grounds that it is difficult to see how the patient's experience can contribute to the learning process. This didactic approach to learning is underpinned by the behaviourist viewpoint that suggests that the educator is able to predict what the student will learn in response to a given situation. There are other educational theorists who would propose a more humanistic approach to psychoeducation in which the patient is able to contribute to their own learning activities. In addition, other cognitive theorists describe a process by which problem-solving is central to the educational strategies and that this could also be incorporated into the psychoeducational process. However, the authors may have proposed this teacher-centred method because of the potentially threatening situations that people with serious mental health problems could find by participating in a more active way. No matter how much we may agree or disagree with the various learning and teaching approaches there will be a need to have, at least in part, a humanistic orientation.

Rogers (1983) advocates that in order to achieve true self-actualisation we need to help individuals to achieve unconditional positive self-regard. This he does because of his belief that the incompatibility of an individual's true feelings with those of the conditions of worth placed on them is a major source of maladjustment. This may seem to be a courageous ideal for patients in forensic health and social care settings, and also for their practitioners. Although unconditional positive self-regard may possibly be achieved in some areas of a patient's life in forensic health and social care settings, it is difficult and challenging to understand how this can be achieved in a more generalised sense. In its pure form, as with many other theories, the Rogerian concept of education, namely learning that fulfils totally the individual's need and does not place restraints upon them, can seem a difficult and almost impossible model to achieve within these settings.

Harmon and Tratnack (1992) further advocate the use of various teaching methods to reinforce and hold the person's interest, such as flip charts, whiteboards, handouts, and checklists. However, to achieve unconditional positive regard, at least in part, learning can be negotiated with patients and carers, learning contracts can be drawn together, individual tutorials can be arranged and pastoral support given. Experiential methods can play an important part and can include buzz groups or other group methods. On the other hand, there may be a need to promote conditional positive regard in some areas of the patient's lived experience in forensic health and social care settings. Attempting to achieve behavioural goals, completing assessments and formal teaching methods may all lead to the conditions of others being placed upon the individual. Positive self-regard can be achieved from the acquisition of group values from either influential individuals or from the expectations and rules of societies and organisations. These processes must be monitored and dealt with by those who facilitate psychoeducational interventions in forensic health and social care.

Harmon and Tratnack remind psychoeducational programme designers:

o to explain knowledge in plain English, in a way that is compatible with the patients' or carers' backgrounds, excluding jargon

o to use good humour

o to provide break times – after every 30 minutes of lecture, a 15-minute break can be provided, a good time to practise a skill in a very informal manner

o to recognise the importance of the setting, e.g. 'breaks' should be in a separate lounge area.

DEVELOPING COMPETENCE THROUGH PSYCHOEDUCATION

Education for the mentally disordered offender is currently in the process of becoming a standard part of the milieu. The family psychoeducational model has had a positive effect on the quality of life for those with serious and enduring mental health problems by providing useful information. However, Viggiani (1997) considers that independence and self-management still remain a goal for this group of people and that the forensic health and social care practitioner as an educator will need to consider the strategies from all other specialities to meet the challenge of teaching mentally disordered offenders. A conceptual framework of competency is, therefore, proposed as a psychoeducational strategy for forensic health and social care.

It is suggested that this competency development could be built upon the triple foundations of patients' and carers' knowledge, skills and attitudes towards the management of their mental health problems. For instance:

Knowledge and understanding of:

o mental health, wellness and illness; patients and their families want to know more about the nature of mental illness and know how to cope with it

o public attitudes, moral values, ignorance and stigma

o psychological aspects of impaired cognitive ability and distorted thinking

o medication, its uses and its side-effects

o social skills and inter-personal relations; patients may need to learn social skills to establish and keep human contact and to co-operate with others in an acceptable way

o empowerment and paternalism; patients and their families may need to learn self-management skills and self-application of therapy.

Skills to:

o combat shame, guilt and mistrust

o interact with members of the role set

o talk about feelings, emotions and problems

o counter hostility and ignorance

o self-manage their mental health problems to their highest potential

o identify resources

o create self-esteem and self-worth

o make early identification of risk and relapse signatures

o learn or relearn activities of daily living that include how to dress, wash and cook, and even to communicate with others.

Attitudes that result in:

o adherence to prescriptions

o willingness to collaborate in care with carers and practitioners

o a commitment to risk assessment and management

o a willingness to co-operate in their care.

A proposed model

Once an appropriate level of motivation is achieved, a four-stage model is proposed to develop a strategy to achieve appropriate competencies in patients and carers.

Stage 1: Reflecting on life experiences

This is a complex stage. Helping patients to identify learning from their life experiences can be a demanding task; it requires considerable sensitivity in teasing out information. Many of their experiences may have been unpleasant ones, and although learning may have taken place, there may still be unpleasant feelings attached to them. It is important that both patients and carers feel in control of this activity, which can seem of doubtful relevance or especially threatening. They must clearly understand its purpose and that they alone will determine what experiences will be discussed.

Some patients may discount their experiences and what they learned from them to such a degree that they do not recognise the experiences as valuable, or even that they took place. It takes some time before they realise that they are using skills and competencies in forensic health and social care settings. Providing patients and carers with the opportunity to identify useful learning experiences from life is a crucial stage in the process of the assessment of need. The idea is to help them become aware of the learning experiences they have had and, therefore, of the competencies they already possess, and how these competencies can be developed and extended.

The process of identifying and reflecting on life experiences is the first step in starting to identify competencies they have acquired. It can be a positive learning strategy, and can boost confidence; it is often made easier by group work and can itself help group cohesion.

In supporting this activity, the practitioner/facilitator should provide sufficient time for the process to take place. This may sound facile, but the urge is often to discount experience and move on quickly to the next activity. In doing this, much is missed. Since this is a time of reflection, it should be seen as a valid activity in itself. The facilitator should be non-judgemental, accepting and supportive, particularly focusing on positive experiences, whilst recognising and not discounting negative ones. They need to remain patient- or carer-centred, allowing them to develop the skills of recall and reflection, and therefore to recognise their own learning experiences (and eventually what they have learned from them).

Here are some techniques, which can be used with patients and carers. They could be encouraged to:

- o make a chronological list of events that have occurred in their life

- o identify good and bad times in their mental health care

- o do some sort of 'life-line' activity, possibly mapping out most recent events first and moving back to those in the past

- o use the life-line to organise things they have done or experienced under particular themes, e.g. relationships, communication, medication management, etc.

- o identify immediate experiences by keeping a reflective diary or journal

- o focus on experiences they have had

- o write a short autobiography

- o draw a bubble chart of their current activities

- o think and talk about situations in which they learned successfully and those in which they failed to learn; investigate the reasons, focusing on the features of the situation.

Stage 2: Identifying actual learning

Having identified experiences in which learning took place, it is then necessary to work towards identifying what this learning is. One way that patients and their families can achieve this is by writing freely about a particular experience. Initially this may be difficult for some, particularly those who did not develop this skill at school, or who have not used it for some time or whose cognitive skills are impeded by their mental health problems. So in conducting this activity practitioners/facilitators should:

- o be particularly aware of their supportive role

- o introduce the activity gently

- o allow individual privacy initially, but move towards gentle disclosure; this will help confidence building

Once patients and their families have an overview of what might be the areas worth investigating further they should look at these in more detail. When doing so, a combination of writing individually, in pairs and small groups is both supportive and productive. When writing about and discussing learning experiences, patients and their families should be encouraged to concentrate on these kinds of questions:

- What was the experience and which feelings were associated with it? This helps to release the full details of the experience.

- What knowledge was used?

- What skills were involved?

- Were any aspects of these useful in subsequent situations? Could any of them be applicable to future or long-term goals?

The purpose of this is to help them to identify what was learned, not simply to write extended accounts of the life and learning experience. In referring to life experiences, tasks or roles they have experienced, they may find it useful to:

- list exactly what was involved, e.g. what they did, responsibilities, etc.

- focus on the above and identify what was learned as a result; providing them with a selection of skills checklists may assist this.

Stage 3: Forming competence statements
The next stage involves forming competence statements. By this stage, patients and carers should have identified various skills, areas of knowledge or 'items' of learning specific to situations in the past. It now becomes important to begin to move towards rephrasing in terms that might be more generally applicable to future situations. The intention is to indicate the extent to which acquired learning might be transferable to other life situations. This involves translating the statements of skills, knowledge, attitudes or learning already listed into 'can do' statements.

The term competence is defined as a blend of skills, knowledge, aptitudes and attitudes which can be successfully applied, e.g. to complete a task or achieve a demonstrable goal. Competence statements are therefore statements of what a patient or member of their family can do as the result or 'outcome' of a learning process. They should refer to:

- knowledge used and acquired

- skills used and acquired

- aptitudes/attitudes where appropriate.

Stage 4: Developing a strategy

While defining the competencies gained from prior experience, patients and carers should be encouraged to develop a realistic psychoeducational strategy. The process of determining future goals should occur as soon as possible if they are to utilise this knowledge before it begins to fade. Once goals or intermediate goals are identified, this helps to:

o identify competencies required for progression

o guide their self-assessment in relation to intended goals; they are then able to identify and state 'strengths' as competencies possessed and 'weaknesses' as those needing development in order to progress

o influence the content of 'on-course psychoeducational' learning negotiated on the basis of weaknesses identified.

Helping patients to establish realistic goals may prove difficult. They may have little idea about what they want or need to learn, or may be unable to choose from the possibilities open to them. Any of the following approaches may help them to focus on some clear and realistic goals:

o Working individually or in small groups, ask them to write down any goal they might have and carefully identify the steps or strategies by which it might be achieved.

o Give them a range of options and ask them to eliminate the ones they do not wish to use, giving reasons why.

o Identify the knowledge, skills or attitudes required through experiential methods.

They should be provided with guidance and opportunities to obtain information about resources and knowledge, involving, for example:

o learning resources, people who can help, agencies, etc.

o discussions with members of the multidisciplinary team, other patients/clients, advocates and carers

o access to policies, procedures and standards of care

o open learning packages.

Newell (2000) states that effective goal-setting is defined by the patient or carer, and represents some significant change in the patient's or carer's well-being. Effective goals are realistic and are representative of improvements in other areas of the patient's or their families' life. Effective goal-setting involves allowing the patient, carer/family member/advocate and practitioner to agree the appropriateness of goals or sub-goals, and to agree when those goals have or have not been achieved. Effective goals will contain the attributes of the desired activity; frequency, duration, setting and other criteria.

ACHIEVING ADHERENCE TO PSYCHOEDUCATION PROGRAMMES

In order to achieve effective learning and growth in patients and carers health care 'professionals must have a fund of knowledge to impart and the ability to communicate, picking up verbal as well as non-verbal cues to identify appropriate times to provide information' (Macleod Clark 1983, p.25). Just giving information even when patients or carers seem receptive does not guarantee adherence. Becker (1974) provided five major influences that are seen to affect the level of motivation. Within the context of this text, Becker's Health Belief Model has been utilised within the forensic health and social setting, thus further demonstrating its universal applicability:

- The individual patient must believe that he or she is susceptible to mental health problems.

- The individual patient must believe that these acknowledged mental health problems will have serious consequences. These consequences relate to offending behaviour, involving danger to the public and self.

- The individual patient must believe that action to counter the mental health problems will be effective.

- To be motivated, the individual patient must believe that action is possible: barriers to taking action must not be perceived as too great.

- Even when all four criteria described above have been fulfilled, there often still needs to be a cue for action. Nurses, health professionals and advocates can normally provide a prompt or added persuasion for patients in forensic health and social care settings. For those who still maintain contact and links with the wider society this can also include relatives, advocates, friends and partners.

THE FACILITATOR'S COMPETENCIES IN PSYCHOEDUCATION

Vaughan and Badger (1995) point out that mentally disordered offenders are not a homogeneous group but that they do share certain commonalities. They propose that professionals working with this group need to develop some commonalities of approach even though their forms of training, professional identities and employing agencies may be very different. They discuss this approach under the headings of attitudes and values, knowledge and understanding, and skills.

The values are centred upon concepts such as user, consumer choice, partnership and empowerment. Working with the mentally disordered offender, even in the community, though depending upon co-operation and a sense of partnership, can never be a truly equal partnership. However, facing this inequality and disparity in power is an important starting point for anyone who becomes involved with working with this group of people. The knowledge and understanding relates to facts about psychiatry and the mental health system, and to the law and criminal justice system. The skills discussed by Vaughan and Badger (1995) centre on making relationships, which are at the heart of all forms of personal helping and form the bedrock of working with mentally disordered offenders.

Self-awareness is the key to working in this way as the practitioner's own responses to the client who may have committed serious offences is a major concern. Being aware of the possibility of being prejudiced against this client group to which many are hostile presents a great challenge. It is critical for the success of a psychoeducational approach that a therapeutic alliance between practitioner and patient is established. This is particularly important for a client group that may be very defensive owing to previous encounters in the forensic health and social care setting, or psychologically inaccessible because of their mental health problems.

In Chapter 12 of this book, Kirby and Cross propose a five-phase therapeutic alliance continuum, which has been designed to support and underpin care strategies. They state that the foundation work for this is the creation of a dynamic mutual learning environment that will allow the patient's experiences to be shared and understood within the context of mutual growth. This alliance for mental health care is depicted by a continuum from the patient's first contact with mental health services, to a state of improved self-management with increased levels of autonomy and engagement (appropriate to their environment) in preparation for eventual discharge. In order to achieve progression along this continuum Kirby and Cross propose the following phases (these are further described Chapter 12 and in Kirby 2001):

- survival

- recovery

- growth

- reconstruction

- reintegration.

In the main, patients and their families in forensic mental health and social care have to make some meaning out of what they discover about themselves and their environment. This is what gives them insight and the power to modify and change their lives so that the patient enjoys better mental health. Psychoeducation is used actively to help patients understand their present life in terms of their past experiences and the part their families have played. Gardner (1997) suggests that many psychotherapeutic approaches are formulated, more or less explicitly, around a narrative model: that is to say, our lives can be seen as lived stories and the process of psychological therapy as involving the telling, retelling, editing and exchanging of those stories.

The stories need to be heard by practitioners in forensic mental health and social care, and understood in terms of their own stories. The degree to which these stories are accommodating of others' experience will influence the subtle and not-so-subtle ways in which the practitioner prompts, edits and validates the patient's and family member's story. Thus, practitioners need to be sensitive to their own stories and the ways these may affect their patient's freedom to find their own voice.

The practitioners' stories operate at various levels. There are their own stories that may contain experiences similar to or very different from those of patients and their families, and which are usually grounded in a more recent historical context. The importance of being aware of personal stories and the ways they may act for, or against, the patient's interests is well understood in psychotherapy. In the psychoeducational approach, practitioners may need to look again at their own life stories and the ways of telling these is affected by one's current life context. In beginning a psychoeducational strategy with a problem, dilemma, diagnosis or pathology, there is an inherent danger of forcing a retrospective evaluation of a life constructed in terms of vulnerability, weakness and failure. If practitioners are sensitive to the way their retrospective evaluation may be influenced by their current life situation, they will be more likely to help patients and their families 'free up' their own perspectives on their pasts.

PRACTICAL APPLICATION

Vignette 1: Jenny's admission

Jenny is a 32-year-old admitted from a local prison where she was serving a custodial sentence. She has a history of schizophrenia with associated disturbed and aggressive behaviour. She was admitted to the medium secure unit following an incident where she set fire to her cell, endangering not only her own life but that of her cell mate. Upon assessment it was evident that this was in response to 'command hallucinations'. Prior to this incident she was noted, by the prison health care staff and visiting medium secure unit staff, to be withdrawn and had been seen to be talking to herself.

o *survival* – maintaining existence and surviving risk associated within critical times of acute mental distress

o *recovery* – developing an increasing level of functioning to allow the person to take more involvement and responsibility for their own mental health care.

On admission to the medium secure unit she commenced a programme of psychoeducation that addressed the survival and recovery phases of the therapeutic alliance. This was focused on learning about her new environment and the immediate management of her condition.

Vignette 2: David's continuing care

David is now 39 and has been in the medium secure unit for three years following a transfer from a high secure hospital where he had been since he 25. He has come to the medium secure unit to develop his practical rehabilitation skills, having had limited experience of the practical applicability of these in his previous hospital. At this point in time, there is no mention of him being discharged. During this phase David will be addressing his self-worth, confidence and social skills aspects of his life which are deemed to be integral to this practical rehabilitation preparation programme and are essential for any consideration for eventual discharge. These will focus on the growth and reconstruction phases of the continuum:

o *growth* – a time of increasing self-knowledge, greater social awareness and understanding relating to the person's mental health problems

o *reconstruction* – a time of personal change, where the person finds new ways to live and cope more effectively with their mental health problems through the development of new interpersonal skills and problem-solving approaches.

Vignette 3: Tony's rehabilitation

Tony is 36 and has been in the medium secure unit for nearly seven years with a history of psychosis and a serious assault on a female. In the time he has been within the service, his psychosis receded quickly once a beneficial psychopharmacological regime was found, and there has not been any indication of his previous violence towards females. In fact, he is very remorseful; and, at times over the years, he has been quite preoccupied with the severity of his index offence and the damage and impact it had upon his victim. He has been considered for discharge on a couple of occasions in the past, but never reached the point of actually leaving the rehabilitation ward as he has 'sabotaged' his rehabilitation regime with his feelings of guilt and desire not to be discharged for fear of recrimination and revenge from his victim's family.

He is now, once again, at the stage where discharge to a community residential accommodation is appropriate and a great deal of psychological work has gone into preparing Tony for this stage. By focusing on the reconstruction and reintegration phases of the continuum of therapeutic alliances the multidisciplinary team prepared a programme of psychoeducation. This addressed his coping abilities with his new (community) environment as well as dealing with any stigma and discrimination he may encounter and practical issues around his transition and transfer from secure service back into the community.

- o *reconstruction* – a time of personal change, where the person finds new ways to live and cope more effectively with their mental health problems through the development of new interpersonal skills and problem-solving approaches

- o *reintegration* – this is the final phase, when the person is able to demonstrate their full potential relating to self-management skills and optimum levels and methods of empowerment to safeguard their mental health and rejoin their social world.

CONCLUSIONS

Throughout this chapter, a strategy has been described to help practitioners engage and work with forensic service users who experience serious mental health problems and their families. This chapter argues for an educational approach in forensic mental health and social care and identifies methods that will be effective if the practitioner is able to work in a supportive multidisciplinary team where identified therapeutic approaches are integrated into a long-term plan. Practitioners are urged not to work in isolation: they need to be surrounded by team members who are willing to change and reflect upon their behaviours and assumptions.

Individuals with serious mental health problems in forensic mental health and social care settings can benefit from a psychoeducational approach that is integrated into such a therapeutic psychological framework. The authors acknowledge that there are many difficulties and challenges in working with this client group and their families using educational interventions. However, they consider that under the professional responsibility of high-quality clinical supervision many qualified forensic health and social care practitioners will be able to utilise their teaching and facilitative skills for the benefit of patients and their families.

The authors are aware of the danger of making sweeping generalisations about patients and of having inappropriate expectations of what can or cannot be achieved. Putting these educational ideas into practice will be an ongoing challenge and will need to be monitored and developed by teams.

Furthermore, engaging patients in treatment in forensic health and social care can be very difficult, for example those that have come from a prison regime may not view themselves as either needing or requiring treatment. Additionally, within high security forensic health care, engaging relatives can be very difficult. For instance, the relatives may have no wish to see the patient because of the criminal act in which they were involved or implicated; or the large physical distances and visiting arrangements within high security may not lend themselves to regular contact with relatives.

FUTURE DEVELOPMENTS

The future of psychoeducation lies in it being promoted and accepted as an integral part of a therapeutic process in which it is crucial for individuals and their support network to be able to design their own relapse prevention plans and strategies. These developments, for the clinical setting, would require a fundamental understanding and acknowledgement that psychoeducation provides a strategic tool that promotes and aids recovery and strengthens the coping abilities of our patients within the forensic setting.

Psychoeducation is not a treatment. It should be seen as part of a wider, integrated, approach to care; this should see psychoeducation as an ongoing process, being both a formal and informal part of the recovery process. This complements the notion of an integrated and dynamic mutual learning process as proposed in Chapter 12. Throughout the psychoeducation process, families will also (wherever feasible) need education regarding the nature of the illness, the range of treatments the patients will or could be offered, which agencies and personnel will be involved in the treatment process, and the likely or potential outcomes of the integrated treatment process. Families can be helped to understand how environments can maintain or aggravate symptoms, behaviour patterns and relapse signatures. The family should, therefore, be considered an important part of the collaborative therapeutic alliance treatment team. The contribution made by psychoeducation programmes in diminishing distress is determined by many factors, but chiefly by how well the information is understood by the patient and their family. To have maximum value, psychoeducation programmes must be developed where the information is accurate, is in a language accessible to the average person, and is sensitive to the person's beliefs. This can only be achieved by providing information in a meaningful way and presented in an appropriate manner.

In the past ten years or so, there has been increasing emphasis placed on the importance of psychoeducational work with both relatives of patients as well as patients with psychotic illness (Kingdon and Turkington 1994). Despite the evidence supporting the importance of psychoeducation to families, there has been relatively little research focused on the psychoeducational needs of patients that clinicians can use to guide their treatment approaches (Smith, Birchwood and Haddrell 1992). McGorry (1995) states that clinicians have been unable to see the potential value of psychoeducation to the patient, where it fits into the broader therapeutic approach, and, more fundamentally, how to do it in practice.

CHAPTER 6

Nursing Interventions and Future Directions with the Severely Mentally Ill

Paula Ewers and Paul Ikin

INTRODUCTION

This chapter will explore the development of psychosocial interventions (PSI) for the severely mentally ill. It will discuss the benefits of using PSI in a forensic setting for patients and staff, and for the wider organisation. It will then explore the concepts which underpin the PSI approach, the potential challenges to implementing this approach in a forensic setting, the research applications for forensic units, and a potential service model for implementing and integrating PSI. Finally, it will focus on education and training issues. To illustrate the above topics, the authors will draw on clinical case studies.

BACKGROUND

In psychiatric services in general, clients suffering from severe and enduring mental health problems potentially exercise the highest demand upon mental health services. Up to 70 per cent of the client population within high security services are likely to have a diagnosis of severe and enduring mental illness. Despite this, services across the board have been criticised for failing to give the needs of this client group sufficient priority (Sainsbury Centre for Mental Health 1997a). Recent official and media interest has focused on these services, largely because of a few well-publicised incidents in the community that have provoked a series of formal inquiries (Department of Health 1992; Ritchie, Donald and Lingham 1994). More general criticisms of services are found in other government-sponsored reviews such as the Reed Review (Department of Health and Home Office 1992). In-patient services have been a particular target for criticism. For example, in the report on the National Visit to acute psychiatric wards

(Sainsbury Centre for Mental Health 1997b), it was reported that hospital-based mental health nurses were poorly trained to meet the needs of this client group.

The overwhelming recommendation of these reports is that mental health services must become more systematic and focused in their delivery of care. There is agreement that effective assessment and treatment of these patients is of principal concern and should include the delivery of a range of psychosocial interventions adhering to sound case-management principles. Meeting the needs of the severely mentally ill is now a national priority and this is reflected in the new National Service Framework (Department of Health 1999a).

COGNITIVE BEHAVIOUR THERAPY AND PSYCHOSOCIAL INTERVENTIONS

Prior research has demonstrated that cognitive behaviour therapy (CBT) and psychosocial interventions (PSI) are beneficial in the management of schizophrenia (Wykes, Tarrier and Lewis 1998). Investigations into a broad range of programmes have shown improved outcomes for patients with serious mental illness in the community under controlled conditions. These intervention programmes involve detailed assessments of clients and their carers, education about schizophrenia, the utilisation of communication and problem-solving strategies to reduce stress, and specific cognitive-behavioural treatments designed to improve symptoms.

There has been extensive research focused on the influence of family interactions and the concept of 'expressed emotion' (EE). EE is a term used to describe hostility, criticism or emotional over-involvement that can occur between carers and patients with severe psychiatric disorders (Brown et al. 1962). High EE has been shown to have a solid association with the increased probability of relapse (Brown, Birley and Wing 1972). Studies involving the use of intervention to reduce EE in identified families have confirmed a consequent reduction in relapse rates, along with many other associated benefits for the patient and their carers (Barrowclough and Tarrier 1992).

A range of cognitive-behavioural interventions have also been investigated. They have been shown to be effective in the reduction of the symptoms of serious mental illness and their associated distress (Sellwood et al. 1994). The interventions have included the use of focusing and other strategies in the management of auditory hallucinations (Bentall, Kinderman and Kaney 1994; Chadwick and Birchwood 1994). Belief modification strategies have been focused on delusions (Chadwick and Lowe 1990). A number of small randomised controlled trials demonstrating the merit of this approach have been published (Garety et al. 1994; Tarrier 1992; Tarrier et al. 1990). Wykes et al. (1998) have shown the value of adding CBT to the routine care given to acute inpatients. A succession of larger-scale trials have been initiated, and initial results appear to be positive (Tarrier *et al.* 1993; Wykes *et al.* 1998).

Despite the overwhelming evidence, there has been a failure to influence psychiatric services. Although some excellent training programmes exist, these interventions are not widely available in routine practice. The benefits of these programmes are, therefore, applied almost exclusively to research participants or have been offered on a segmented basis. For this reason, further studies have examined training nurses to apply these treatments with their patients in the community, so that they have a better chance of becoming a part of standard practice (Wykes *et al.* 1998). The most notable of these is the Thorn Nurse Initiative, based at the University of Manchester and The Institute of Psychiatry. Diploma and degree-level training courses are provided that aim to train psychiatric nurses to provide such specialist care for people who have a serious mental illness (Gamble, Kidence and Leff 1994). One limitation of the Thorn scheme is that training is delivered away from the environment in which psychosocial interventions are carried out. This has created difficulties for many Thorn-trained nurses who have returned to institutions that have been poorly organised to make the best use of their skills.

The Sainsbury Centre for Mental Health (1997a) report contained a review of what training and education was needed for the mental health workforce. It stated that 'unless staff are educated, trained and developed to meet the needs of service users within the currently emerging models of care, services cannot work well or meet the challenges ahead'.

SECURE IN-PATIENT CARE

These initiatives are almost entirely aimed at improving the practice of community-based nurses in mainstream (i.e. non-forensic) services. Nevertheless, there is a real need to adapt this body of research and apply it to in-patient settings, particularly in secure services. Although there has been a move to retract institutional care for this client group with the modification of care in the community policies, there are still large numbers of people who spend appreciable amounts of time as in-patients or in residential facilities staffed by professional carers. Though the particular configuration of services may change, there are no grounds for assuming that this picture will alter significantly in the future.

Systematic psychological interventions are rarely provided within in-patient settings, and clients frequently complain about the inadequacy of the therapeutic environment (Lavender 1985). Several studies have examined EE as exhibited by staff in institutional settings, demonstrating that staff/patient relationships influence the course of schizophrenia (Moore, Ball and Kuipers 1992) and that benefits to patients, staff and the organisation might, therefore, be realised if interventions were implemented to improve staff/patient relationships and reduce environmental stress. A trial of cognitive-behavioural interventions with acute psychotic in-patients has shown the value of this approach in terms of faster and more complete recovery from psychotic episodes and a sustained reduction of symptomatology at follow-up (Wykes *et al.* 1998). Taken together, these observations indicate that substantial improvements in patient outcomes are likely to be achieved by the thorough and systematic implementation of psychosocial interventions in in-patient settings, and particularly in secure settings, where the clientele are invariably in-patients for some considerable time.

POTENTIAL BENEFITS OF USING PSYCHOSOCIAL INTERVENTIONS IN A FORENSIC SETTING

The provision of PSI within the forensic setting provides several potential benefits for patients, families, staff and the wider organisation. Many forensic patients have ongoing distressing residual symptoms that are medication resistant. Often these symptoms are linked to their index offence and contribute to the patient being an ongoing risk. For example, the first author worked with a young man called Paul. Paul had been admitted to the service after very seriously assaulting another man in a hostel. Paul had been convinced that this man wanted to harm him and that he had to do something to stop himself from being killed. Whilst in the unit, Paul continued to exhibit paranoia towards other young men. If anyone new was admitted to the ward, he immediately asked to be locked in his room and to be given PRN medication. He frequently complained of being bullied and was very distressed. He was prescribed various different combinations of medication, which did not seem to reduce his paranoia. His ongoing misperceptions of threat and his resistance to medication meant that the threat to his distress and potential risk to others was high.

The therapist worked with Paul in several ways. First of all, the therapist helped Paul to see the links between his thoughts, feelings and behaviour and helped Paul to develop some initial coping strategies to reduce his anxiety and arousal when he felt threatened. They looked at how Paul's own body language and interpersonal skills contributed to the problem (e.g. always giving cigarettes away, eyes down, hunched shoulders, looking vulnerable). This was helping to maintain the problem by serving to attract people who saw him as easy prey to get money and cigarettes from. This consistently reinforced the feelings that he was being bullied and inferior. To change this, the therapist, Paul and a male health care assistant carried out a series of video role-plays. This gave Paul the opportunity to see how he came across to others, and he practised appropriate assertiveness skills. These increased his confidence and improved his engagement with the therapist.

The therapist helped Paul to see where his beliefs about himself and others had developed (e.g. always the new kid at school, picked on by peers, etc.). He was enabled to begin challenging whether that was how people saw him now and to modify his beliefs about others; for instance, instead of automatically assuming a new patient was a threat, he would 'give them a chance' and attempt to get to know them.

By working with Paul in this way it was possible to demonstrate through repeated assessment that his distress had reduced considerably. This meant that he was far happier and enjoyed a better quality of life. Also, his paranoia was diminished, which meant that his risk to others was reduced. His symptoms were better controlled and trigger factors, which were identified through therapy, were made known to everyone involved in his care.

PSI has consistently been shown to reduce distress and symptomatology, and increase life quality for patients (Chadwick and Lowe 1990; Garety et al. 1994, Wykes et al. 1998). The above case study illustrates that not only is PSI needed as a treatment option for this client group, but that for forensic patients it can also contribute significantly to risk assessment and case management. By identifying the patient's early warning signs of relapse, it is possible to prevent relapse or shorten its duration (Wykes et al. 1998). This, again, not only contributes to a reduction in distress for the individual and family, but can also reduce overall risk by reducing the occurrence of symptoms associated with violence to self and others. Another advantage of implementing PSI in a forensic setting is the fact that, generally speaking, the patient's stay is much longer than in an acute in-patient setting. This provides the opportunity to work closely with the patient and family over a longer period of time providing more opportunity to enable them to make progress. This can enhance the likelihood of discharge.

It has been demonstrated that having a relative with schizophrenia can create exceptional stresses within a family (Barrowclough and Tarrier 1992). This increased stress can often demonstrate itself through EE (Brown et al. 1962). This involves families or individuals displaying criticism, hostility and/or emotional involvement (Barrowclough and Tarrier 1992). These aspects often arise out of a family struggling to make sense of and live with a complex and demanding illness. An example of this is where a family member, who wants the best for their recently diagnosed 19-year-old daughter, nags and criticises her when she won't get up in the morning, thinking that this will help to restore a more 'normal' life to her. However, as people with schizophrenia are sensitive to stress, anything that increases this can lead to increased symptomatology and, therefore, relapse. Consequently, in this situation it is quite likely that the relative will actually contribute to an escalation in the individual's symptoms.

This is why family intervention programmes have been set up: to equip families with the additional knowledge and skills required to live with this illness.

These programmes have been shown to reduce the burden of caring, the levels of minor psychiatric morbidity for carers (Barrowclough and Tarrier 1992; Falloon, Boyd and McGill 1985) and relapse rates for patients. It could be argued that these programmes are essential for families of forensic patients. Not only do these families face exceptional stresses, they also have to deal with the stigma and isolation which can arise from having a son or daughter who not only has schizophrenia, but who often has committed a violent act which the newspapers and community are only too aware of. If the violent act has involved a family member there are additional issues to work with.

Paul's family were referred to the therapist owing to his frequent complaints about bullying. His mother was understandably concerned and she would get very distressed making repeated telephone calls and visits to the clinic, which seemed to contribute to and maintain both her stress and Paul's belief in his paranoia.

Although the family's knowledge of the illness was quite good, it was often not applied to their son's situation. The therapist helped the family to explore their situation and to discover that they were not the cause of their son's problems. This was done primarily by explaining the stress-vulnerability model – for example, in the development of schizophrenia there is a biological disposition that is exacerbated by stress. This was particularly important for Paul's mum, as it became clear during the therapy that she felt totally responsible for his illness and index offence. Her over-involvement was her way of trying to compensate for this and make everything all right for him. This feeling of total responsibility often leads to feelings of stress, and she sacrificed her own life (no time for hobbies, etc.). By helping her to see that it was not all her responsibility or her fault and also helping her to understand her son's symptoms more clearly she was able to step back more. This enabled her to begin to develop her own life again. The repeated assessment measure showed that her stress had decreased and quality of life had improved. She also said that she felt less alone and isolated.

Recently, it has been suggested that staff who spend considerable time with patients (e.g. nurses) can have similar difficulties and reactions to those of families (Ewers 1999). Working with these patients over a long period can often lead to frustration as staff cannot see change. This is often because they understand change in 'black-and-white' terms (e.g. patients are either completely well or they are ill). This can produce unrealistic expectations, which compounds the sense of pessimism in staff (Moore *et al.* 1992). Negative symptoms can be misinterpreted as laziness and result in staff criticism and nagging towards patients. All staff, like families, need training and education to make sense of the illness and to enable them to learn ways of coping and helping patients to cope. PSI training can provide staff with an effective framework. It helps to increase the understanding of what symptoms are, how they are maintained and how to help patients cope with them. Equipping staff with the skills necessary to enable them to reduce patient distress can enhance their feelings of satisfaction. It helps them to feel useful, and as if they have made a difference. A small study by Ewers (1999) showed that equipping staff with a PSI framework in a forensic setting not only increased knowledge levels but also reduced 'burn-out' in staff. This may be because one aspect of burn-out is reduced, that of a lack of personal achievement. By increasing the ability to work effectively, a sense of personal achievement will ensue. Since burn-out has been linked to greater sickness and absence rates (Chirboga and Bailey 1986), then anything that can reduce this is clearly of financial benefit to the wider organisation (Duquette, Sandhu and Beaudet 1994).

Further benefits to the organisation from PSI are the reduction in relapse rates and hospital days (Wykes *et al.* 1998). This reduces the overall treatment costs (Cardin, McGill and Falloon 1986; Wykes *et al.* 1998).

ROLE CONFLICT

Nursing care in secure settings has been beset by difficulties for nursing staff relating to the problems of trying to maintain balance. The demands of maintaining a secure environment and the imposition of the restrictive aspects of managing mentally disordered offenders (e.g. locking doors) can often seem to be in conflict with the delivery of therapeutic interventions that often encourage individuals to pursue self actualisation (Department of Health 1992). Indeed, much of a nurse's activity can, at times, involve the widespread use of risk assessments, which are often being used to address organisational requirements rather than individual or clinical needs. This can include such practices as seclusion (Alty and Mason 1994). The contradictions felt by nurses in such circumstances can lead to role conflict or ambiguity, and can result in staff adopting a custodial approach to care. This is because it is often seen to be the way of least difficulty or confrontation.

To deliver effective nursing intervention to patients who are experiencing high levels of psychiatric or emotional distress can place nurses in situations of great risk. At the same time, not doing so can hinder or obstruct the programme of the individual, leading to longer hospitalisation and often more intense psychiatric difficulties. In turn, this can lead to feelings of hopelessness and helplessness amongst hospital inhabitants, whether they are staff or patients. However, it is inevitable that the delivery of evidence-based practice will necessitate the use of risk assessment in secure environments. This is necessary to minimise the risk of harm to patient and others. Nevertheless, it often facilitates the development of coping systems, leading to a long-term improvement in the mental and behavioural presentation of the sufferer. This in turn contributes to a reduced level of risk: described as a 'Risk Management Cycle' (Mason and Chandley 1999).

A MODEL OF PSYCHOSOCIAL INTERVENTION

In order to cascade the skills and philosophy used with the PSI model it was decided to train one person who would act as an agent of change. This person completed MSc training in CBT for individuals and families with psychoses. Their title was given as *nurse therapist*. This was politically advantageous because the vast majority of the work force are nurses, and it was felt that this title and role would engender a sense of ownership among the nurses. This person was freed from ward responsibilities and was able to concentrate on four main components:

o providing, via referral, specialist CBT for patients and their families

o setting up and providing education and training for staff

o providing supervision, so that staff could utilise CBT and PSI in a safe and competent manner whilst gaining confidence

o carrying out research in this field.

By working with patients and their families the nurse therapist was able to demonstrate, through the use of validated assessment tools, that CBT could effectively reduce people's distress and enhance their symptom management. This increased the clinical team's confidence in this way of working. The nurse therapist also spent a lot of time with key people (e.g. senior nurses, influential ward members and other members of the multidisciplinary team) selling this model and emphasising that this wouldn't replace anybody but would complement the current way of working.

The next stage was to develop the knowledge and skills of the in-patient staff with the objective that eventually all staff involved in patient care could offer all patients basic interventions using validated assessments and fundamental PSI interventions to enhance coping strategies. More complex interventions were to be referred to the nurse therapist. The nurse therapist was involved in teaching at Manchester University and through this link started to develop validated training courses. Currently there are three modules running which have been validated. These are:

o Introduction to PSI and CBT

o Managing Challenging Behaviour

o Core Skills with Psychoses.

Individuals from the multidisciplinary team can pursue one or all three modules. This provides the flexibility for the individual to learn basic skills or go on to build up Level 2 university credits, which for those who wish to develop skills further can be used to gain access to Level 3 courses (e.g. BSc in psychosocial intervention at Manchester University). It also provided the opportunity to offer external places to outside agencies, which generated funds for further investment in the courses (books, outside speakers etc.). All these courses incorporate clinical supervision, which is focused on clinical cases and the development of an action plan to work with patients. To pass any of the courses, the participants have to reach both academic and clinical competencies. This ensures the development of both academic knowledge and the clinical skills necessary to carry out the fundamental interventions. Several participants have gone on to undertake further in-depth PSI training. This has made it possible to ensure that every forensic ward not only has the majority of staff trained to a basic level, but also has at least one individual trained to an advanced level. They are still able to access the nurse therapist as a further resource. In order to provide access to this training for all members of the team, a further course has been developed for health care assistants and new starters. This course again focuses on the philosophy of PSI and places emphasis on engagement and communication skills. By completing the course, participants can achieve certain Level 2 and 3 competencies for NVQ.

The forensic pre-discharge ward is now operating a system where all patients prior to discharge have their individual relapse signature identified. This information is shared, after patient consent is gained, with relevant carers and agencies. This not only gives the patient a greater insight into their illness but also helps other agencies to have the confidence to contact the service before a crisis takes place.

FUTURE DIRECTIONS

This chapter has considered how PSI can significantly enhance the lives of service users and their carers. It plays an important role in risk management and equips staff with the skills needed for this work. At present, these interventions tend to be seen as 'advanced' and are offered (if at all) unsystematically. It is critically important, if forensic services are to evolve effectively, that these interventions become systematised and are widely integrated into routine day-to-day care.

To achieve this, several changes within organisations must take place. All levels and disciplines require fundamental education and training in the philosophy and working of PSI. This way, support workers and others can assist in the implementation of this approach. It will enable them not to hinder its development by indirectly undermining the interventions. For example, it is agreed as a short-term coping strategy that if a patient's arousal reaches a certain point in relation to paranoia, they take some time out in their room to calm down. A member of staff who is not aware of the rationale behind this may insist that the patient come out of their room when it is time for rehabilitation activities. Basic understanding can greatly help all staff to understand why patients do what they do. This understanding can often reduce both negativity, and the frustration that occurs from not understanding a patient's problems, often feeling helpless to help them. This can also help staff to feel more empathy towards patients when they grasp an appreciation of the individual's internal state and how this impacts on their life. All members of the clinical team also require this basic awareness. This will enable them to know when a patient should be considered for these interventions. This basic awareness training is ideally provided in-house by clinicians who have been trained and regularly use this approach. This can lend clinical credibility by offering clinical examples that staff can relate to in their own work. To build on this, key people should receive further training and offer supervision to others.

The assessment tools and an account of the interventions should be recorded and integrated into the care programme approach meetings. Each patient prior to discharge should have a written copy of their own early warning signs of relapse together with a copy of an action plan outlining what to do if these signs re-emerge. This would help fulfil standard 4 of the National Service Framework for Mental Health (Department of Health 1999a), which recommends written care plans that anticipate and deal with crises.

Individuals should receive routine access to standard assessments and interventions. Part of any such assessment package must, where appropriate, contain family assessments to examine their needs. Sometimes it is easier and more fruitful to work with the family whilst their relative is an in-patient. During this time, the family often find it easier to be honest and to plan for the future before problems arise again. This again fulfils standard 6 of the National Service Framework, which talks about the need to assess carers and plan for their needs.

Finally, there must be a greater dissemination of information that enhances and promotes good practice relating to PSI. This can be achieved through conferences, publications and networking together. Sharing information also encourages individuals by demonstrating that this approach can and does work. Sellwood *et al.* (1994) state that 'specific details on individual therapy may in the end be less important than a shift in professional attitudes that this kind of work is possible and can show improvements' (p.214). A person will not climb a mountain unless they have a desire to do it and a belief that it will be a positive experience, and they are sure that they have the skills to achieve it. It is essential that every means necessary is utilised to equip forensic nurses with the skills and motivation to use PSI effectively with this client group. This will involve training, education, dissemination, clinical supervision and clinical example.

CHAPTER 7

Nursing Interventions and Future Directions with Severely Assaultive Patients

Mark Chandley

INTRODUCTION

This chapter attempts to take an alternative look at some issues for those who are at the forefront of managing the most violent and difficult mentally disordered offender in-patients. This nurse–patient interface is riddled with difficulties, and although not exhaustive some salient points from a clinical perspective are raised for debate. Writing a text on good practice principles at the expense of a more creative perspective that addresses some taboos would have been easier. Covering every issue in depth has not been possible, but where this is a particular problem, guiding principles or recommended texts are included.

The chapter considers whether any special skills are required, important conceptual underpinnings and practical steps. Staff resources are an important variable as well, which are reflected upon before discussing some frequently used interventions. The current problems are then discussed before moving on to how this important area of forensic nursing can progress.

This specialism can hardly be compared with contemporary nursing. However, nurses are the greatest resource, and as such, the social dynamic is at the core of the nurses' work. The skills of this group of staff are often referred to at any senior level in the managerial coffee rooms at an informal level, but even here any compliments are shrouded within doubt. Any apparent success is viewed with sceptical reservation, and any admirable practice set within a context of potential over control. The difficulty is that these reservations are occasionally well founded, and if left unchecked can escalate to ill-treatment and abuse (Department of Health 1992). Abuse can be well hidden and skilfully camouflaged. On the other hand, lay skills appear to form the mainstay of day-to-day operation, while conversely a strong academic underpinning should meet the extensive bureaucratic needs. Working in a forensic environment, therefore, is particularly demanding on many fronts.

More often than not there is little thanks, but the practice has to be beyond reproach and the supporting documentation superior to that in other areas of psychiatry. While altruistic intent remains a dominant feature, a socio-political sideshow competes for equal attention. I suggest that this phenomenon is not an institutionally bound notion but pervades every heath care worker's psyche, and is a particular issue working with this group of patients, adding to the complexities of the social dynamic. Clearly, therefore, the dominant attraction to such a unit can only be in the challenges it offers at a professional level. Debates abound about whether special skills are required. The view adopted here is that there are skills required beyond the usual psychiatric skills that are worth commenting on, but that the knowledge(s), critical minds and the creativity required are in very short supply. Even the skills acknowledged are generally considered hidden and not really open to assessment or appraisal. Further, they may be the same qualities as would be required elsewhere, but imbued with a fundamental qualitative difference (Kettles and Robinson 2000b).

Of particular importance is teamwork. It is held up as a central tenet of practice, but the collective nature of such a principle points to the importance of sociological issues. Imbalances in power can be exaggerated if the teamwork principle is not bound within a conceptual approach addressing the collective nature of the context.

Conceptual tuning: teamwork

Teamwork is often only used at a shallow and rhetorical level, and when one delves deeper there is little but a bureaucratic apparition of collective working to match organisational expectancy. Teamwork should however be an integral and crucial part of the world of managing the most difficult patients in a forensic environment. The team concept here closely relates to the dual notions of accountability and professional survival. Multidisciplinary care teams are at the forefront of this idea, acting as a touchstone for daily practice standards and decision-making. It is in the most open and honest use of this forum that daily practice standards are assured. Furnishing the team with the difficult dilemmas and conflicts means those attending members are bound to contribute significantly. The wisest of staff who have grown with changing health care provision describe passing every issue on to the care team as one of their most valuable resources.

Previously, nurses working with this group of patients preferred to dominate decision-making processes and in many facilities would hold on to clinical information. Nurses put limits on the availability of knowledge and could and would sometimes hide any practice they preferred not to discuss. The withholding of knowledge is a powerful tool that increases personal importance, but correlates with dysfunction and inappropriate care delivery.

Perhaps the willingness, or not, to discuss sensitive or delicate issues in a multidisciplinary setting is a measure of whether any unidisciplinary clandestine team culture exists. At a managerial level, this could be a major clue on practice and cultural values. At a practice level, discussion means early reflection and self-regulation in an environment where values and beliefs can easily become deviant to recognised standards. Of course, a team alliance should include everyone as valued members who have important contributions, and there should be management to ensure that everyone can be heard.

The wisdom of the mountain: Chinese parables and management

The team concept in this context requires every member to contribute positively and meaningfully. The setting needs to support this target. Addressing this concept, Pinkerton (1993) describes *the wisdom of the mountain*, which has at its core the notion that the view at the top of a mountain is different from the view at the bottom. To gain an overall view from the mountain, both views are necessary. All too often the lay views of assistants not conversant with psychiatric discourse and explanation are considered illegitimate and are therefore neglected. Mason and Chandley (1999) note this very point. While this is clearly a problem in itself, it is also a misuse of staff resources. Meanwhile, a large contingent of important staff are ignored, while their dilemmas never get aired at any meaningful level.

It follows that significant people at the clinical interface never contribute and are rarely heard. Marry this with the idea that it is these very people whose personal safety is brokered at higher levels and a seriously dangerous and volatile situation arises where staff are often frightened. Then they will usually manipulate a situation to address that important personal value of physical safety and will not follow team decisions whatever the supporting rationale. In short, involving the risk-takers in the risky decisions and listening to their non-clinical descriptions of their world, however unpalatable, is a pivotal conceptual underpinning to continuing support and appropriate teamwork. This requires strong and confident individuals in the team who are not threatened by alternative interpretations in an otherwise purely clinically ordered world.

There are other powerful qualities to this approach, of which the best is in terms of a symbiotic learning mechanism and the development of two-way respect. A multidisciplinary team that listens to the real issues for the ward domestic is also a team that can influence through debate. Another essential property that develops is information and practice transparency. The most totemic issues should be

discussed and be up for negotiation with rules of engagement that should be collectively recognised.

Dalglish and value: getting the best out of staff

This idea is related to the above concept and again has as a central value the notion
that every member's opinion is respected. Treating the staff well is linked to this
value, and Dalglish (1996) noted this in his experience at Liverpool Football Club.
He noted that the players were treated well, but it was not because they were successful; in fact, it was the contrary – treating the players well brought success.
Dalglish noted the importance of the backroom staff also, including the cleaners
and the kit staff.

The metaphorical kit staff in the forensic nursing arena are equally important,
and a similar conceptual approach is needed to attain and maintain a feel-good
factor throughout the team. Those important staff at the patient–staff interface
must be valued and their contributions taken seriously in this way. Frankly, to
expect these staff to follow clinical plans, to respect each other and to follow their
leaders, it is essential to have a representative, bureaucratic (Gouldner 1954) management style that reflects these principles. Treating the staff well is clearly not the
complete answer. Technically justified rules and accountabilities that are commensurate with appropriately qualified staff are also important. It also seems fitting to
introduce further rules of engagement in the shape of more bureaucratic canons.

The special importance of an evidence base for practice

The need for an evidence base initially appears at odds with the above principles.
However, these approaches actually complement each other, and nursing care
provision exemplifies the value of using a strong evidence base (Le May 1999).
Gaining a practice base that is within this framework is held up as a panacea full of
riches. Unfortunately, the position is less ideal than this with several dominant
problems. These include the ability of average staff to gain access to the appropriate
information, often accompanied with an inability to interpret results. The skills are
just not available in the numbers required. The next major issue is that the literature
often simplifies clinical responses to a single event, not taking into account the
complex clinical variables and social constructions associated with the particularly
violent patient.

Nevertheless, an evidence base for practice aids individual practitioner safety,
and appropriate, effective care. In an increasingly litigious environment, with
competing restrictions and many external and internal stakeholders of practice, it
is crucial to operate with plans that reference appropriately published literature and
research. Wards of this nature require access to a nurse who is academically minded

and acts as a resource to others who have skills in advanced areas of practice. Clearly, the most violent patients should need the most academic resources to guide practice and inform on new ideas and on practice development. Grounded knowledge and evidence usage therefore helps (although it does not assure) both best practice and protection for staff who are otherwise vulnerable to legal challenges and patient complaints. The importance of knowledge appears to have a value based in the idea of self preservation rather than the importance of improving care delivery. The idea of *backup* in psychiatry has historically been restricted to the physical support required in the violent crisis. What is new is the importance of negotiating the bureaucratic process and the administrative threat.

Following on from this notion is the importance of a large knowledge base among the whole team. This means that many perspectives, including lay theory, which usually has little legitimacy, are embraced along with contemporary and innovative professional theory. Conversely, there is a necessity to filter ideas from the field and to be aware that (according to Maier *et al.* (1987)) over-reliance on theory will actually produce gaps in practice.

Evidence and other guidelines

The idea that a text is always appropriate is clearly wrong. The academic literature is but one important condition of practice. To operate safely, this condition must be supported by compliance with several other fundamental guiding principles. These include a consideration for national and local policy. The position is very straightforward. It is irrelevant whether they appear appropriate to practice; they demand compliance, they are safeguards that complement published literature.

The next issue is compliance with the Code of Practice: Mental Health Act 1983 (Department of Health and Welsh Office 1999). It is true that this code has the limited status of being a guide only. What is rarely referred to is the fact that this code will be held up in court as a minimum standard of practice. This does not mean that compliance is an edict, just that there would have to be a very good reason for non-compliance (for example, an alternative evidence base). It is usually recognised that the legal aspects of care require respect; however, of equal concern should be the ethical issues that underpin the decision-making process. Restraint and the management of severely assaultive patients is fraught with ethical issues that require unravelling and recording. So, apart from being a nurse, it is also more than useful to know how the above principles influence care delivery.

Finally, the power nurses hold over those in their care is exceptional. Positive and conscious steps are required to facilitate the views of patients and provide a responsible tether to professional power. That balance should therefore be advocated for by dedicated professionals. Patient views are also a form of evidence and should be carefully considered as such. Navigating these principles, and recording patients' views as rational, commands special skills and dedicated time, which is generally just not available in the clinical field. This brings us nicely to staffing as a resource.

STAFFING RESOURCES

The number of staff in an environment is often an issue for staff on the wards. The evidence is not as clear though, with some reports suggesting that too many staff can actually increase the likelihood of aggression (Geen and O'Neil 1976). Others report that more staff reduce levels of aggression. What is reasonably consistent is that crowding increases aggression (Palmistera and Wistedt 1995; Stevenson 1991). The greater issue is that extra staff should be available for short periods, to contain and control the violent incident, preferably before it occurs.

Staff qualities

A good staff is traditionally considered to have a set of particular skills and values and to be aware of the extent of their respective roles. This conventionally means staff having a strong professional identity. However, there are some excellent staff without this professional identity who operate socially with little psychiatric or forensic knowledge. They appear to behave on broader skills and on other abilities, which means they can identify with patients and reflect sound social values with origins in the wider society. Forensic units are full of these staff who are underused as a resource and limited in their ability to offer their opinion. When staffing resources become an issue, these people are rarely talked of in any positive way, though they are the people on the ward most likely to be at the patient–staff interface. Another interesting point is that these people cannot offer much as to contemporary evidence for their practice, a virtue extolled above, nor are they usually very well qualified. Their opinions, therefore, have low status with qualified practitioners who are more confident and able to debate clinical principles, a point made by Mason and Chandley (1999).

Using staffing resources, therefore, takes on a different approach with the message that valuing all staff is crucial to the management of aggression. Experience has often been overstated, though it remains an important feature if the skill mix is balanced. Determining the qualities required in this unique environment is a nebulous idea that is difficult to reduce to a core set of attributes. This makes recruitment particularly difficult. There are often bungled selections that end up employing the wrong people for long periods of time although they are next to useless. Sometimes it seems they require development plans with a higher level of detail than the patient they are employed to help.

It appears then that the social skills of individual staff members are either primordial, well developed and useful, or a hindrance. Nevertheless, there is often no correlation between qualification and ability. The anecdotal evidence in the field frequently supports this idea. I for one would rather work with good assistants than inadequate qualified staff.

Given the politics of knowledge and the investment in education and training, it is ironic that the greatest attribute a member of staff in this setting could hold for his or her colleagues is common sense. Patience, humour and stamina are often held to be essential as well. Humour deflects all sorts of trouble before it even begins. The requirement for colleagues to be assertive is married on occasion with staff often warning that 'a staff member saying no for no's sake can cause more problems than they are worth'. This ties in with the idea of 'noxious staff', typified by their unhelpful interactions with patients and their propensity to escalate situations into aggression. Other qualities that are considered important include objectivity, ethical and legal knowledge, knowledge of human rights, and being aware of the balance of control, therapy and safety.

Noxious and difficult staff

People are the major resource required to manage severe aggression appropriately. It follows that the major problems can also be people. Several other variables are also important. For instance, while the professional ethic (Seedhouse 1988) dominates, values unfit for health care can lie just beneath the surface. Under a long-term threat, where adrenalin constantly trickles, staff values are ripe for changing. Further, nursing staff in this context are undoubtedly in an unusually powerful position, with control potentially being a dominant feature of any plan. When danger is high and support is diminishing casual, informal leaders emerge. These people classically have little official authority, but surface as culturally important. Morrison (1990) notes their influence upon other staff and their ability to alter a team's beliefs and values such that a toughness quickly emerges that is subtle but destructive.

In practice, these individuals can be either very productive or extremely destructive. At their worst, they appear to relish confrontation and are detectably motivated completely by self-interest. They are also elusive and astute people who can avoid detection. Usually, the only evidence is an abusive patient and an escalating situation that is indistinguishable from a genuine episode. Often, small clues are evident which require subtle interpretation. These clues are available in voice intonation, eye contact and a lack of tolerance that suggests a lack of interest, an attitude-informing behaviour. These staff often focus on less assertive patients, as a demonstration of their power, but conversely they do latch on to more assertive patients. The general staff dynamic should demand compliance from these staff to the appropriate norms, and single individuals tending towards this approach are more often than not governed by the many.

The importance of one's perception being accurate in these instances cannot be overestimated. Providing negative consequences to a staff member who is strong and assertive will destroy team work, morale and the overall approach. Allowing one destructive staff member to amble about causing problems is actually an issue as far as a duty of care is concerned (UKCC 1996a), and so a charge exists to manage the situation. On the other hand, if the problems are more evident then the interventions range from moving the cultural leader to another environment to disciplinary action. Dunn and Sommer (1997) note the potential destructive nature of interactions that these people offer and recommend assertiveness training. The staff member who has been an asset but tends to cause more difficulties than he or she resolves might alternatively be suffering from burn-out. The signs of both are difficult to separate, but either way there are at least clear developmental issues. Observation is important in terms of this issue and is a central tenet of psychiatric nursing that is worthy of further explanation.

OBSERVATION, COMMUNICATION AND DE-ESCALATION

Observation

Observation is traditionally viewed as a fundamental principle of psychiatric nursing, and a level of informedness about what is being observed is vital. A summary of the clinical and risk issues should be given before delegating someone to the role of observer, and this should be accompanied by guidance on the frequency and depth of documentary reports. Appropriate levels of observation for any individuals usually rest on the perceived risk to either the patient or others. The intensity fluctuates along a continuum from continuous observation by one to several staff in a predefined area to close or general observation in the general ward environment. With very aggressive patients, other variables should be included in the assessment of the circumstances of observation. Table 7.1 suggests some of these.

The significance of local policy compliance cannot be underestimated. In what may appear a very useful technique, a note of caution should include the potential destructive nature of intensive observations and balancing this control with therapy and safety of the observer(s). Van Rybroek (2000) addresses this interactive balance in more detail. More recently, the importance of the interactional nature of focused observation has been emphasised. As for those who have the potential to be very aggressive, the idea of using answers from observation to shape immediate intervention is central to the avoidance of critical incidents. In terms of more intensive observation, three further advanced methods are used in practice.

The first is described by Kinsella, Chaloner and Brosnan (1993) and is called an *intensive care area*. The fundamentals are that part of the ward is sectioned off to include one or two potentially aggressive individuals along with staff. The idea is that the environment, the amount of stimulus and other variables are controlled in an area away from the main population. Geographic restrictions are also an option used about the main ward area. Usually this manifests whereby the patient is confined to graded parts of the general area of the unit, limiting risk. The amount of space available for associating with others can be increased or decreased along with perceived risk. Finally, Van Rybroek (2000) notes the importance of special units where staff become 'more familiar with effective, safe management'.

Table 7.1 Resource variables and interactive observation

- Manipulation of stimulation
- Use of the qualities of the environment
- A structure to the time on increased observation to include diversions, assessment
- Maintenance of space between the aggressor and other patients
- A regard for dangers that may increase due to the aggressor having access to significant others
- Maintaining a space between the aggressor and those at specific risk
- Monitoring for specific stress indicators and acting accordingly
- Staff selection

Communication and de-escalation

Communication is a vast subject that can only be touched upon here. Suffice to say that the finer details of interaction are almost continuously held up for examination with very aggressive patients. These skills are probably the single most important attribute of every practitioner. These skills are informed however by attitude that reflects a negative or positive regard for patients, thus the noxious staff and the de-escalating staff. It is not an attitude that causes problems, but the communication of that particular disposition.

Organisations have many support mechanisms in place for this situation. Nevertheless, in terms of this group of staff under particular pressures the literature suggests supportive closed group activity in the form of 'me-time' to deal with counter-transferance (Van Rybroek et al. 1987). Me-time has a dual purpose. On the one hand, it is a reflective period for considering whether violence could be managed more effectively. On the other, the group should be supportive and expressive and provide for the ventilation of personal feelings. Exposing one's feelings before the peer group requires support and a guide who is willing to express their fears first. The atmosphere can become charged. Therefore, it is vital that all the members of the group are clear that the freedom to talk, sometimes in a non-professional and even insulting way about situations cannot, under any circumstances, go beyond the bounds of the group session.

Matched with me-time must be the option for therapeutic non-availability. This means that in the aftermath of a violent incident the staff involved have time out to calm down before having any prolonged exposure to other patients. In practice, staff usually have a cup of tea away from the patient population. Staff who may be angry are, therefore, out of the clinical area in the immediate aftermath of the violent incident. There are advantages both for patients and staff members. Patients are not exposed to staff who are at minimum charged with adrenalin, and staff are not left professionally vulnerable at a very difficult time. Those who assess need also have needs. It is in addressing these issues that the social dynamic and appropriate communication are maintained.

De-escalation is the skill of using communication to resolve a potentially violent incident before it occurs. Knowing the patient and listening to the patient's concerns are crucially important. In the face-to-face interaction, the aggressor will require up to six times the amount of personal space generally required. The staff member must appear calm, in control and confident. After that, voice intonation is important. Speak clearly and attempt to negotiate.

Many have commented on the central roles of both communication and attitude, but for specific guidance the author points to some literature that deals specially with aggressive people (see Table 7.2).

Table 7.2 Observational and de-escalation practices

- The subtleties of communication
- The role of verbal de-escalation
- Talkdown
- Negotiation, knowledge of patients

(see Mason and Chandley 1999)

INTENSIVE SUPPORT AND SPECIFIC ASSESSMENTS

Intensive support

Central to this concept are the notions of safety, control and therapy (Mason *et al.* 1996). Safety of others, including staff, is a charge bound within a duty of care. Control is essential because of a utilitarian ethic and the above duty. Care facilities for very aggressive individuals fall short when they fail to provide a therapy component which is likely to move the patient from being dangerous to being safe and in providing self-help skills to aid self-control. Sharing this problem with colleagues helps provide potential solutions.

Some useful interventions used with this group include increasing the space. This is based on the principle that aggressive people require more personal space than the regular person, in terms of attempting to assure everyone's safety. Other interventions are included in Table 7.3.

Table 7.3 Useful interventions

Spatial techniques
- Low stimulation environment
- A time-out facility (DOH 1999)
- Interim plans
- Decompression (Monroe, Van Rybroek and Maier 1988)
- Special units (Van Rybroek 2000)
- Intensive care areas (Kinsella *et al.* 1993)

Theoretical notions
- Aggression cycle theory (Maier *et al.* 1987)
- Stress-coping strategy (Whittington and Mason 1995)
- Phases of aggression (Mason and Chandley 1999)

Practical steps from practice
- Post-incident discussion and support
- Post-incident clinical team reviews
- Judicious use of PRN medication
- Programmed activities, e.g. exercise and use of diversion
- Special environments, e.g. snoezelen. This is a specially provided sensory environment. It encourages participants to explore their environment offering security and allowing participants mental and physical relaxation.
- Achievable objectives for patients
- Continuity and consistency of care approach

Specific assessments

Short term

The key to the short-term assessment of violence is knowing the patient, their individual stressors and stress indicators. Occasionally these are blatant, while often they are more subtle and can be accurately described as micro-cues. Short-term risk assessment is, therefore, a key notion to managing the extremely violent patient, maintaining duties of care and protecting others. Principally, this means predicting what will happen next by observing what has previously happened. This notion underpins most assessment but is used as a 'best' indicator in day-to-day practice. This involves spotting individual signs and symptoms as well as personal and social cues. This should be structured through a multidisciplinary team where safety should be embedded within therapeutic plans. Using behavioural approaches can be an advantage in identifying early behaviours through a functional analysis. Then, behaviourism provides for a consistent approach to care delivery before the crisis emerges. Structured assessment and shared plans through formalised risk assessment form the basis of sound practice.

Longer term

In the longer term, assessment of risk is a more nebulous issue. Many risk assessments aim for longer-term ratings, and specific papers should be sought for in-depth knowledge. However, the focus of assessment with the most aggressive is more focused on the immediate future. Longer-term appraisals have been developed by each discipline to one degree or other and hold the values and opinions of that profession as central, while some risk assessments are multidisciplinary in nature. Opinions vary, with some believing that we are chasing a holy grail and that accurate long-term risk assessment will always be an illusion. Having said that, specific multidisciplinary assessments include the Behavioural Status Index of Woods *et al.* (1999), who comment on an acceptable test/retest reliability and the importance of key social and communicative skills.

Meanwhile, the emergence of the HCR–20 risk assessment is commented upon by Belfrage, Fransson and Strand (2000). They state that the 'total score has a highly significant predictive validity' (p.170). These tests are not used as widely as they should be, but then the difficulties associated with reliability in specific cases remain a source of concern. In summary, the claims of validity, reliability and accuracy should be reviewed with a critical mind.

Nurses are often vulnerable

Nurses are often their own worst enemy in this sense. Their understandable value attached to their personal physical safety usually means that sufficient attention is paid to this element of practice. However, when it comes to the other interventions highlighted above in evidence bases and other guidance they are often vulnerable legally, or in terms of their job. They simply do not act at a standard defined in law as reasonable (see UKCC 1996a). This is partially because of a lack of awareness and also because many guides available are taken to be what Gouldner (1954) would call a 'mock bureaucracy' and as such are just not observed. Gouldner's sociological unravelling of an organisation highlighted the directive of *no smoking* as a mock rule in that everyone understood that it was a rule that nobody really observed. Actual practice is often outstandingly good, but this is almost by chance as guides, policies, laws and ethics are sometimes not respected as such and are taken as a mock bureaucracy.

Other problems are also home grown. Occasionally an organisation's ability to manage this group of patients is dubious. This may be based in a lack of clinical knowledge at senior managerial level and a consequent inability to be able to assess the technical justification for appropriate, but contentious, practice. This is perceived by ward staff as a lack of trust by senior managers, but more importantly the effect on the socio-clinical aspects of work and on physical safety are too destructive to contemplate.

Practice in this area of health care must continuously be beyond that elsewhere. With constant surveillance from a range of visiting stakeholders the finer details of performance are potentially held up for inspection from a variety of perspectives. After that, legal conflicts from litigious patients are a constant threat, and the arrival of the human rights legislation will potentiate this issue because of the levels of restraint used with this very difficult group. What requires demonstrating is that restrictions and restraints are both reasonable and proportionate, and with which the guidance on offer is complied.

CURRENT AND FUTURE DEVELOPMENTS

Current problems

Criticisms from outside bodies and ill-informed clinicians and managers are a key issue. It seems that myths can surface about the likely cultures that dominate in these areas. This is potentially damaging at an individual professional level, and there are concerns for effective treatment delivery. It takes an assertive and energetic team to maintain a clear, unequivocal approach that is consistently within the parameters of good practice.

From another perspective, the generation of administrative procedures that are primarily about data collecting for others is a major problem. Associated with this phenomenon is the notion of the bureaucratic world. The social world appears secondary. It is recognised both by staff and increasingly by litigious patients who use bureaucratic avenues to convey their own power. Record-keeping is essential but the result of this phenomenon is an ever-growing paper chase that goes beyond the bounds of sense. Organisational audits promote this diversion, and at one level the criticism could be that neglect is legitimised because audits most often measure and monitor the bureaucratic record as opposed to measuring any actual clinical or nurse–patient activity. Staff often aim for a positive audit at the expense of nurse–patient activity. In this arena, the consequences can ultimately mean further detention for the patient. For the staff and patients, a lack of clinical activity can result in physical danger.

Related to this is a fashion for moral rhetoric. Armchair observers often take the moral high ground. Working with this group of patients, therefore, offers jeopardy at several different levels. Staff are often reluctant to work with these individuals. The argument at the ward level goes that they pay the same to work with less difficult individuals. This fact leads to the often-asked question: What is the sense in aspiring to work with a group that will place significant challenges and danger in the way of day-to-day practice?

Dumping grounds?

Because of the ethical and legal issues that accompany the very aggressive patient and their exacting needs they are perceived by other facilities as problematic and draining on resources. Several problems emerge from this departure point, including therapeutic opportunities being denied or refused. This manifests as bed-blocking, a problem usually observed between the social services and the NHS, where the one does not appear to provide an adequate level of service thus being unable to admit patients in need. In this relationship, bed-blocking appears to be grounded in funding issues. When it comes to very aggressive individuals, the issues appear to be social as well. They include staff fear and exaggerated staff self-interest, with attitudes typified by comments like having enough on their plates. Patients who are particularly violent are known institutionally at a mythical level, and their reputation precedes them.

Other facilities frequently misconceive the role of expertise and expect a purely holding role, and there are often hints that retribution is part of the overall approach. These misplaced attributes and the suspicions of managerial stakeholders mean that the maintenance of a clinically minded approach is vital as situations suddenly descend into dramas with consequential inspection of the microscopic detail of practice.

Saturation

Environmental balance is a recently used idea in units that manage the most difficult patients. With the trend towards units of between six and twelve patients being the norm, the idea is that an environment has limits on its ability to remain therapeutic, and this is proportionally related to the number of very difficult patients. This is despite the quality and quantity of staff in the same environment. Because of this, admissions are managed according to whether the unit has the therapeutic capacity bearing in mind the current population and the needs of the intended transfer in. In essence, staff will ask themselves whether the unit can tolerate another very aggressive individual. Going beyond the capacity means that therapeutic ideals collapse, the ward organisation becomes ineffective. This is the point recognised as saturation. It is at this point that there is a significant risk of the values of the unit warping as personal safety eclipses all other matters.

Retaining beds on parent wards

Retaining beds on parent wards has long been an approach to attempting to manage this difficult group. Clinicians in the field resign themselves to the idea that these types of contracts are worthless and that no bed will be available when required. There may be no clinical accountability by the original ward, which results in counter-therapeutic placements. In other countries, some facilities are combating this with several approaches, including having a facility in larger institutions for as short a stay as possible for the very aggressive patient in an intensive support area. This is on a controlled self-referral basis. Other facilities are using a cross-charging facility, while others use independent stakeholders and patient advocates, to push the issue as a complaint. However, it remains a general phenomenon in a social world where dangerousness is at best in the eye of the observer, and therefore open to interpretations when personal interest of staff is the dominant priority.

A system of complementary unbroken health care provision for violent patients should be organised as they are seen through a different conceptual framework. It should be organised at a strategic level and with an element of governance monitoring clinical rationales and accountabilities with an overall assessment of clinical argument and judgement.

Deficiencies and scarce resources

Many options are available here, but the idea that intensive units are under-resourced financially is largely unsupported if expressed in terms of staffing numbers. In addition, there is generally a flexibility in this respect, particularly when increased needs dictate further staffing.

Resource issues do emerge, however, in other areas and have a direct clinical impact. Increasingly, less skilled people are being employed as cheap labour. With this patient population, the slightest of flaws in social skills or negotiating ability can ruin a whole plan and send clinical success into a rapid downward spiral. Staff in these areas require a special aptitude, as highlighted above, without which they are a liability and deleterious to clinical achievements, team work and everyone's safety.

At another level, although relatively inexpensive, organisations overlook the significance of the environment and the behavioural expectations conveyed through the setting. With a multitude of aesthetic, decorative and furnishing changes, the environment can be used to its fullest to meet the significant challenges of maintaining safety and control while attaining a permanent therapeutic setting. Both managers and clinicians are to blame in this respect. Clinicians, for example, need to be aware that it would take an unwise manager not to provide resources for an established clinical need. Providing clinical evidence is an underused instrument by clinicians who often have more clout than they realise in the pursuit of change.

Philosophical approaches at a clinical and managerial level to managing the most aggressive patients require a fundamental rethink. They are treated within a generally biomedical frame of reference. This significantly reduces the options for both management and treatment. The potential of alternative therapies set within other health belief models has never been realised. Very many opportunities exist that are relatively inexpensive.

THE WAY FORWARD

Despite the propensity of organisations to send ever-increasing numbers of nurses on degree courses and the surfacing of the Project 2000 nurses on wards, any emerging traits of criticality are limited. This lack of potential (for whatever reason) to dissect one's own practice and the practice of others in the same organisation is a problem. It means that the only time one is rigorously forced into reflection is in terms of a major internal or external review. Despite initiatives to encourage reflection including reflective practice, clinical supervision and more structured annual reviews, critical self-regulation exists only in the best of facilities.

There are two issues here. The first is a widespread disposition of nursing staff to meet the managerial bureaucratic demands of their social world while meeting the monitoring requirements. Meanwhile, they almost never challenge any status quo and preoccupy themselves with the demands of day-to-day practice. New managerial initiatives are, however, seen as primarily advancing the personal interests of the promoter. Second, nurses on the wards complain that the above support mechanisms do not meet their needs. Ironically, their impressions are that such support mechanisms are invasive; they are often perceived as suppression or surveillance and paternalistic in nature. Improvements in practice are distractions, of no value and a waste of time in an otherwise busy schedule. In a social world, solutions should adopt a sociological underpinning.

As for the very violent, there are some key issues. Primarily, because of their violent history they often adopt the role of prisoner as opposed to patient, consequently they often perceive the nurses as prison officers. Second, when the violent patient reaches these persistent levels of severe aggression, they are classically in-patients at the time and psychiatric interventions such as drug and therapeutic interventions have helped fuel their degeneration into the violent crisis. Frequently, this population have issues with what they term the 'system'. They talk of over-control, of frustration and anger towards an unjust and unpredictable system.

There is a commonly held view, holding the politically comfortable ground, that some facilities are too big. This does not hold up to deeper scrutiny. For example, none of these critics explains how they are too big; is it by patient population, by area of the campus, by total number of employees or by bureaucratic capacity? How does this concept match with big business ventures, all with a structure that supports their respective corporate goals? And therein is a clue. It cannot be merely size of an organisation that is the deciding variable on whether it will or will not be a success. If it is the structure that supports the goals, then perhaps the structures are at fault. By this I do not mean purely the internal management arrangements but the whole conceptual approach that revolves around NHS policies and values, and around the conceptual frameworks that dictate the overall structure. In turn, in most healthcare facilities the author asserts that the published organisational structures with their order and Newtonian-type reductionist frameworks do not admit the social interpretation. The suggestion is that there is a need to challenge the national representation of managerialism, to confront the contemporary health-related frameworks of which the patient is clumsily made to fit and suffer at the hands of. Nursing staff in particular could contribute through both their latent power in sheer numbers and an unchallenged clinico-social proximity that delivers them a unique qualitative perspective.

Patients who are extremely violent typically have no earliest date of release. Their detention is open-ended and not purely dependent on getting better. There are many variables that affect the length of time detained, and it is extremely difficult to attribute any sense of predictable future. To help counter this, patients ought to be contracted, not to definite periods of clock time in detention, but to identified achievement that promotes their health career. Chandley (2000) makes this point about high security hospital patients overall. This may or may not reduce time detained, but would provide markers against which individual patients could measure themselves.

At another level, units that manage the most aggressive can assume an elitist status with clear boundaries that limit their availability to the wider patient population. Two clear initiatives could be used here. The first is about formalised outreach to other less intensive facilities who would benefit from the specific recommendations. The second is concerning a facility for a very short stay (hours) at the patient's request. The benefits to individual patients and organisations could outweigh the potential difficulties.

At a philosophical level violent patients need to be viewed differently by organisations. They can be viewed as problematic and draining of resources. However, they are people in deep crisis and as such they should receive the best skills and the best resources.

Finally, research must always be a recommendation. As has been stressed, evidence is crucial; and the units involved with such care should be contributing to the new theory. This theory should be open to various competing paradigms of other Western academic thought and to theories beyond contemporary health beliefs.

CHAPTER 8

Nursing Interventions and Future Directions with Exercise Therapy

Lesley Adams

INTRODUCTION

Participation in exercise activities is known to be good for you, and the vast majority of the population are more at risk from doing too little exercise rather than too much (Bird 1997). In the case of psychiatric patients, their stamina and endurance have been documented for some time to be problematic in carrying out everyday living activities (Dodson and Mullens 1969). But the question arises as to how exercise can be used in forensic nursing environments for the benefit of the patients. Other chapters of this book focus on practical and innovative clinical approaches and evidence-based forensic nursing practice in such areas as therapeutic alliances. This chapter aims to extend the parameters of the forensic nurse's role by introducing a concept of health promotion, facets of patients' health, and the role of exercise therapy in forensic rehabilitation.

The concepts considered and highlighted here include the nature of chronic mental illness, the effects of medication, the controlling environment and the practices leading towards holistic nursing care. The main theme is the effects of these factors and how they often lead to the physical degeneration of the patient. There is little doubt that the mentally disordered offender who is being nursed in secure environments, and being cared for by the multidisciplinary team, who focus on psychiatric symptoms and offending behaviours, tend not to incorporate other interventions, such as exercise therapy, into the care programme of the patient (UKCC and University of Central Lancashire 1999). 'The physical health care of people with mental illness can often be ignored while treatment for the mental illness is provided' (Wallace and Tennant 1998, p.82).

In this developing area, forensic nurses need to find the balance between the effects of custody and long-term stays in secure hospitals and community settings.

The forensic nurse's aim should include reducing levels of ill health, through the facilitation of health promotion approaches of nursing care, using exercise as an adjunct therapy to promote positive mental and physical health outcomes.

The evidence about the physical health of the mentally disordered offender is of concern, as an area that is not given much attention. This chapter contends that it should become one of the priorities of forensic clinical governance.

PHYSICAL HEALTH OF THE MENTALLY DISORDERED OFFENDER

Physical degeneration can be seen in mentally disordered offenders who gain body weight, start smoking or smoke to excess, who have a sedentary lifestyle taking little or no active exercise. The Nursing in Secure Environments Study (UKCC and University of Central Lancashire 1999) highlighted physical illness, such as obesity, respiratory disease, cardiovascular disease, hypertension, diabetes and musculoskeletal complaints in the mentally disordered population in secure environments (Wallace and Tennant 1998). These health factors may not seem very important, but they are considered health risks, which are partially caused through inactivity and can have profound implications in the rehabilitation of the mentally disordered offender (Hutchinson, Skrinar and Cross 1999).

The Scottish Executive's White Paper *Towards a Healthier Scotland* (Scottish Executive 1999) highlights the main health priorities such as cardiovascular disease, stroke, cancer, the elderly and mental health. These health risk areas or populations are not entities in themselves, but should be considered as interlinked. Rates of serious physical illness in the psychiatric population as high as 60 per cent and mortality rates 2.5 times higher than the general population are cited by Hutchinson *et al.* (1999) and Berren *et al.* (1994). People with mental health problems, and those nursed in secure environments, may be more at risk than the general population of falling ill to these lifestyle diseases. There is a growing body of evidence that links an increased risk of certain diseases to a sedentary lifestyle and general lack of fitness (Bird 1997).

THE HISTORY AND RESEARCH EVIDENCE OF EXERCISE THERAPY IN THE PSYCHIATRIC NURSING ARENA

Exercise or sports therapy is not new to psychiatry. As early as 2000 bc the Greeks, Egyptians and Romans considered 'exercise and the arts' as having healing powers (Fortinash and Holoday-Worret 1996). In the 18th and 19th centuries, activity therapy was used frequently in therapeutic settings by nurses who recognised its therapeutic value. Florence Nightingale was involved in the birth and evolution of recreational therapy, introducing theory and practice and developing it into a specialised area of nursing (Fortinash and Holoday-Worret 1996). Late in the 18th century, Dr Adolf Meyer and the American Red Cross during the First World War recognised the 'curative' nature of activity therapies, which were used to 'meet specific medical goals and objectives' often with neuropsychiatric patients (Fortinash and Holoday-Worret 1996).

Much of the current literature refers to using exercise intervention with patients with mild and moderate depression and anxiety (Burbach 1997; McEntee and Halgin 1996), as well as with more recently recognised disorders such as chronic fatigue syndrome (Fulcher and White 1997) and post-traumatic stress disorder (Ochberg 1991). However, there is little on its use with schizophrenia and other thought disorders (Plante 1996; Smeaton 1995). A recent small study by the author (as yet unpublished) provides some evidence that exercise can alter the negative symptoms of schizophrenia. Exercise therapy has been used not only to enhance psychological functioning, but also mood and general well-being (Plante and Rodin 1990).

Exercise has been shown to improve body attitude (Martinsen 1988), self-awareness (Pelham and Campagna 1991) and self-concept (Collingwood and Willer 1971). Exercise therapy also enables treatment-resistant individuals to respond better to other therapy interventions (Layman 1974). Exercise and other movement therapies, such as dramatherapy, have been shown to reduce aggressive behaviours often seen in patients (Reiss et al. 1998) and emotionally disturbed adolescents (Munson 1988; O'Kelly et al. 1998).

THE SECURE ENVIRONMENT VERSUS THERAPY, AND THE SECURE ENVIRONMENT'S EFFECTS ON PATIENT HEALTH

The effect of treatment and care in secure environments is an area that is relatively unexplored (Whyte 2000). 'Therapy versus security' is a topic of contention, especially where the mentally disordered offender's physical health is of concern. Collins (2000) states that forensic psychiatry is not therapeutically restrictive, but the opposite; and Swinton (2000) suggests forensic nursing should try to provide 'forms of care which can maintain and creatively work within the critical tension between therapy and security' (p.114).

Many forensic texts contend that secure environments are areas where the issues of physical control and security restrict the patient's mobility. They also describe that controlled, skilled supervision and interaction is required in secure settings so that deterioration in the patient's behaviour and the development of different attitudes, feelings and anger does not occur. However, none specifically mention the skilled supervision and interaction required to prevent the deterioration of the physical status of the patient.

Control of their own physical health is often removed from the individual patient as a result of the restrictive living environment. Holistic health care considers not only the psychological and spiritual but also the physiological aspects of the individual (Fortinash and Holoday-Worret 1996). Prior to becoming ill, the mentally disordered offender may or may not have led an active lifestyle. However, on admission, the freedom or choice to participate in various activities may be removed because of the differing levels of security that have been implemented in the care plan at that time. The patient in a high security environment, when not on parole, cannot just go out for a long walk as you or I may, because of the risk assessments and the security procedures. The sedentary lifestyle and control induced by the secure environment may act together to debilitate the patient (UKCC and University of Central Lancashire 1999). It is a problem that our nursing and medical care allows for this kind of physical degeneration.

Health promotion in nursing is well established, being accepted as an element of nurses' daily clinical practice. There are many explanations of health promotion and the World Health Organization (WHO 1984) defines health promotion as 'a unifying concept for those who recognise the need for change in the ways and conditions of living...a mediating strategy between people and their environments synthesising personal choice and social responsibility'. This description emphasises the dual prominence of both lifestyle and living conditions on health (Delaney 1994).

The forensic nurse should consider the lifestyle and living conditions the patient is subjected to. The holistic health care model and the WHO definition, where the individual has 'supposed' choice and self-responsibility in the promotion of their health, is not always the case for those in secure settings.

The creation of a therapeutic milieu seems appropriate as it is designed to promote health (Fortinash and Holoday-Worret 1996). Florence Nightingale defined her work as 'organising her environment to allow the body to heal', and Maxwell Jones in the 1950s aimed to create a therapeutic community, milieu or culture that might promote healthy personalities. There was recognition that the environment could affect the progress, symptoms and behaviours of patients. The therapeutic milieu is an environment thought to provide corrective and healing experiences, and which attenuates patients' coping abilities and maintenance of health. An important factor is that the patient plays an active part in their care, is responsible for their own behaviours and environment and should be involved in the management of all three (Fortinash and Holoday-Worret 1996).

Both the Nursing in Secure Environments Study (UKCC and University of Central Lancashire 1999) and the Scottish Needs Assessment Programme (Office for Public Health in Scotland 1999) paint a picture of an unhealthy mentally disordered offender population in NHS secure environments and prison settings. Both studies highlight that many of the people admitted to secure environments often come with an abundance of physical health problems. The provision of medical and nursing interventions to meet these health needs can be successful, substantiating the health care model's effectiveness in secure settings. Multiple disciplines provide treatment and supportive measures, which enable the mentally disordered offender to maintain their health or recover from illness. The Scottish Needs Assessment Programme shows that some prisoners report improvement in their health as a result of their stay in secure environments. This is because they are removed from their often chaotic lifestyles, and as a result receive proper health care, regular meals and opportunities to exercise and improve their physical well-being. There are no research reports of comments such as these from patients in NHS secure environments (although it may happen). The Nursing in Secure Environments Study (UKCC and University of Central Lancashire 1999) high-lights that the majority of secure settings have policies in relation to physical health. For example, the *Marsden Clinical Handbook on Physical Care* (UKCC and University of Central Lancashire 1999) has been adapted and implemented in the Scottish Prison Service and Ashworth Hospital Authority in Merseyside.

The provision of a therapeutic community having access to fitness or recreational facilities, appropriate therapists and equipment are environmental issues. Current traditional nursing environments tend to have fitness equipment, but this is not always used to promote health specifically, rather such equipment tends to be for diversional use. This situation is not only current in psychiatric areas in Britain but also in Canada, as evidenced by the author's experience during visits to Canadian facilities. The UKCC and University of Central Lancashire (1999) state that mental health units often do not have the guarantee of 'therapeutic and recreational facilities that are a necessary part of good care' (p.29). There are a few unique settings in both Scotland and England where fitness facilities are on-site within the secure setting, where the nursing staff, with a recognised fitness qualification, carry out therapeutic exercise interventions. This is a very positive resource; however, access to the fitness facility depends on the availability of the nursing staff.

There is an argument that if forensic patients become physically fitter and thus stronger, then risk is greater for violence and aggression towards staff and other patients. There is no evidence in the literature that this is the case. The opposite is to be found in the literature (Bell and Cooney 1993; Chamove 1986), which shows that after exercise there is a decrease in irritability, tension and anxiety, fewer psychotic features, a more positive mood through the increased output of endorphins and active seeking of physical and cognitive diversions to cope with thoughts.

THE MENTALLY DISORDERED OFFENDER IN SECURE ENVIRONMENTS

The forensic nursing ward environment can provide well-documented (Collins 2000) restrictions for the mentally disordered offender. Different levels of security may directly affect what a patient can undertake in terms of exercise. The main reasons for confinement to secure environments are the offending behaviours and accompanying mental illness symptomatology, which determines the individual as a risk or danger to others in society or themselves.

Of the population being nursed in secure environments, many of the patients have serious mental health or behavioural problems. The diversities of chronic or enduring mental illness create problems for any professional who offers a clinical intervention. The UKCC and University of Central Lancashire (1999) state that the patient population in secure settings suffering from mental illness increased from 79 per cent to 92 per cent between the years of 1987 and 1997. Schizophrenia and treatment-resistant psychosis, depression, dual diagnosis and behaviour disorders are the main conditions presented. People with psychopathic personality are included in these figures.

Various symptoms of mental illness and challenging behaviours often make it difficult to engage with the mentally disordered offender, such as the negative symptoms from psychotic disorders, the depressive personality and the secondary symptoms derived from neuroleptic medications. Lack of motivation, inertia and passivity may be considered the symptoms of disengagement in care planning and therapy programmes. Motivation is often one of the most challenging aspects of working with patients with enduring mental illness. Motivational approaches should focus on the present and the future physical health of the patient and not only on mental health or behavioural issues.

EFFECTS OF PSYCHIATRIC MEDICATIONS AND PREDISPOSITION FOR WEIGHT GAIN ON PHYSICAL HEALTH

Obesity, in both general psychiatry and secure environments, is an area that tends to be given little attention (McConnell and Duncan-McConnell 1999). Although drug therapy allows the mentally disordered offender to take up psychological and social therapies and often improves their quality of life, the debilitating side-effects of medications can reduce both the feelings of control over physical health and other effects of 'holistic' care.

Clinicians may monitor or observe any weight change, possibly even ignoring or tending to dismiss the problem, because it is one of the 'expected' outcomes for many patients who are prescribed neuroleptic medications. Weight gain may also be considered an outcome of 'complex interactions of genetic, environmental and psychological factors' (Campbell 2001).

The health of the mentally disordered offender is threatened by the primary and secondary side-effects of the many medications and regimes prescribed. Primary effects are the anticholinergic effects of the antipsychotic medications, such as dry mouth, blurred vision, hypotension, constipation, sexual dysfunction and sedation. The more serious side-effects, such as muscular spasms, rigidity, tremors and abnormal body movements (extrapyramidal side-effects and tardive dyskinesia) and restlessness (akathisia), are very distressing and can reduce self-esteem, treatment outcome and compliance with drug therapy (Brazire 2000).

Secondary effects include the well-recognised lack of motivation and apathy. These side-effects play a major role in lack of adherence to therapy regimes and engagement with everyday living skills, such as dietary control. Brazire (2000) states that patients medicated on antipsychotics can incur a weight gain of 7 per cent or more over baseline weight; this is usually gained in the first 16 weeks of therapy, and can often continue well after that. Patients can become as obese as the general population through taking medication, even if they were not obese on admission. Female patients taking antipsychotics especially can be more obese than the female general population (Allison *et al.* 1999).

The taking of medication and weight gain are related in various ways:

o *Sedation* causes drowsiness and lethargy leading to reduced activity in general, as well as decreased interest in participating in sports and exercise activities (Brazire 2000).

o *Dry mouth or thirst* leads to polydypsia, mainly of sweet coffee or tea or sugary drinks increasing the calorie intake (McConnell and Duncan-McConnell 1999). Research evidence (Wirshing *et al.* 1999) indicates that taking anti-psychotic medication affects the appetite centre of the brain, initiating appetite stimulation, resulting in increased food consumption. There are also changes in food preference, with an attraction towards carbohydrates (McConnell and Duncan-McConnell 1999).

o *Motivation to participate in activities and exercise* is diminished by the negative symptoms of schizophrenia and the secondary effects of medications. Thus, high calorific consumption versus low energy expenditure leads to weight gain.

o *Environmental factors* include minimal or poor support by staff, and not having access to nutritious food and helpful advice on dietary control. In addition, not being warned of the effects of their medication and having little or no access to exercise or the freedom to carry out everyday living activities increases the problem.

Weight gain caused by psychiatric medications is reversible and can be treated and managed by diet, education and exercise programmes (McConnell and Duncan-McConnell 1999; Wirshing *et al.* 1999).

THE ROLE OF THE FORENSIC NURSE IN PROMOTING THE HEALTH OF THE FORENSIC PATIENT

Health promotion and health education are important components of the role of the nurse (Norton 1998). Health promotion in psychiatric or forensic nursing, however, tends to focus on educational areas such as healthy eating, sex education, alcohol misuse, drug misuse and addiction. There is less focus on the promotion or the maintenance of physical fitness.

Motivation, or the lack of, can be a facet of some mentally disordered offenders' make-up, which often makes them unreliable in taking up therapeutic interventions. Motivation may be considered as the manifestation of purpose or the striving to achieve an end and concurrently the mark of behaviour (Hargie 1991). Motivation occurs on two levels. The first is the intrinsic level and belongs to the patient; whereas the second, the extrinsic level, includes the influences of the environment, the staff and the exercise therapist. Prochaska and DiClemente's (1984) trans-theoretical model of health-related change has focused on working with people with addictions and eating disorders such as obesity (Smith, Heckemyer *et al.* 1997), and can be used to change behaviours in physical activity (Pert 1997) with the aim of changing lifestyle or health-related behaviour habits.

For behaviour change to occur, and in this instance to change behaviour towards increased physical activity, the patient needs a reason for change (intrinsic), for example, to maintain or lose body weight or to achieve a feeling of well-being. Prochaska and DiClemente (1984) describe the process of behaviour change in five stages. The pre-contemplation stage is the first stage, where the patient may not have considered their lifestyle or become aware of any risks to their health behaviour (e.g. not being physically active enough to promote health). The second stage is where there is contemplation, consideration or awareness that the lifestyle is not conducive to optimum health. However, at this stage the individual is not ready to seek advice or help. The third stage is where there is realisation that behaviour change may have benefits (e.g. being more active may reduce weight gain). Preparation to change then occurs. When the fourth stage occurs, work in making the change in behaviours becomes evident. Where the individual has made the decision to 'become more active', goals, realistic plans, support and rewards become important for this stage and the next. In the fifth stage, the maintenance of the new behaviour is sustained and the mentally disordered offender continues a healthier lifestyle.

The exercise therapist, however, can be a positive influence on the mentally disordered offender's motivation. Exercise therapists have a dual role as both specialist forensic nurses and exercise specialists. Physiotherapists have a more remedial therapy role dealing with joints and muscles that have suffered injuries or suffer from disease, whereas the exercise therapist takes a more active role in enhancing the health status of the patient.

From the five stages of the Prochaska and DiClemente (1984) model the question becomes 'How can the patient be engaged in a more active lifestyle?' The first two stages of the model, the pre-contemplation and contemplation stages are relevant to the educational approach of health promotion (Naidoo and Wills 1994). At this stage, the exercise therapist may help to make the patient more aware. For example, monitoring their body weight may reveal weight gain. The exercise therapist may then offer advice and give information on healthy eating, maybe even involve the expertise of a dietician and offer information on the benefits of participating in a regular exercise programme. This approach may not be enough to persuade or motivate the patient to change their health behaviour. The therapist might involve other members of the multidisciplinary team to identify the possible motivators that may help the patient.

In the third stage, where the patient is preparing to change, the exercise therapist may intervene by giving extra support, possibly suggesting a realistic exercise programme to follow. The fourth stage of making the change not only requires positive decisions from the patient, but positive, enthusiastic support from the exercise therapist. Realistic plans might be set so that rewards can be gained. Rewards include weight loss, changes in body shape and psychological changes such as body image and attaining programme goals. The rewards may build intrinsic motivation to continue with the programme and the extrinsic support may enhance adherence. Patients who are involved in the planning stages of their programme are more likely to be motivated. Lastly, the maintenance stage is when there is less need for motivation for the exercise therapist as the patient is wholly self-motivated. Motivation or adherence to programmes is enhanced when the patient is fully involved in the continuous monitoring of, and changes in, the exercise therapy programme. It must be remembered that this is only a guide to behavioural change, and it is likely the patient will move backwards as well as forwards through the series of cycles of change.

Other extrinsic factors such as the attitude of the forensic nursing staff and the secure environment itself may result in a negative force in the motivation of the patient, mainly owing to the restrictions placed upon them. Forensic nurses' perceptions of which clinical interventions were part of their nursing role and the level of importance ascribed to the interventions were investigated (UKCC and University of Central Lancashire 1999). The results showed that forensic nurses perceived their main roles were to 'contribute to raising awareness of health issues' and to 'enable individuals to address issues which affect their health and well-being'. The following are considered to be secondary components of their nursing role in order of importance:

1.   contribution to the joint implementation and monitoring of programmes of care for individuals

2.   contribution to the provision of effective physical, social and emotional environments for group care

3.   implementation of specific therapeutic interventions to enable nurses to manage the behaviour of patients.

This evidence suggests forensic nurses have awareness of the health needs of patients, and it could be surmised that they offer health promotion information on health-related issues under the auspices of 'educating the patient', although health promotion is not actually mentioned. The implementation and monitoring of therapeutic interventions are the failing of the health care process. Naidoo and Wills (1994) highlight that raising awareness and education as a mode to promote health-related behaviour change is not sufficient. Therefore, the attendance at and compliance with interventions such as exercise therapy, or social and recreational therapies in secure settings, may be dependent on staffing levels or assessments on the individual's mental state as to whether or not they can participate. These influences can have an effect on the patient's arousal or motivation to participate in exercise activities and it may seem to the patient that there are too many obstacles to be overcome.

Rask and Holberg (2000) investigated psychiatric nurses' views regarding their areas of responsibility and work content. The study reported similar findings to the UKCC and University of Central Lancashire (1999) study, in that it was not clearly stated that physical health and health promotion were focal nursing care tasks.

Educating and motivating the patient to make health-related behaviour changes by taking more control over their own health needs, by using exercise to control their weight gain or feelings of well-being, is conducive to the therapeutic milieu. The exercise therapist has knowledge that clinical interventions, such as medications, will have a diverse effect on health, and could use the Prochaska and DiClemente (1984) model. Assessment, planning and implementation of a programme of prevention is important so that the patient avoids the distress of weight gain and refraction of self-image and self-respect, as well as the conglomeration of additional health risks that are associated with weight gain. Focusing on sports and exercise in a health and recreational sense can be appropriate, so that productive and enjoyable activities can be used as part of everyday living activities and possibly offer a better quality of life.

Exercise therapy may not be an intervention option for all patients, because of the attitudes that medical staff and other professionals sometimes have towards exercise and the perceived lack of adherence by the patient to this therapy. This attitude may arise because there is little empirical research evidence to support the benefits of exercise and mental health. Although there is an abundance of literature, most of the studies (Jin 1994; Li and Wang 1994; Thornley and Adams 1998) have small samples. In a study by McEntee and Halgin (1996), where they investigated psychotherapists' attitudes to exercise, it was found that it depended on their work environment whether they promoted exercise therapy in their psychotherapy sessions, and on the therapist's personal history or keenness to participate in exercise habits themselves.

The author carried out a study evaluating the outcome of an activity nurse intervention in a community rehabilitation setting. Preliminary results indicate that staff attitudes to the activity nurse were positive and supportive; however, their views on incorporating exercise into the patients' care programmes were not considered to be a priority. They also did not consider the benefits of physical exercise on the physical or psychological well-being of the patient, but saw the exercise intervention more as a social interaction. The attitudes of staff towards social and recreational therapies in institutions have often been seen as diversional activities and a therapy which 'gets the individuals off the ward'. Like McEntee and Halgin (1996), the author observes that it is nursing staff who are interested in exercise or sports personally who promote exercise therapy. What needed to be ascertained was the attitude of the patients.

The author consulted patients prior to their entering into a research study, involving exercise therapy, as to whether they would prefer to participate in the exercise group or control group interventions. Somewhat surprisingly, eight out of nine preferred to be included in the exercise group. The reason for this was that they wanted to become more active 'to lose weight'. Since coming into hospital, they had put on weight and missed having the freedom and opportunity to do the type of exercise that would benefit them. Some felt the restrictions of the secure environment and not having access to facilities did not maintain or enhance their fitness levels. The effects of their medications and sitting around the ward were also factors that were of concern to them. These reasons, or intrinsic motivators to participate, were only identified because the patients were asked. The patients' preference did not affect adherence to the study interventions which is often a problem when patients' choice is taken away with the Randomised Controlled Thai Design.

As forensic nurses, we have a duty and responsibility to discharge this population back into the community as healthy and functioning as possible (UKCC and University of Central Lancashire 1999). No matter what the patients' mental state, their physical functioning will have a relation to their sense of well-being and rehabilitation. Exercise therapy may not be appreciated as a treatment focus for all patients, but those who want to use this as a vehicle in their rehabilitation, can reap the benefits.

Care planning, patient assessments and programme interventions often cover many of the attributes of everyday living skills, encouraging nurses to practise holistically practical care, but not necessarily including physical fitness in the equation. Without strength, stamina and a sense of well-being, how can the individual cope with the activities of daily living? Many interventions provided by occupational therapy and physiotherapy support the patient in ways such as having someone to accompany them shopping, help carry their groceries home, give them a lift to and from the supermarket. Is this really beneficial to the patient? Such 'parental intervention' may be a condition for the patient to go out at all, but will the patient be fit enough or able to carry out these acts of daily living on discharge home? However, it may well be that risk-management strategies demand that certain patients may always need this level of supervision. With many patients, the problems occur at the beginning of their reintegration into their community, where lack of stamina and endurance causes them to discontinue daily commitments such as work or activities such as shopping (Dodson and Mullens 1969). Working together, the various professionals involved in this kind of care could devise an appropriate programme to deal with such issues.

CASE STUDY: TREATMENT-RESISTANT SCHIZOPHRENIA

Many of our patients may present with treatment-resistant mental illness, and Adams (1995) describes how exercise can initiate changes in daily living skills, psychiatric symptoms and physical fitness for patients with these problems.

> Alan is a 28-year-old who presents with a long-standing treatment-resistant schizophrenia. Alan came in contact with the forensic services after assaulting a member of his family. His offending behaviour resulted from his auditory hallucinations and delusional thought processes. He was selected by staff to take part in the study because he was making little improvement with his treatment regime. Alan presented as flat in mood, socially withdrawn with little spontaneity, poor personal appearance and self-esteem; he slept most of the day and when awake appeared physically irritable, lacked concentration and tended to pace the floor.
>
> The case study used a before-and-after method of measuring change. After giving his consent to participate, Alan underwent physical fitness tests. Valid and reliable psychological testing, using the Brief Psychiatric Rating Scale (BPRS) (Overall and Gorham 1962), and observational measures using the Nurses' Observational Scale for Inpatient Evaluation (NOSIE) (Honigfeld, Gillis and Klett 1966) were used. The study included a 12-week exercise

programme, where Alan increased dimensions such as duration, intensity and frequency. Initially, he exercised for 30 minutes twice a week increasing to four times a week for 50 minutes.

The outcome of the study indicated changes in his physical fitness in areas of strength and flexibility, as well as a reduction in body weight, body measurements and composition. There was no improvement is his cardiovascular fitness, but the programme focused on weight training so this was not expected.

The psychological change, as measured by the NOSIE, showed improvements in social competence, social interest and personal neatness. During the study, he showed no signs of psychosis and fewer signs of irritability and motor movements. The BPRS revealed lower ratings in motor retardation and bodily tensions, and Alan appeared less withdrawn and more alert. He did, however, score higher on his post-intervention ratings, suggesting that he was less well mentally.

This study shows that exercise therapy can be used to alter physical fitness levels, and to cause behaviour changes and changes in psychiatric symptoms. Alan, who was living at that time in a forensic rehabilitation hostel, was able to progress to more independent living accommodation, partially as a result of his improvements after having exercise as an adjunct intervention in his treatment regime.

RESEARCH EVIDENCE OF THE EFFECTS OF EXERCISE ON THE SYMPTOMS OF SCHIZOPHRENIA

Empirical evidence of the effects of exercise with the schizophrenic population is not in great abundance. The author carried out a before-and-after pilot study (as yet unpublished) to investigate whether there were any measurable changes in mentally disordered offenders' schizophrenic and other psychiatric symptoms. The local research funding committee were interested in whether mentally disordered offenders could be recruited and whether they would adhere to the research interventions.

The small-scale study population was targeted from a medium secure forensic unit of a Scottish psychiatric hospital. The pilot study recruited nine participants, of whom three dropped out. All six participants in the pilot study followed the inclusion criteria of having a schizophrenic diagnosis, being medicated on psychotropic drugs, living in the same environmental circumstances and being deemed medically fit enough to participate. The participants were randomly allocated to either a non-exercise control group or an exercise intervention group. Each group participated in their interventions three times per week, over a period of 12 weeks.

Pre- and post-scales and tests were used to measure any change in the participants' psychiatric and fitness recordings. The scales used were the Positive and Negative Syndrome Scale (PANSS) (1987), the Hospital Anxiety and Depression Scale (HADS) (1983) and static and dynamic fitness tests. The results of the study showed no statistically significant differences in mental health status between the two groups after the 12-week intervention programmes; this was probably due to the small sample size. However, there was an indication of change when mean scores were used to analyse the differences between before-and-after scores of each group individually and comparatively. Mentally disordered offenders can be recruited and do have the staying power to adhere to challenging interventions such as exercise therapy. However, many projects using small sample sizes often fail to meet statistical recognition; in this case it is suggested that a study of a larger sample size will show promising outcomes.

THERAPEUTIC BENEFITS OF EXERCISE ON THE MENTALLY DISORDERED OFFENDER

A number of authors (Bird 1997; Johnsgard 1989; Pert 1997) have identified the following therapeutic benefits of exercise therapy:

Physical health

o   aerobic benefits – improved cardiovascular function and alleviation of respiratory disorders

o   strengthening benefits – improved strength of muscles, tendons and bones; increased maximal strength; improved muscular endurance, motor movements, muscular tone and posture; prevention of loss of muscle mass; and reduced risk of osteoporosis

o   flexibility benefits – improved economy of movement; enhanced range of movement; and maintained mobility of the joints

o   additional benefits – maintenance of optimal body weight or composition; and reduction of obesity and obesity-related disease.

Psychological health

o   Enhanced psychological functioning – improved mood; reduction in anxiety; improved memory and intellectual functioning, and self-esteem and self-concept; reductions in stress; improved perception of capabilities and limitations; reduction in anger and hostility; and improved social functioning and skills

○ Additional benefits – increased behaviours in self-care and daytime
activities; improved sleep patterns; and relief of boredom.

CONCLUSION

It should be noted that the focus of this chapter does not really fit with the traditional underpinnings of accepted nursing practice. It needs to be asked 'Who
considers the physical fitness of the patient and the therapeutic value of exercise
therapy?' However, highlighting clinicians' views of the importance of differing
and innovative interventions, focusing on the patient is the crux of this book.

The author's main objective was to raise awareness of the physical health status
of the mentally disordered offender population, the effects the environment might
have on their health, including the effects of psychiatric medication, and the role
an exercise therapist might have in promoting patients' health. This chapter has
highlighted the evidence that mentally disordered offenders have the potential to
be an unhealthy population. Apart from the effects of their lifestyle before entering
into secure settings, there is a good probability that the secure environment can
affect the health of the patient. This includes staff attitudes, staff prioritisation of
clinical tasks, the effects of neuroleptic medications and security restrictions on
patients' freedom to attend therapies or take regular exercise.

Trying to motivate this population, with often serious mental health and
behavioural problems, is not an easy task, and can prove to be very challenging for
the forensic nurse. The use of exercise therapy has many benefits for the mentally
disordered offender, both physiological and psychological. These offer many
rewards for the individual – relief from debilitating side-effects of medications,
such as weight gain; inducing feelings of well-being; and reducing the boredom
and frustrations of living in secure environments.

THE WAY FORWARD

Future directions for clinical practice using exercise therapy will need to take
account of recommendations for health initiatives for this population living in
secure environments. There is a need for a focus of health promotion initiatives
within the secure environments aiming to encourage exercise activity (Scottish
Executive 1999). Innovative and creative nursing practice should be promoted,
allowing nurses to develop their therapeutic skills in imaginative ways, such as
exercise therapy, as an adjunct treatment in the holistic care of the mentally disordered offender in secure settings (UKCC 1992b).

Evidence-based practice is necessary for forensic nursing practice to develop,
as Gibbon and Kettles (Chapter 2) identify. Much of the research in the area of
exercise therapy is subjective and opinion-based. We now know that exercise is

good for your physical health and mental health, but why or how? Research is very challenging and not for the faint hearted, but it is also rewarding personally and professionally. Nursing today with the emergence of clinical governance expects all clinicians to take the responsibility to evaluate our interventions and practise evidence-based care.

CHAPTER 9

Nursing Interventions and Future Directions with Women in Secure Services

Anne Aiyegbusi

INTRODUCTION

Though easily recognised by forensic clinicians, a population of mentally disordered women offenders remain poorly defined in any formal sense. A high concentration of such women are detained in high security psychiatric hospitals, where to a large extent they continue to be clinically ill-defined, that is, not fitting neatly into any existing diagnostic category or conforming to traditional theories of psychological dysfunction. Nevertheless, they have an extreme range of needs, which are hard to meet.

This population of women tend to present severe challenges to services. Historically, they have proven to be especially difficult to manage in those mental health services offering less than a high level of security. With few exceptions, they are nevertheless badly placed in high security where they tend not to fulfil the admission criteria laid down in the NHS Reorganisation Act 1973, which requires compulsorily detained patients to be in need of special security on the grounds of their dangerous, violent or criminal propensities. As most women do not fulfil this requirement, they are regarded as inappropriately placed in the high security psychiatric hospitals. Recent policy suggests that something other than the existing range of secure provision is required for women.

When exploring why so many women mentally disordered offenders with complex clinical presentations have ended up detained within the high security psychiatric system, it seems clear that their extreme behavioural disturbance, as opposed to, say, their index offences, is the main contributing factor. Lack of any coherent, workable formulation compounds the difficulties professionals have, while virtually sealing the patients' fate in terms of long-term detention in condi-tions of high security.

This chapter aims to clarify some of the patients' clinical needs. By integrating clinical experience with existing academic theory, a putative clinical formulation is described. By delineating specific, though overlapping, clinical characteristics, some insight into the significance of trauma re-enactment should be gained. There is a need for much additional research into clarifying needs and establishing effective and evidence-based mental health nursing practice in relation to women detained in secure services, but this seems a weak excuse for not beginning to redress the very raw deal these patients and their caregivers have traditionally had.

WOMEN IN SECURE SERVICES – A BRIEF REVIEW OF THE HISTORY

It is almost a century and a half since the first secure psychiatric facility was opened in England. However, it is only during the past ten years that mental health profes-sionals have begun to clarify the needs of mentally disordered women offenders and to start accepting that their needs are different from the larger, more dominant group of male mentally disordered offenders. Appreciating that women require something other than the currently available mainstream, male-oriented secure mental health provision is therefore not too great a leap to make.

The Report of The Committee of Inquiry into Complaints About Ashworth Hospital (Department of Health 1992) (hereafter referred to as the Ashworth Inquiry Report) provided a first public description of the kind of care and treatment provided for women mentally disordered offenders. The account given was a harrowing one. It described an impoverished, harsh and grossly disempowering regime, where relationships between patients and professionals were characterised by abuse, including the sexualised abuse of women patients by male professionals. Shockingly, it was also felt that many women did not need to be there but were detained in conditions of high security because of a lack of appro-priate provision at lower levels of security. This observation has been echoed many times since then, highlighting the failure of the national regional secure unit programme to evolve in a way that was as responsive to the needs of women mentally disordered offenders as it was to the needs of their male counterparts. Most specifically, these facilities, which operate at the level of medium security, have a predominance of mixed-gender wards.

Women patients' severe psychiatric disorders could be understood as the con-sequence of their traumatic histories, the most extreme of which would include prolonged and severe physical and sexual abuse by disturbed men. These women, when detained in regional secure units, were expected to recover from the long-term sequelae of traumatic antecedents in the shadow of disturbed, sometimes abusive, males. Furthermore, as the minority gender, it was not unusual to find only one female patient on a ward with anything up to 14 males.

Threats and possible traumatic re-enactments have not only emanated from male patients. The picture of the Women's Services at Ashworth Hospital as a brutal psychiatric backwater has also been portrayed elsewhere. Potier (1993) reports that during her work as a principal clinical psychologist working with women at Ashworth Hospital, she received accounts from women patients of being stripped, secluded and frightened by male staff. Barnes (1996) reports how women patients at Ashworth Hospital made complaints to the Mental Health Act Commission about abuse by carers. Abuse allegations took the form of sexual abuse, voyeurism, restraining, secluding and stripping women patients by male nurses. Stevenson (1989), in a paper referring to the treatment of women in the three English high security psychiatric hospitals, makes the following comments:

> The women talk of being strip searched by men, and of being forcibly put into seclusion. The men are used as a threat if they don't behave. The talk is of abuse of power and sexual favours. (p.16)

It is widely known that large numbers of women detained in the English high security psychiatric system have endured severe and prolonged sexual abuse during childhood and adolescence. This is especially the case among women with a Mental Health Act classification of psychopathic disorder (Bland, Mezey and Dolan 1999; Department of Health 1992; Maden et al. 1995; Potier 1993; Stevenson 1989). In the light of this, the situation at Ashworth, and also perhaps in other high security psychiatric hospitals according to Stevenson (1989), was closer to recreating those devastating antecedent conditions than to providing a safe facility from where recovery could safely take place. Suggestions to correct the dismal picture have been made. These include the need to integrate into the overall treatment facility an understanding of how the women's early histories of sexual, physical and emotional abuse inform their current mental health and clinical needs. This will mean both properly preparing those who will work with the patients and examining the overall design of services (Adshead 1994; Adshead and Morris 1995; Bland et al. 1999; Gorsuch 1998, 1999). For example, Adshead and Morris (1995) note that the 'substantial impact of working with behaviour such as deliberate self-harm should not be ignored'.

Since the Ashworth Inquiry Report was published, a number of attempts have been made at policy level to describe the needs of women patients and indicate the types of services they require (Department of Health and Home Office 1992; Mental Health Act Commission 1995, 1997, 1999; Special Hospitals Service Authority 1995). In 2000, a project group commissioned to review secure services for women by the High Security Psychiatric Services Commissioning Board (purchasers of secure psychiatric care for England and Wales) announced the outcome of its work. Central to the recommendations was a principle that responsibility for providing effective, women-centred services should be devolved down to specialist commissioners of mental health services at regional level. This development informs the current reshaping of women's secure mental health services now taking place in England and Wales.

TRAUMATIC EXPERIENCE AND LINKS WITH COMPLEX CLINICAL PRESENTATIONS

As already mentioned, the clinical needs of women detained in secure mental health services remain to be clearly defined. This creates a problem, in that to proceed with the development of services there needs to be a framework in place that underpins the way the services are shaped. This is especially so in the light of the complexity of need and clinical presentation associated with the population of women in question.

It has already been established that what currently exists is inappropriate for women. In the absence of sufficient conventional research findings for guidance, clinical experience will be relied upon as a method for shedding some light on the needs of women in secure services. This approach is not unique in mental health care and treatment. For example, contrary to the tradition of force-fitting patients' needs into existing clinical frameworks, the forensic psychotherapist Estela Welldon (1997) has stated: 'I believe the only way to make any working theoretical hypothesis about how the mind works is through clinical observations' (p.31).

It is through extensive clinical observations during therapeutic work with women patients in a high security psychiatric hospital that a theoretical hypothesis about their needs has been made. The intention is for this hypothesis to inform future practice, research and service design. The most critical aspect of the formulation hinges on the repeated observation that patients' backgrounds reveal extreme tragedy, terror and trauma. Because much of this has occurred repeatedly during key developmental phases (i.e. infancy, childhood and adolescence), personality and health have been profoundly affected with a tendency for patients to recreate adverse conditions internally and within their environments. The personal histories of many women patients contain cumulative episodes of psychological trauma as a result of repeated exposure. To provide any service to women mentally disordered offenders, the very first stage is to understand that any professional endeavour will involve working through massive psychological trauma. Therefore, it seems essential to understand the picture of traumatic experience that the patient population are likely to have endured and how this impacts on their current presentation. The following account is an attempt to clarify key aspects. For ease of presentation, elements are described under a series of subheadings but in reality, the various elements are likely to overlap.

Hereditary and vulnerability factors

There is often a family history of severe mental ill health. This may include a recognisable psychiatric disorder for which the family member concerned has sought and received formal interventions. Just as likely, severe mental ill health may be suspected on the basis of the family member's behaviour. Of particular concern would be substance abuse, perpetration of domestic violence, or child abuse or neglect.

Where details of the patients' biological mothers are available, a striking number are described as alcoholic, which raises questions about the quality of the uterine environment during foetal development.

Many patients' mothers are described as engaging in prostitution, suffering domestic violence or otherwise living traumatic lifestyles, which may have an adverse effect on their children prior to their birth.

Perinatal conditions

Many women patients had complications directly associated with their birth. For example, significantly pre-term births are commonplace as are life-saving, medical interventions.

Attachment system

Negative early life events damage women's attachment systems and, therefore, their capacity to form and sustain healthy relationships with other people over the rest of their life cycle, unless specific interventions are available.

Some women patients have been relinquished at the time of birth for adoption, others have experienced abandonment during their first few months of life, and yet others later in infancy or childhood. The experience of early separation from family during some point in infancy or childhood is commonplace amongst the women patients. Nevertheless, the experience of early separation or abandonment may be less significant than the conditions within which the child remained. In the case of the women patients, the norm is for them to have not experienced good enough surrogate care. They are more likely to have experienced a traumatic environment, overshadowed by marital discord, emotional deprivation and various forms of pathological caregiving.

Childhood deprivation and abuse

The result of sustained early deprivation and abuse in the context of an already damaged attachment system results in a young person who has failed to internalise a sense of security and containment. This fundamental position can be found amongst most women who are detained in secure services. Hence, they tend to report feeling a chronic lack of safety. This may be expressed in terms of persistent worries, which are likely to revolve around fears of harming others, or that harm to self might occur at the hands of others.

Adolescence

It is during adolescence that most women mentally disordered offenders present with serious mental health breakdown with behavioural disturbance, possibly including offending. Destructiveness, including self-injury, substance abuse, interest in offensive weapons and fire-setting, is likely to have first been evident during adolescence. Additionally, many women describe their first experience of marked psychotic symptoms at this stage in their development. A sense of identity is sought through identification with a criminal subculture or Satanism, and the self is conceptualised as 'evil' or 'bad'. There is a high probability of psychosexual disturbance becoming evident during adolescence.

Offending

The patients' offence-related behaviours usually link with what they report as their own traumatic experiences, either in literal or symbolic ways. While the range of offending is relatively large, the majority have been convicted of fire-setting, or interpersonal violence or threats to attachment figures. Destructive or violent behaviour towards professional carers or to their own children may have occurred without leading to any criminal charge or conviction.

Relationships and attachment behaviour

The patients have an impaired capacity to relate with others. This is particularly evident in the interpersonal domain where giving and receiving care is concerned. Such is the magnitude of their relational disturbance that professionals often feel drawn into scenarios with the patients that they feel uncomfortable with. Hence, among nurses, they are not a popular patient group.

Significant stress is conveyed through social relationships, and a key factor in understanding the most negative subjective feelings associated with working in secure services for women lies in the relationships patients have with their care-givers. Patients' damaged attachment systems form the basis of maladaptive relationship patterns and the affective disturbance that dominates the clinical picture. Difficulties establishing therapeutic alliances can be predicted as many patients simply cannot trust. An inability to conceptualise trust may be evident in overtly paranoid symptoms, possibly directed at a specific group or 'type' of person, reflecting the patient's internal working model for relationships. Those who are targeted represent 'bad objects' from the past.

Patients regularly test caregivers' ability to withstand their 'badness' and 'unworthiness' with acting-out behaviours unconsciously designed to counteract rejection and neglect of their needs as they perceive them. This in itself presents an enormous challenge because counter-transferentially, it is experienced as punishing and invalidating. Caregivers feel rejected and neglected as patients powerfully project these feelings on to them. As an attachment paradox, it is amongst the most emotionally stressful interpersonal exchanges clinical staff face. The patient feels an intense desire for care, but at the same time fears care because psychic pain originating from earlier rejection and loss is associated with it. Through anxiety, rage and fear of abandonment, the patient attacks the potential source of caregiving, while at the same time continuing to crave their care. In a chapter entitled 'Violence in the family' Bowlby (1988) describes how difficult it is for any caregiver to respond positively to this type of disagreeable attachment behaviour. Sudden unprovoked attacks of anger and violence are particularly hard to take. These violent, angry attacks, including self-harm, may aim to ensure the compliance of those targeted. They may also aim to increase the proximity of a favoured carer by posing a threat to everyone else. The significant carer eventually feels hijacked.

While not really trusting as such, some patients may appear compliant and even seductive. They are unable to protect themselves from re-trauma because of an inability to maintain or even understand appropriate interpersonal boundaries within relationships. However, where this pattern is observed, anxiety, fear or rage are likely to be expressed in more indirect or passive ways such as preoccupation with fire-setting, damage to property, self-harm and attacks on the service's ability to provide care and treatment by not responding to, or by rejecting, planned interventions. Both Main (1957) and Menzies Lyth (1988) describe the agony experienced by caregivers when their attempts to 'cure' are thwarted by patients who refuse to get better. It is nonetheless necessary to withstand the pressure and contain patients' fears and negative expectations in order to progress therapeutically.

The relationships between people who work in the services require special attention. Consistent and secure attachment relationships between team members are vital for protection against traumatic symptomatology and for effective role functioning. When attachments are interfered with and relationships are inconsistent or unhealthy, stress increases, effectiveness reduces and the workload can eventually become traumatic.

Some colleagues have complained about high levels of psychological stress caused by perpetual and intense anxiety. A sense of emotional hard labour associated with the task of developing and maintaining therapeutic relationships with patients results from this. In such circumstances, the patient does not seem to have a limit to the commitment caregivers are required to demonstrate and does not appear to be soothed by interventions. This phenomenon has been described by Main (1957), who also recognised how clinical teams can act out patients' projections, typically by splitting, whereby colleagues, having adopted an oppositional stance about the patients' needs, begin to fight between themselves. These dramas mirror patients' internal worlds and can be understood dynamically in terms of projective identification. Unless these dynamics are understood for what they are and appropriately worked through in staff supervision, a predictable gulf will emerge between colleagues. Splitting will result in perpetual conflict between colleagues rather than constructive team working. In the long term, the atmosphere created will be experienced as unbearably stressful.

Further examples of relationship problems have been described by Adshead (1997), who discusses how the patients' need for a fantasised, idealised caregiver leads to denigration of less-than-ideal care, which is perceived as abuse. The patients can unconsciously coerce professionals to attack colleagues' caregiving attempts on their behalf. An important function of clinical work in the services involves discontinuing these entrenched cycles of dysfunction and danger.

Given the centrality of interpersonal relationships to the nursing role, the negative feelings generated by these patients can perhaps be understood. In addition to disturbance when receiving care, the women patients' interpersonal disturbance extends to their own caregiving, and may be manifest in their parenting style where this is relevant. Their relationships with their own bodies are also significant, in the sense that their bodies are often experienced as detached, and it is with their bodies that the non-verbal narrative of their traumatic history is expressed.

For those women currently in secure care who have been able to spend at least some of their adult lives at liberty as opposed to in some form of continuous detention, their history of trauma is likely to extend into their adult relationships. Severe, prolonged domestic violence, often including sexualised assaults, is a frequently reported experience amongst women patients who have been married or who have cohabited with men. It may therefore be unsurprising to find that many vulnerable women detained in high security psychiatric hospitals drift towards relationships with some of the most sadistic and dangerous male patients.

Somatisation

The way the patients use their bodies, often in a violent way, to express and communicate what they cannot manage with words, immediately marks them out as a population. In broad terms, various forms and degrees of self-harm, disturbances of physical health and more traditional forms of conversion whereby emotional distress is unconsciously expressed in the form of physical symptoms, are considered here within the category of somatisation. The extreme and unusual way the patients use their bodies corresponds with their experiencing massive, repeated violation of their psychic and bodily integrity and with its obvious link with objectification during their early development.

Associations between bulimic and self-mutilating behaviour have been explored by Farber (1997) who describes the psychosomatic functions these behaviours serve for those who engage in them. Farber describes how acts of self-harm represent a bodily narrative. They are used to express unspeakable psychic pain where verbal expression of emotion is absent. Each patient's repertoire of behaviour can be understood as representing the fixed script of their own traumatic histories.

Severe, life-threatening forms of mutilation are frequently repeated by patients for reasons that they cannot easily explain. Caregivers feel this subjectively as a form of psychological torment. Their attempts to prevent such acts are continually attacked. Simultaneously, the none-too-subtle message is of blame, should one of these episodes turn out to be lethal. This often unfathomable and irresolvable conflict occurs in a minority of women. Their attachment to the destruction of their bodies, and tendency to project all responsibility for life on to their caregivers, can be viewed in terms of the pathological organisation that Joseph (1982) describes as an addiction to near death. This group present particular challenges, as the focus of care drifts towards merely keeping them alive. Meanwhile, they fill their carers with alarm and dread, continuing to deteriorate gradually regardless of how much energy is invested in care and treatment.

Most women patients who report exceptionally severe abuse for prolonged durations while their brains and personalities were still developing re-enact this in frenzied and violent self-injury. Intrusive emergency and surgical procedures related to self-injury can also be understood in terms of traumatic re-enactment. A sense of their bodies being knocked about and brutally violated at the hands of past abusers is relived. The dissociative dimension seen to accompany this kind of scenario would undoubtedly approximate the patient's state of consciousness when abused as a child. The severe pain and the physical force involved in these re-enactments may delineate internal and external body boundaries. Often, attention is drawn to, or actually involves, the regions close to internal genital organs, again recreating the physical pain of childhood sexual abuse in the context of unbearable emotional numbing (Farber 1997). This paradigm may explain the predilection for enemas, laxatives and diuretics that some patients have. The retching and discomfort associated with bulimia can be considered in this light too.

Psychosis

Despite the psychiatric diagnosis of borderline personality disorder, and the Mental Health Act 1983 classification of psychopathic disorder being attached to most women who present to secure services with complex psychopathology (Gorsuch 1998, 1999), clinical experience suggests that most are also psychotic. The psychosis they experience may be conceptualised as the final common pathway of repeated traumatic experience. The symptoms are often overlooked by formal diagnostic tools and differ phenomenologically from conventional psychiatric categories of psychotic illness. The psychotic symptoms link with reported traumatic experience. Therefore, the presentation is in keeping with the observation of Davidson and van der Kolk (1996) that psychotic symptoms in trauma victims are different from the psychotic symptoms in other disorders because of the re-experience of actual events, which may or may not have been distorted.

Examples of the women patients' psychotic symptoms include hallucinations and delusions. Hallucinations tend not to have been believed by clinicians in the past. As a result, the patients are often reluctant to talk about them unless asked directly. Hallucinatory experiences can cover the full range of visual, auditory, olfactory, gustatory and tactile. However, the content of hallucinatory experience, again, tends to link directly with what the patients report of their traumatic pasts. Concrete representations of those who have victimised them are frequently experienced in hallucinatory form as demons, devils, monsters, reptiles or vampires. This may link with abuse that allegedly took place in the dark during childhood and that, typical of childhood memory, has been encoded in a disguised way.

Auditory hallucinations include abusers' voices denigrating or commanding the patient to do things she claims not to want to do. Additionally, auditory hallucinations communicate thoughts that the patient cannot own. Olfactory hallucinations are usually associated with bodily smells, mostly of an excretory nature and connected with what is reported by the patient of her history of abuse or deprivation. Likewise, gustatory hallucinations tend also to be associated with bodily tastes connected to what is reported of abuse or deprivation. Tactile hallucinations involve insects and snakes, which may also be understood as concretised representations of childhood abuse that has been encoded in the patient's mind in a disguised way. Other forms of hallucinations experienced by the patients through touch involve the direct re-experiencing of sexual abuse, usually during the night. This tends to be reported in terms such as the patient feeling that she has been 'raped by the devil'.

Delusional ideas tend to be about contamination or about other people, usually their current or past carers, plotting to harm or kill the patient. Also, they may believe that they are being spied on, controlled by other people, or that others are putting 'bad' thoughts into their head. The link between these abnormal experiences and reported childhood abuse is quite clear and direct.

Affective disturbance

There is a predominant affective component intertwined within the clinically complex presentation of these patients. Bouts of low or labile mood are experienced. During periods of low mood, patients are frequently at most risk of self-injury, suicide, anger, rage and violence. Psychotic symptoms are likely to be most intrusive and distressing during low mood. So-called antisocial behaviours are often an attempt to regulate mood. Clinical observations suggest that mood may be mediated by attachment relationships and the presence or absence of attachment figures.

Physical violence and destructiveness

De Zulueta (1993) points out that 'by defining an act of violence we are giving meaning to a particular form of interpersonal behaviour' (p.000). She sees violence as a 'by product of the psychological trauma and its effects upon infants, children and adults' (p.000). De Zulueta's thesis states that the invalidation of the sense of self or of sexual identity occurring in psychological trauma is at the heart of humans' violent and destructive behaviour. In other words, psychic pain resulting from the psychobiological changes consequent on early emotional deprivation and abuse can convert to violence and destructiveness under certain conditions.

Like Bowlby (1988), who conceptualised violence as a form of attachment behaviour in violent families, de Zulueta (1993) regards violence as 'attachment gone wrong'. The way some patients are physically violent towards caregivers with whom they are also attempting to form a relationship, has already been discussed in this chapter. Female nursing staff are the most frequently targeted caregivers. Adshead (1994) identifies this pattern in her research about a sample of women referred to a regional forensic service. She links their histories of childhood sexual abuse, later deliberate self-harm and dangerous behaviour with the risk presented to health care professionals. The close approximation of carers' roles to that of 'mother' in patients whose unconscious rage toward their own mothers can often be described as murderous, hypothetically underlies this dynamic, which is typically strengthened by a psychotic transference. In their acts of abandonment, frank abuse, neglect or failure to protect, the patients' mothers have become targets of rage. During childhood, this rage was split off and dissociated from consciousness, but within the environment of a high security psychiatric hospital it is triggered and displaced on to current caregivers.

TRAUMATIC RE-ENACTMENT: THE NURSING EXPERIENCE

Understanding the transference and counter-transference

Chronically traumatised women patients may re-enact their trauma through what they do to their bodies. However, the relational context will be re-enacted through the relationships they have. To nurses attempting to work therapeutically with women mentally disordered offenders, relationships and attachment behaviour, somatisation and violence to others represent some of the most challenging aspects of the patients' presentations. This is because of the nurses' role as caregiver. Where the patients' early experiences of care were characterised by abandonment, betrayal, abuse and deprivation, there is a high risk that in the transference, unconscious emotion associated with those experiences will be expressed towards the nurse. Additionally, in such circumstances, there is a high risk of nurses feeling towards the patient as their abusive caregivers did. This, of course, would be understood as counter-transferential phenomena. Where nurses experience powerful emotional reactions to patients but do not have a framework for making sense of such emotions, there is an increased risk that these nurses will act out on their emotions rather than contain them. Therefore, a re-enactment of traumatic experiences occurs. For that reason, it is important that nurses working clinically with women mentally disordered offenders have a good working understanding of transference and counter-transference as these are likely to be intense with this population.

Herman (1992) gives a detailed account of the traumatic counter-transference. She makes the following, important point:

> Trauma is contagious. In the role of witness to disaster or atrocity, the therapist is at times emotionally overwhelmed. She experiences, to a lesser degree, the same terror, rage and despair as the patient. This phenomenon is known as the traumatic countertransference or 'vicarious traumatisation'. (p.140)

According to Herman (1992), traumatic counter-transferential reactions may include an underestimation of the caregiver's own expertise while the patient is experienced as entirely helpless; as such, therapeutic relationships are seen as being of no value to the patient. Another powerful counter-transferential reaction described by Herman is that of the caregiver experiencing strong feelings about rescuing the patient. This can eventually lead to undermining multi-professional colleagues' decisions and working outside professional boundaries. Where the caregiver identifies more strongly with the perpetrator than with the patient, there is an increased risk of behaving in an abusive way towards the patient.

The important practice issue is that nurses, along with professionals from other disciplines, require close emotionally oriented supervision when working with a population of severely and chronically traumatised individuals, such as the women patients detained in secure psychiatric services. As Adshead (1997) reminds us in relation to forensic patients who self injure: 'The clinical team may not be able to deal with the patient's feelings, but they can (and must) make an attempt to deal with their own' (p.114).

In essence, feelings are intense, with potential for provoking destructive acting out. This is so for patients and for their caregivers. A further important practice issue pertains to models for organising nurse–patient relationships. In particular, the practice of having one allocated nurse responsible for meeting individual patients' care needs through the medium of the nurse–patient relationship (for example primary nursing) is inappropriate with this population. Rather, a small team of nurses working together with the patient is more effective, as the emotional labour can then be distributed between a number of people rather than concentrated in the direction of one sole carer. Essential supervision could be provided for the team by another clinician who holds an overview of the patient's pathology.

Establishing a secure base

Adshead (1998) describes the first step of treatment for patients who are traumatised and whose attachment systems are damaged, as providing a secure base. The term 'secure base' is derived from the work of John Bowlby and has its theoretical roots in attachment theory. In the context of secure psychiatric care for women, it can be understood as referring to a physically and emotionally containing space that enables growth towards increased interpersonal effectiveness. Therefore, the purpose of establishing a secure base is to promote the recovery of the patient within the context of physically and interpersonally safe and secure conditions.

Gunderson's (1978) criteria for a therapeutic milieu provide a useful framework for organising the clinical environment. Criteria include containment, support, structure, involvement and validation of feelings. These criteria could also be provided for nursing staff who by virtue of their role also require a secure base from where they work with patients.

It is important that all interventions occur in the context of a secure base and relationship management could be considered as a principal factor of therapeutic work. Herman (1992) suggests that all the relationships traumatised people have should be assessed for their potential degree of support or abuse. This principle is valid for women in secure care for whom the re-enactment of abusive relationships is often central to understanding their presentation. Often, abusive relationships will be presented as though they are positive and healthy. Importantly, progress is rarely made when the patient is engaging in destructive relationships; for nursing staff, this offers an important marker for establishing whether progress has been made.

DISCUSSION

When services for women are talked about, gender issues, such as the way all women tend to be socialised to consider the needs of others first and foremost, are usually the most obvious factors to consider. They are, of course, entirely appropriate and important factors. However, experience in a high security psychiatric hospital suggests these women also present complex clinical challenges in terms of delivering even the most basic care. In fact, the very act of caring has often proved to be highly problematic, even dangerous to the patients and to those who try to deliver it. Such everyday challenges seem to predict long-term detention in conditions of high security. This is compounded by the fact that the forensic psychiatry community has no established clinical framework to support their care and treatment. In dynamic terms, it could reasonably be argued that this absence arises from a counter-transference. As such, the pattern of turning a blind eye to the events that at least contribute to their psychopathologies is perpetuated. Experience suggests that when all other factors are taken into account, it is severe, repeated psychological trauma during their early development which marks the patients out as a population, predicts their bizarre phenomenology, and causes such a high level of risk to caregivers.

The contention of this chapter is that when services for women who use forensic provision are thought about, means of effectively meeting the profound clinical challenges presented by their complex needs ought also to be thought about and planned for. The traditional medical model underpinning most forensic psychiatry services has proved ineffective with this population, who have been largely designated to the long-stay wards of high security hospitals, or indeed to prison, in the absence of any better way to meet their needs for care, treatment and security. Their index offences tend not to be amongst the most severe crimes committed by forensic populations. It is their behavioural disturbance within the hospital setting and the day-to-day management problems caused by it that leads them to high security. It seems likely that this pattern will continue until services are organised with their needs in mind.

FUTURE DIRECTIONS

By understanding chronic psychological trauma and the way past traumatic experience is re-enacted, a framework becomes available for making sense of how the most challenging women patients who use forensic mental health services present clinically. It should be the starting point from where appropriately designed services can eventually evolve. This position would be in keeping with recent policy statements about the development of secure mental health services for women; that is, with an understanding of the centrality of chronic psychological trauma and interventions to address the related, complex symptoms women mentally disordered offenders present with. However, in so doing, special attention to the needs of professionals providing therapeutic care for the population in question would also need to take place. The emotional labour associated with caring and treating mentally disordered women offenders can be intense to the point of being extreme and, therefore, aversive. An explanation, it may reasonably be argued, is that women have been force-fitted into services designed with the needs of men in mind; these have, therefore, been virtually useless in terms of providing them with meaningful therapeutic experiences. In fact, there has been a high chance of re-enacting past traumatic experiences as inappropriate models eventually break down in the face of women's complex needs.

The legacy of inappropriate service provision has no doubt included present-day stress associated with professional work with women mentally disordered offenders. Future services would therefore need to be committed to discontinuing rather than perpetuating the cycle of abuse, both in terms of that which has its roots in early life and that which is rooted in the provision of inappropriate secure mental health care. Revising the taken-for-granted, male-centred view of service design and delivery would be a fundamental step in that direction.

One practical way of discontinuing cycles of abuse and deprivation would be for clinical interventions to focus on the interpersonal rather than simply the intrapersonal domain and for a developmental world-view to be adopted as a way of explaining the disturbed interpersonal behaviours characteristic of women mentally disordered offenders. Thus, nurses may be provided with a viable framework for understanding their patients.

Support, training and supervision of nursing staff in relation to the clinical framework would be essential. Critical components of such a model would include recognising sequelae of chronic psychological trauma from the perspective of the patients' clinical presentations. Perhaps equally important, any model would need to accommodate the relational context, providing nurses with an understanding of the psychodynamics of trauma as they impact on the emotions and behaviour of individual patients, groups of patients in residential units, individual professionals, professional teams and the organisation. Through regular learning opportunities, including supervision, nurses would need to be able continually to reflect on their experiences. In addition to a well-organised therapeutic milieu, which combines structure, predictability and containment with empowerment, involvement and emotional validation of patients, the aspects of care provision mentioned represent a good foundation for providing a secure base from where the process of recovery for this population can commence.

CHAPTER 10

Nurse Therapy in Forensic Mental Health

Paul Rogers and Kevin Gournay

INTRODUCTION

Over the past 30 years, forensic mental health nursing has strived to establish itself as a specialism, and to a large extent it is now recognised as such. Additionally, over a similar period cognitive-behavioural nurse therapy (CBNT) has developed and become recognised as a specialist area of nursing. However, it is only lately that we have seen the incorporation of CBNT within forensic services, which is surprising considering the evidence base it provides.

Traditionally the application of specific therapies within forensic mental health settings have been viewed as being *owned* by psychologists, however the last five years has seen a shift away from therapy ownership determined by profession towards a more pragmatic approach to therapy provision. Consequently, some forensic mental health services have begun developing nurse therapists who are trained in the assessment and treatment of mentally disordered offenders using a particular therapeutic model.

Cognitive behaviour therapy (CBT) has been one of the main therapies where this trend is evident. The training of nurses to use behavioural and cognitive-behavioural approaches has been through the English National Board 650 course. Professor Isaac Marks set up this 18-month course in 1972 at the Maudsley Hospital, with additional sites at Sheffield, Eastbourne, Plymouth, Chichester, Guildford, and in Northern Ireland and the Republic of Ireland, setting up similar training. The therapeutic outcomes of those nurses trained on the ENB 650 course have been rigorously evaluated. It is known that the therapeutic outcomes of clients treated by nurse therapists compares equally to those treated by psychologists and psychiatrists (Marks, Bird and Lindley 1978; Marks, Hallam and Connolly 1975; Marks 1985), and their selection and management decisions match those of psychiatrists (Marks *et al.* 1977). Furthermore, it has been shown that clients treated by nurse therapists use less health care resources after one year, compared with an increased use of resources for those treated by GPs (Ginsberg, Marks and Waters 1984). A recent follow-up study by Gournay *et al.* (2000) identified that to date 274 nurses have undergone this training since 1972.

The development of CBNT in forensic settings has been relatively late compared with non-forensic services. Newell and Gournay (1994) reported on 113 nurses who had completed the ENB 650 course over a 20-year period. The focus of such nurses' work was clearly on anxiety-disordered out-patients, with little if any forensic perspective. This is not surprising, as the course was specifically designed to train nurses in the treatment of anxiety disorders in out-patient settings. However, with recent research suggesting that CBT may offer benefits for patients with severe and enduring forms of mental illness (e.g. CBT for acute psychosis: Drury *et al.* 1996), the potential of CBNT in forensic settings becomes apparent.

Rogers (1997a) reported on the successful utilisation of a CBNT service at the Caswell Clinic over a two-year period. This service offered assessment and treatment to in-patients and out-patients as well as advice to other agencies on a range of clinical management issues. Clinical referrals included post-traumatic stress disorder, schizophrenia, sexual offending, morbid grief, anger control problems, morbid jealousy, social phobia and borderline personality disorder. In the two-year audit, this two-and-a-half-day clinical service received a total of 76 referrals for assessment and treatment from consultant psychiatrists. At present, there are CBNT nurses in a number of medium secure units and all four high security hospitals have at one time employed 'CBNTs'. This development has been extended into prison health care centres, with HMP Parc in Bridgend employing a full-time CBNT (e.g. Kitchiner 1999; Kitchiner 2000).

This chapter will identify the potential that CBNTs have to offer such services from a clinical perspective. It is impossible to cover every aspect of CBT, therefore, a specific focus on three prevalent clinical areas where CBNT is being utilised will be provided with supporting case studies. Finally, a brief discussion of service and training issues will be given.

COGNITIVE BEHAVIOUR THERAPY

CBT may be defined as any mode of therapy that attempts to change clients' thinking, behaviours and affect through the use of the pragmatic implementation of sound evidence. This form of therapy, which is practised in many psychiatric hospitals today, has been ever increasing in its popularity since the techniques were first developed in the 1960s. They have since been expanded to encompass many problems within both the psychiatric and medical fields. The techniques themselves, mainly through constant evaluation, have been greatly refined. CBT does not attempt to interpret behaviour or cognitions as symbolic consequences of hidden problems (cf. psychoanalytical approaches), nor does it necessarily search for the origins of the problem behaviours. Primarily, it attempts to assist clients to change current problems, which they identify in the *here and now.* The core principle underlying CBNT is that of evidence-based practice. As such, we do not advocate the evangelical application of CBT techniques without an evidence base, as was seen during the 1980s when nurses used counselling approaches as a main intervention for a range of disorders, regardless of supportive evidence. On the contrary, we advocate the need for all nurse therapy to be evidence-based. Therefore, if the evidence supports another treatment approach (e.g. systemic family therapy or analytical therapy) then this should automatically be the first treatment approach.

EVIDENCE BASE OF COGNITIVE BEHAVIOUR THERAPY

Currently, CBT is the most effective treatment for a wide range of mental health disorders (Blanes 1994). It is seen as the treatment of choice for the following problems: phobic disorders, obsessive compulsive disorders, sexual dysfunction, alternative sexual practices, habit disorders, social skills deficit, panic disorders (such as generalised anxiety disorder) and post-traumatic stress disorder. Many of these problems are seen within forensic settings, and treatment can be adapted for some of the special needs of the service. Additionally, the range of disorders where CBT is developing good evidence-based success is widening: new evidence has shown it can be effective in the treatment of somatic disorders (Salkovskis 1989), chronic fatigue syndrome (Deale *et al.* 1997), body dysmorphic disorder (Gournay, Veale and Walburn 1997), some biological disorders such as hypertension (Patel, Marmot and Terry 1981) and chronic pain (Philips 1987). Furthermore, the developing evidence base relating to the adjunctive benefits that CBT attains when provided with medication in serious mental illness has many potential benefits for mental health and forensic mental health nurses and their clients.

CRITERIA FOR COGNITIVE BEHAVIOUR THERAPY

When assessing a client for suitability for treatment the following criteria are used to ensure that the characteristics of CBT are met:

o The problem can be defined in terms of observable behaviour. This is done by obtaining a detailed assessment of the client's behaviour, thoughts and feelings before, during and after problem situations.

o The problem must be current and predictable. Current means that the problem is currently affecting the client's lifestyle. A client may have had intrusive sexual thoughts two years ago, but not since that time. How much is this a problem?

o The CBNT and client can agree on clearly defined behavioural outcome goals. This is agreed prior to treatment starting and progress to achieving these goals is measured throughout treatment as an indicator of the progress that is being made.

o The client understands and accepts the rationale and treatment offered. This is crucial to the process of treatment. The therapy is unlikely to be successful if clients do not understand why they are supposed to carry out the various treatment exercises.

CLINICAL APPLICATIONS WITHIN FORENSIC SETTINGS

CBT has many benefits to offer clients. However, apart from Rogers (1997a) there has been no systematic study of the clinical- and cost-effectiveness of such services. Additionally, it is unknown how favourably such services fare against traditional psychology services. However, it is our experience that CBNTs can work effectively within settings where established clinical psychology services exist. Primarily, we have found that the role and demands on clinical psychologists to provide risk assessments and detailed psychometric evaluation of clients, as well as managerial requirements, means that their ability to provide therapy is diminished. CBNTs can supplement such therapy gaps as well as having the added advantage of being cheaper to employ. This section will highlight some of the areas where CBT can offer benefits. This is but a mere outline and not an exhaustive list.

Anger management

A common problem for forensic clients is anger control and aggression. Anger may often be the reason why some clients are in a secure setting. Traditionally, forensic personnel have focused on the control of aggression (e.g. Cahill *et al.* 1991), while little if no attention was paid to the treatment of anger (especially in those with a serious mental illness). Thus, methods of controlling aggression focused on identifying causes for such behaviour or on adapting the environment to reduce such problems, for example by removing stressors, or imposing some consequence (e.g. time out for anger or aggressive behaviour). However, over the last 20 years CBT has developed a good evidence base for anger intervention. Additionally, Rogers and Vidgen (2000) provided examples of how anger can be a greater problem for those with serious mental illness through the experience of:

o *auditory hallucination* – which can in itself be irritating and a stressor

○ *delusional systems* – which can be paranoid, suspicious and loaded to look for threat

○ *the impact of symptoms on lifestyle* – for example, hospitalisations

○ *the psychiatric 'system'* – with issues such a disempowerment, lack of autonomy and control.

A number of descriptive models of CBT for anger exist; however, the work of Novaco (1975; 1976a; 1976b; 1979; 1985) is probably the most well known. Novaco views anger as a dyscontrol phenomenon made up from three loosely related components:

○ *physiological arousal* – activation in the cardiovascular and endocrine systems causing somatic tension and irritability

○ *cognitive structures and processes* – antagonistic thought patterns such as attention focus, suspicion, ruminations and hostile attitudes

○ *behavioural reactions* – such as impulsive reactions, verbal aggression, physical confrontation and indirect expressions.

This model of anger is explained by suggesting that anger is caused by thoughts related to behaviour, and that faulty appraisals of this behaviour and future expectations will determine the cause of anger. Anger is viewed as one response to the demands of the environment (stress) and that continual exposure to these without the necessary coping skills induces stress reactions. These reactions then affect psychological and physical well-being.

Anger management aims to assist clients either to control their anger when activated or to reduce the triggering cognition that evokes the physiological and behavioural responses. Treatment invariably involves a combination of relaxation techniques and cognitive therapy, which assists clients to identify anger-evoking cognitions and looks for ways to cope with or alter such thoughts and behavioural strategies (e.g. assertion training, role play exercises, social skills training).

Case study: Anger management

Mike was a 42-year-old in-patient on the intensive care unit at a medium secure unit. He had a 20-year history of paranoid psychosis and assaulting others. However, even when his paranoia was well controlled with medication he still had a tendency to become assaultative. He was admitted after having attacked his local psychiatrist who wanted to increase his medication.

The basis for all future CBT for Mike depended on engagement, as he had a good relationship with his primary nurse, who was involved in therapy as a co-therapist. Initially, Mike was reluctant to view his anger as problematic and instead blamed others for his circumstances. CBT did not dispute this, however, it assisted him to examine why he attacked his psychiatrist. Mike said that he felt as if he had no control over his treatment. Further analysis of other assaults all had a similar theme. Thus, it soon became apparent that Mike's history of assaultativeness was due to feeling angry over having a lack of control.

Treatment involved four sessions of assertiveness training and four sessions of behavioural therapy aimed at helping him to react first by walking away despite feeling provoked (through agreed provocation exercises), and four sessions of examining his thinking in relation to control and the consequences of losing control. Additionally, it became apparent that Mike required assistance in his nego-tiations with mental health teams; therefore, the area advocacy service was contacted and an advocate arranged. Formal measurement of his anger showed a 60 per cent reduction in anger at the end of treatment, and at two-year follow-up there had been no further admissions or assaults. Prior to this, the longest he had remained as an out-patient in the last 20 years had been nine months.

Unfortunately, there is no randomised controlled evidence to demonstrate the effectiveness of anger management in those patients who have a severe mental illness and who have also offended. However, a controlled study is under way. Some single case studies do suggest that anger management with this population provides good clinical benefit (e.g. Rogers and Gronow 1997).

Post-traumatic stress disorder

Post-traumatic stress disorder (PTSD) is consequent on experiencing a traumatic event outside the range of normal human experiences. It is characterised by three clusters of symptoms: re-experiencing, increased arousal, and emotional numbing, which must be present one-month post-trauma. It is estimated that between 1 per cent and 1.3 per cent of the general population have PTSD (Davidson et al. 1991; Helzer, Robbins and McEvoy 1987). However, it is increasingly being recognised that there is a greater prevalence within forensic populations. Hryvniak and Rosse (1989) examined concurrent psychiatric illness in in-patients with PTSD and found depression, alcohol abuse, atypical psychosis and intermittent explosive disorder occurred significantly more frequently, whilst Riggs, Dancu and Gershuny (1992) found that increased anger was related to PTSD in female crime victims. The question of co-morbidity should be addressed in forensic clients who have a major mental health problem and have experienced trauma. Freyne and O'Connor (1992) reported on six prisoners who observed a cell mate's death in prison: three developed full PTSD, and the other three developed some PTSD symptoms. In a separate case, they report how one prisoner developed PTSD after an assault by other prisoners leading to his attempted suicide. They go on to advise that owing to the high co-morbidity in this study all prisoners should be screened for PTSD after witnessing an attempted suicide. Within the constraints of the chapter, we cannot report on all aspects of PTSD work within forensic settings. However, we will report on two areas of clinical work where CBNT has been useful.

Male rape

Huckle (1995) reported on 22 male rape survivors who had been referred to a forensic psychiatric service over a six-month period (representing 12.5 per cent of male referrals). Of these, nine (41%) had a diagnosis of PTSD. Thus, rape-induced PTSD accounted for approximately 5 per cent of all male referrals. Huckle also described the long-term emotional effects. Common problems were embarrassment and shock, rape related phobias, increased anger, irritability, conflicting sexual orientation, and sexual dysfunction. Rogers (1997b) reported on the psychological consequences of male rape in a single case. The client had flashbacks and intrusive memories seven times a day, lasting up to one hour, when he felt he was being raped again. He was anxious and angry when remembering. He had nightmares twice a week. His PTSD was worse when he was in the bathroom, when bathing and when alone in bed at night. His worst fear was that he would be raped again. He avoided talking about the rape, going out alone, being touched, public lavatories, public houses, groups of men, and reading papers in case there were any sexual crimes reported. He also avoided television programmes when sexual scenes were shown. His sexual behaviour had changed and he no longer masturbated or entered into relationships.

King (1995) suggests that where PTSD develops following male rape then cognitive-behavioural therapies that use imaginal and real-life exposure may be helpful. (For a detailed description of exposure see Richards and McDonald (1990, pp.65–83).) The benefit of exposure with female rape survivors has been clearly demonstrated by Foa et al. (1991). In a study of 45 female rape survivors with PTSD, they found prolonged exposure to be superior to other therapies at follow-up on all PTSD symptoms.

PTSD consequential to offending

The traumatic effect of killing has, to date, primarily focused on combat veterans or police officers with little research pertaining to mentally disordered offenders. Two studies that examined the experiences of Second World War veterans found that guilt from killing enemy soldiers was a common emotion (Bartemeier et al. 1946; Futterman and Pumpian-Mindlin 1951). Kruppa, Hickey and Hubbard (1995) studied the prevalence of PTSD (relating to all causes) in a sample of 44 in-patients diagnosed as psychopathic who were detained in a British high security hospital. Seven (16%) met criteria for a lifetime diagnosis of PTSD related to their index offence. Hambridge (1990) described three cases of grief in perpetrators.

One case of a 28-year-old man who had strangled his wife fulfilled DSM-III diagnostic criteria for PTSD. However, although a detailed description of symptoms was provided no assessment procedure was described.

If, as is suggested, PTSD can develop after the killing of another person, then what are the treatment implications? Rogers *et al.* (2000) reported on a single-case experimental design where a woman developed PTSD after killing her employer with a knife. The patient had 16 sessions of CBNT and the success of the treatment was evaluated using a statistical technique for evaluating change in serially dependent single-case data (Mueser, Yarnold and Foy 1991). The results clearly demonstrated statistically significant improvements in all measures of PTSD and depression symptomatology at 30-month follow-up. The authors concluded that the prevalence of PTSD in perpetrators of violence outside of combat and policing has not yet been studied and warrants further research. Additionally, it was suggested that the development of PTSD may also vary as a function of pre-crime intent. Specifically, post-trauma reactions may differ as a function of whether the crime was premeditated. Finally, the authors hypothesised that when PTSD is co-morbid with another serious mental illness (e.g. depression or schizophrenia), then PTSD may act as a chronic stressor and relapse indicator.

These findings open a range of possibilities for understanding the severe psychopathologies that exist within some clients in forensic settings. They may also suggest one explanation why some clients' schizophrenias are treatment-resistant.

The most effective treatment for PTSD remains the subject of a historical and ongoing debate with a variety of interventions claiming success. There is no definitive treatment of choice for PTSD. Sufferers often present with a multitude of symptoms, and their treatment may also vary depending upon the extent and duration of the disorder. Undoubtedly, the most efficacy as demonstrated through randomised controlled treatment trials (Foa *et al.* 1991; Marks *et al.* 1998) comes from cognitive behaviour therapy using exposure and cognitive techniques, with such treatments requiring on average only 8–16 sessions.

Exposure, the easier treatment of the two, involves the gradual facing of feared situations and memories in order to reduce the associated anxiety and distress. Exposure techniques were first used to treat PTSD in the US on Vietnam veterans (Cooper and Clum 1989; Keane *et al.* 1989) with some success. Foa *et al.* (1991) treated rape victims in a randomised controlled trial with prolonged exposure or stress-inoculation training, which included elements of exposure, and cognitive restructuring with significant improvement in PTSD symptoms. In a more recent controlled trial, Marks *et al.* (1998) treated a mixed trauma group with exposure or cognitive restructuring alone and in combination, which resulted in significant improvements of PTSD.

Case study: PTSD

Martin was a single, 19-year-old unemployed man referred to the medium secure unit by the local prison where he was on remand for assaulting another man. He was referred because he was severely depressed and had attempted to hang himself within three days of being remanded. He was assessed by the CBNT after the assessing consultant psychiatrist identified symptoms of PTSD prior to his attempted suicide. The CBNT assessed Martin and reviewed his known history.

Martin's PTSD was considered as a direct consequence of killing his father three years earlier. He was convicted of manslaughter for this offence, but did not receive a custodial sentence as he stabbed his father in an attempt to stop him attacking his mother. On assessment, Martin had very clear symptoms of PTSD. These included daily flashbacks where he would see his father falling to the ground, and intrusive memories and nightmares. He avoided all trauma-related stimuli and had extreme feelings of guilt and a desire to be punished. When remembering or talking about the trauma he was clearly distressed. Onset of PTSD was after the offence and had become gradually worse over time. Coping strategies used were avoidance of all triggers, drug abuse and self-punishment. There was evidence that in the past he had attempted suicide and self-harmed during difficult times. On interview, he was severely depressed with low mood, guilty thoughts and ideas of self-punishment. He had initial and middle insomnia. He did not feel refreshed on waking, had lost all interest in sex and had regular suicidal thoughts. He was planning to act on these. There was no evidence of psychosis. He also reported a major drug-use problem, with the polydrug use of cannabis, amphetamines, crack cocaine, heroin, LSD and diazepam. Administration included oral and intravenous routes.

Martin was admitted to the local medium secure unit, where his immediate risk of suicide was managed through nursing observation and care planning. Therapy was then instigated and lasted 23 sessions, totalling 15 hours of treatment time.

Sessions 1–4 involved a detailed individual assessment of his PTSD, depression, desire to die and polydrug use. Sessions 5–10 involved examining his reasons for feeling guilty and his need to self-punish. These sessions targeted 'hindsight bias' by encouraging Martin to look at the options he had at the time of his offence and the likely result had he not intervened. Martin was soon able to identify that if he had not acted then his father would have probably seriously hurt his mother and that he was in a catch–22 situation. Martin also disclosed that he felt that his family missed their father and blamed Martin for his death. Martin had never discussed what had happened with his family and had no idea how they felt. He had assumed instead that they blamed him. Behavioural targets involved him asking his family about their feelings over what had happened and whether they blamed Martin. Previous to doing this, contingencies were discussed as to what Martin could do if they said they did blame him. Martin completed this target and found that the family did not blame him and had actually welcomed the opportunity to talk about it, and they had avoided previous discussion for fear of upsetting Martin.

Sessions 11–22 involved imaginal exposure to the death of Martin's father. This involved the CBNT assisting Martin in recalling what happened on the night of his father's death. At first, this was in the past tense; however, by session 15 this was changed to present tense. These sessions were audiotaped, and Martin listened to them daily through a personal stereo and headphones as homework. Session 23 involved relapse prevention, which identified potential future problems. During this time, his risk of violence and self-harm increased, so carefully designed collaborative care plans were developed to ensure his safety and the safety of others at all times. These care plans encouraged Martin to inform staff when he felt *destructive*, and a range of previously identified coping strategies was offered (e.g. applied relaxation, listening to his own previous challenges to his guilt that were recorded and on audiotape).

A range of individualised and standardised measures was used to evaluate change, and the effectiveness of the interventions was assessed using a single-case study design. The measures (Impact of Events Scale, the Posttraumatic Symptom Scale and the Beck Depression Inventory) demonstrated a significant decrease (i.e. above 70 per cent) in PTSD symptomatology and depression. At the end of therapy, he was reassessed by the consultant forensic psychiatrist who agreed that he no longer had PTSD or depression. Additionally, these improvements were supported by his family. The client was discharged from medium security and at three-year follow-up reported no further post-traumatic stress symptoms and had not been arrested for any further offences during that time.

COGNITIVE BEHAVIOUR THERAPY FOR SERIOUS MENTAL ILLNESS

The recent emergence of CBT interventions for serious mental illness offers many opportunities. Nurses are increasingly being called upon to ensure that they focus their interventions on such clients (Gournay 1996). Traditionally, CBT interventions have had limited application with psychotic disorders. However, this has changed significantly in recent years with randomised controlled trials demonstrating significant evidence in support of such approaches. Although much research is in its infancy, the evidence to date cannot be ignored.

Interventions for acute psychosis

Drury *et al.* (1996) demonstrated that cognitive therapy in acute psychosis was associated with a 25–50 per cent reduction in recovery time. The authors concluded that the impact of cognitive therapy interventions extended beyond positive symptoms to include dysphoria, insight and low-level psychotic thinking. Additionally, interventions aimed at reducing the length of time the client experiences positive symptoms have received considerable study. Areas where interventions look promising are for command hallucinations and delusional beliefs (Chadwick and Birchwood 1994).

Social skills training

Perhaps the most underused but effective intervention is that of social skills training. Smith, Bellack and Liberman (1996) evaluated all the major social skills training studies over the past decade and commented that there is strong evidence that skills training leads to skill acquisition and its maintenance in schizophrenia, especially if such training is intensive (more than two sessions a week) and of sufficient length (at least six months).

Family interventions

The importance of considering the family when treating people with schizophrenia is increasingly recognised. There is a range of interventions based on the expressed emotion model (Leff and Vaughn 1985) and behavioural family management (Barrowclough and Tarrier 1994). While there is current controversy about the efficacy of some forms of intervention (Pharoah, Mari and Streiner 2000), it seems clear that some forms of family intervention may lead to a decrease in the frequency of relapse and hospitalisation and encourage medication compliance.

Considering that a major goal of all forensic services is to detain people in conditions of security for as little time as possible, it would be common sense for the availability of such interventions to become routine. McCann and McKeown (1995) reported on the obvious benefits that developing a forensic Thorn initiative would offer. However, to date such an obvious nurse training development has not occurred.

Coping strategy enhancement

Coping strategy enhancement is a treatment which has developed from earlier research, which found that many clients with auditory hallucinations have a repertoire of strategies that they use (Falloon and Talbot 1981). Coping strategy enhancement involves a very careful and detailed assessment of the client's positive symptoms, involving a problem assessment of the voices (what, who, where, when, frequency, duration). The antecedents, emotional impact, and current coping strategies are also assessed, before the therapist aims to help the client develop a range of effective coping strategies in a step-by-step manner. Controlled studies show that this is a useful intervention for helping people with hallucinations (Tarrier *et al.* 1993; Tarrier, Yusoff and Kinney 1998). (For a detailed text on the principles and practice of assessing auditory hallucinations refer to Chadwick, Birchwood and Trower (1996).)

Case study: Paranoid psychosis

Steve was a 27-year-old single man who was admitted to a medium secure unit from the local remand prison for assessment and treatment of paranoia. His offence involved attacking a neighbour who he believed was sent by the Devil to 'corrupt him' to become evil. He had a one-year history of paranoia related to this theme. He did not know why the Devil wished to do this, except that he was a believer in God. He felt that such 'treatment' was undeserved and, therefore, persecutory. He provided three reasons to support his belief: (1) his neighbour always acted suspicious and avoided eye contact when he saw Steve; (2) his rubbish bags were regularly moved from the back alleyway where he had left them; (3) he had overheard his neighbour saying the word 'Devil' aloud one day when talking to a person in his back garden.

Traditionally, it has been assumed that delusional beliefs are fixed entities that are not amenable to change. However, Garety, Hemsley and Wessely (1991) have demonstrated that this is not the case. Whilst there are various different cognitive-behavioural theories that attempt to explain the development and maintenance of delusions (e.g. Bentall, Kaney and Dewey 1991), no single model has been universally accepted. Nonetheless, consensus supports the view that delusions are judgements that an individual makes when attempting to make sense of internal or external events (Garety 1992). These judgements are considered to be a continuation of normal thought processes. This model allows clinicians to provide clients with a normalising, as opposed to alienating, rationale for their experiences.

Paranoid delusional beliefs have been demonstrated to be associated with people who over-focus on threat-related events, and additionally have an attentional bias of attributing negative events to external influences (Bentall 1992). The focus of therapy is to develop a safe and therapeutic relationship whereby the client can view their problems as worthy of examination and exploration. This can sometimes take considerable time, especially within in-patient settings, as clients may rarely be asked to talk about their beliefs and associated meanings in great detail.

CBNT aimed at assisting Steve in examining his beliefs. He was referred by his consultant psychiatrist as medication alone had not changed his paranoia in any way. He was taking clopixol decanoate 200 mgs weekly.

Treatment lasted for 11 sessions (including assessment) totalling 12 hours of therapy time. Therapy aimed at helping Steve try to identify as many possible alternative explanations for each of the three evidence examples (e.g. reasons why these may have been innocent). It didn't matter at this stage whether he believed them or not. At first, to help Steve do this the therapist offered some explanations that were outrageous but possible. Steve accepted these and found them humorous. He then was able to carry on this process of finding non-threat-related reasons. In all, Steve generated 17 possible explanations. During these sessions Steve informed his therapist that he had been worrying about the Devil coming after him (after reading a book about the Devil) just prior to his neighbour moving in. Thus, evidence as to why the Devil would want to get him was examined.

Steve felt that by reading the book he was allowing the Devil inside his mind and, therefore, began worrying that he would want to 'claim him'. Additionally, he felt very guilty about reading the book. This guilt was examined over a number of sessions; it helped Steve to identify that the only thing he did wrong (his belief) was to read the book. He was encouraged to examine why reading a book alone would give the Devil enough power to control him. Behavioural exercises aimed at getting Steve to do things he didn't want to do (e.g. smoke a cigarette) assisted him in examining whether he was in control of his own actions. These experiments were very useful and soon Steve began to say that 'no one could make him do anything against his will...not even the Devil'. He then was able to challenge his beliefs about his neighbour, which was very successful and relatively straightforward. His strength of belief (i.e. the percentage conviction that his belief was true on a 0 per cent to 100 per cent scale) was 100 per cent prior to treatment and 10 per cent at the end of treatment. These changes in belief were maintained at one-year follow-up when the client was back living at home. Additionally, there had been no further disputes with his neighbour or further readmissions to hospital.

NURSE THERAPY TRAINING

This chapter has examined some areas where CBNT can be useful for forensic mental health services. These are not intended to be an exhaustive list, but they do highlight some of the exciting possibilities for the development of CBNTs within forensic mental health.

However, a major problem of resources and training exists. Gournay *et al.* (2000) reported that there are only 274 trained CBNTs. Furthermore, these nurses are mainly employed to work in out-patient departments with clients who have anxiety and related disorders, and there are serious deficits in the numbers to provide an equitable service nationally. Additionally, there have been growing advances in the development of nurses trained in psychosocial interventions and case management with patients with serious mental illness (Thorn Programme) (see Gournay and Birley 1998). However, again, the majority of such staff are primarily employed to work within the community and not as in-patient CBNTs. Therefore, it would appear that while both the ENB 650 and Thorn training courses offer some options for services and nurses alike, it would appear that the courses are not easily transferable to forensic mental health, because of the focus of such training programmes being out-patient oriented. We believe that a stand-alone course for in-patient nurse CBT applicable to forensic settings is urgently required, that amalgamates the salient aspects of both the ENB 650 and the Thorn Programme with additional necessary aspects of risk assessment and offending treatment programmes.

DISCUSSION

CBT has a great deal to offer forensic mental health, to services, clients and nurses. This chapter has only provided a brief overview of what nurses trained in CBT can offer. Additional to the above are the added benefits of developing systems and providing structured clinical supervision, and setting up and running training courses, as well as providing occupational resources through the use of critical incident stress debriefing.

Additionally, there are the obvious benefits of providing therapy for those clients who have anxiety disorders. Undoubtedly, the vast majority of patients detained in conditions of medium or high security suffer from severe mental illness or personality disorder. It is generally considered rare that a person's anxiety disorder will lead them to offend. However, it is now well accepted that clients with schizophrenia have a high co-morbidity of anxiety symptoms. Moorey and Soni (1994) studied 30 stable clients with chronic schizophrenia living in the community and found that 40 per cent suffered anxiety symptoms, including panic, compared with the general population, where 7 per cent have anxiety problems. Furthermore, clients with borderline personality disorder can also have high levels of anxiety problems. Coid (1993) examined mood states in 72 women with a diagnosis of borderline personality disorder. The results of the women's reported affective symptoms suggest that 90 per cent of the participants had problems with anxiety.

Finally, the National Service Framework for Mental Health (Department of Health 1999) has emphasised the need to prioritise the provision of cognitive behaviour therapy as the central evidence-based, non-pharmacological intervention for mental health problems. Forensic services and nurses could well benefit from taking notice of the evidence base that CBT offers them.

CHAPTER 11

Nursing Interventions and Future Directions with Sex Offenders

Mary Addo

INTRODUCTION

This chapter examines nursing interventions for sex offenders detained in psychiatric hospitals and cared for by forensic nurses. Theories of attachment style and intimacy deficits are used to explain acquisition of sexual offending and the difficulties that it creates for sex offenders (Ward, Hudson and McCormack 1997). The decision to use attachment and intimacy theories to explain the acquisition of sexual offending is influenced by the work of Bowlby (1969, 1973, 1980), Ainsworth (1989) and Ainsworth and Bowlby (1991), and by the importance of the impact of early interpersonal relationships in the development of sexually inappropriate behaviour (Marshall 1989, 1993). What constitutes a sexual offender, sexual offences, the scale of sexual offences as a problem, a case for treatment, the need for multi-agency collaborative working, and implications for future practice are addressed. Unfortunately, it is not possible within the confines of this chapter to discuss all aspects of such a complex social issue. A case within clinical practice is used to illustrate some of the nursing interventions utilised in working with one sex offender charged with lewd, libidinous behaviour and sexual indecency towards under-age girls.

OVERVIEW

Sexual offences are considered a serious social problem and are an important part of the criminal law concerned with behaviours that society recognises as both unacceptable and criminally culpable (Home Office 1990, 2000). Also, the subject of sexual offending is very emotive and compounded with many blind spots and prejudices (O'Rourke 1997; Prins 1990). To understand what constitutes sexual offence in any given society we need to understand the particular society's view of what is right and wrong in sexual relationships, and the social attitudes towards the roles of men and women. According to O'Rourke (1997), an understanding of those who commit sexual offences is closely associated with the wider attitude to sexual behaviour and society's view on that topic. Sexual behaviours deemed normal to one person may be viewed by another as abnormal since not all sexual behaviours deemed deviant constitute a crime. For example, oral sex between two consenting adults could be considered as deviant by some societies but would generally not be a criminal offence. However, the occurrence of HIV has promoted awareness that certain sexual practices can be unsafe, but not deviant. Also, the law only intervenes in private sexual matters when children and vulnerable people are involved, and where opportunities for coercion exist or where public decency might be affronted (Prins 1986).

Sexual experience is a private thing between individuals. The dishonouring by another person of one's personal autonomy and freedom to choose with whom and when one shares sexual experience (Home Office 2000), whether by coercion or not, must be devastating and the lowest form of human degradation. Among those who commit these crimes, some are caught, some are never caught, some are convicted and some are eventually sent to mental health care providers for treatment and care (Fedorff and Moran 1997).

Such crimes raise many different emotions within various sectors of our society. If you ask the average person on the street their views on what to do with people who commit sexual offences, you are likely to hear mixed views: they need help; lock these monsters up and throw away the key; shoot them; hang them; castrate and electrocute them. It is believed by some that nothing less will prevent sex offenders from offending again in the future (Lotke 2000). Perhaps an entrenched belief about sex offenders is that they cannot be treated (Furby, Weinrott and Blackshaw 1989; Soothill and Gibbens 1978). These varied stereo-typical views do not reflect reality in the context of what we now know about offering interventions to sex offenders through specific tailored treatment programmes (Grubin 2000; Marshall 1989; Prentky and Burgess 1990; Scheela 1995, 1997; Spencer 1999).

As health professionals, we are increasingly called upon to assess child sex offenders for treatment and for disposition purposes to legal and social services and mental health care providers (O'Rourke 1997). It may be that we, as mental health nurses, in the course of our work are providing care for perpetrators *and* victims of sex crimes unknowingly (Burgess and Holmstorm 1974; Carter *et al.* 1987; Dunn and Gilchrist 1993; Eby *et al.* 1995; Gilbert 1994; Harvey, Rawson and Obert 1994; Koss and Heslet 1992; Lotke 2000).

Not only do forensic nurses need to have the theoretical understanding of sexual offending behaviour to work with sex offenders, but they also have to confront their own reactions to the nature of the offence alongside working with other agencies in the treatment programme.

WHO IS A SEX OFFENDER?

The problem is that sexual offenders vary considerably in characteristics, abuse and criminal mental health history, social skills, degree of remorse and ability to be rehabilitated (Finkelhor 1986; Hindman 1989; Hollin and Howells 1991; MacFarlane and Waterman 1986; Maletzky 1991; Salter 1988; Scheela 1994; Sgroi 1982). According to Duehn (1994), child sex offenders are evenly distributed across demographic, socio-economic, ethnic, cultural and religious categories. The problem is that it is difficult to pick sex offenders out from the crowd (Spencer 1999). The difficulty in knowing who is a sex offender is embedded in the fact that such crimes take place in private (Lotke 2000), and in most cases the perpetrators of these crimes are ordinary people leading ordinary lives (Spencer 1999). There is also a bone of contention between theorists on how individuals become sex offenders. One school of thought is that this type of offending behaviour stems from having been subjected to sexual abuse when a child (Burgess and Holmstorm 1974; Carter et al. 1987; Dunn and Gilchrist 1993; Eby et al. 1995; Gilbert 1994; Groth 1979a, 1979b; Harvey et al. 1994; Koss and Heslet 1992; Lotke 2000). However, this view is not shared by others (Fedorff and Moran 1997; Perkins 1991), who assert that being abused as a child is not the sole determinant of becoming a sex offender later in life and that a multiplicity of factors have a major role to play in victim outcome. This seems to be the basis for the complexity in understanding this social phenomenon.

WHAT IS A SEXUAL OFFENCE?

In the UK, a wide range of behaviours are officially classified as sexual offences (Home Office 2000; Prins 1990). Sexual offence has many facets and individuals commit sexual offences for a variety of motives. Sexual offences occur when one's autonomy and freedom to decide with whom one shares sexual experience is usurped by another with or without force (Home Office 2000). A broad definition is offered by the Centre for Disease Control and Protection (1997). This states that a sexual offence is:

1. the abuse of physical power to compel a person to engage in a sexual act against his or her will, whether or not the act is complete

2. an attempted or completed sexual act involving a person who is unable to understand the nature or condition of the act, or unable to decline participation or to communicate unwillingness to engage in a

sexual act due to age, illness, disability, influence of alcohol or other drugs, intimidation, pressure and/or abusive sexual contact

3.   any act that does not involve the consent of the other and with the intent to abuse power over another.

Sexual offence therefore has many strands to it, from dabbling in child pornographic materials, child trafficking for sexual exploitation, child prostitution operated by adults for their personal economic gain, abduction and rape and other lewd and libidinous activities. This may, in some cases, involve actual bodily harm, grievous bodily harm, torture, maiming and murder.

HOW SERIOUS IS THE PROBLEM OF SEXUAL OFFENDING?

Sexual offences are nothing new in society, but their acknowledgement as a social problem is a fairly recent phenomenon (Crighton 1995). In North America, the feminist movement was largely responsible for the acknowledgement that sexual abuse of women and children is a large-scale problem (Marshall and Barbaree 1990a), a development followed in the UK (Fisher 1994). The victims of sexual offences are predominantly females and children although males are affected too. There is ample evidence indicating a disparity between the number of sexual offences taking place in society and those reported. This must be considered in order to have a clear picture of the real scale of this problem. However, both victim and offender studies emphasise that official statistics greatly underestimate the true prevalence of sex offences, such that a significant amount of sexual victimisation never reaches official attention (Baker and Duncan 1985; Finkelhor 1984; Groth, Longo and McFadin 1982; Lotke 2000; Morrison, Erooga and Beckett 1994; Salter 1988; Peters, Wyatt and Finkelhor 1986). Nonetheless, the Home Office (1990) asserts that the number of sexual offenders identified by the criminal justice system has risen dramatically over the past ten years in the UK and attributes this marked rise in sexual offending to an increase in reporting rather than offending. Victims of sex crimes have become increasingly vocal and involved in lobbying the attention of politicians, who in turn have become convinced that sex offences constitute a new social pandemic that is calling out for changes in the law (Fedorff and Moran 1997).

Another reason for what appears to be an increase in sexual offences is that people are more informed and intolerant about sexual offences in present times. They know their rights more, and are listened to when they report cases of sexual assault and abuse, as evidenced in the legislative changes taking place to tackle sexual offences (Home Office 2000; MacLean 2000). Enforcement of the sexual offence laws is more aggressive now, and the media coverage and growing social awareness of the ripple effect of such crimes on society have galvanised public attention to the problem (Briere and Runtz 1987).

FAILINGS OF SEXUAL OFFENDERS

Research and theoretical evidence suggests that sexual offenders have intimacy skill deficits that may contribute in the aetiology and perpetuation of their dysfunctional sexual behaviour. The need to belong and to be intimate with someone is arguably as fundamental a human motive as the need for food and sex (Baumeister and Leary 1995). According to Ward, Hudson, Marshall and Siegert (1995), the satisfaction of this need requires frequent affectively pleasant interactions with another person in the context of a stable and enduring relationship. Despite the controversy that surrounds the subject of intimacy, most researchers agree that it involves mutual self-disclosure in relationships, warmth and affection, closeness and interdependency between partners (Fehr and Perlman 1985; Weiss 1973). Other writers, such as Bass and Davis (1988), define intimacy as the 'bonding between two people based on trust, respect, love and the ability to share deeply' (p.223). Intimacy can, therefore, be perceived as an enduring motive that reflects an individual's preference or readiness to experience closeness, warmth and communication. The consequent benefits of a sense of security and emotional comfort that intimacy offers individuals are seen in the fact that individuals in satisfactory close relationships appear to be more resilient to stress, feel better about themselves, and enjoy better physical and mental health (Fehr and Perlhan 1985). As maintained by Marshall (1989, 1993), the quality of early interpersonal relationships plays an important role in the development of sexually inappropriate behaviour, partly as a result of its influence on adult attachment styles, and subsequent fulfilment of intimacy needs in adult relationships.

Similarly, Ward, Hudson and Marshall (1995a) argue that an insecure attachment style has been found to be a vulnerability factor for criminal offending in general, with the various attachment styles being associated with different types of sexual offending. In addition, a consistent observation from the literature shows that sexual offenders are socially isolated, lonely individuals who appear to have few intimate relationships (Tingle et al. 1986). Nevertheless, sexual offenders who have had numerous social contacts paradoxically describe these relationships as superficial and lacking in intimacy (Marshall 1989). Their failure to attain intimacy may lead to the experience of loneliness that indeed appears to be a common experience for sexual offenders compared with other offending groups and controls (Awad, Saunders and Levene 1984; Fagan and Wexler 1988; Saunders, Awad and White 1986; Seidman et al. 1994; Tingle et al. 1986).

It seems that although sexual offenders may desire the need for intimacy, their fear of being rejected may prevent them from attaining it (Bumby and Marshall 1994; Lisak and Ivan 1995; Seidman et al. 1994). Again, failure to develop secure attachment bonds in childhood according to Marshall (1989, 1993) results in a failure to learn the necessary interpersonal skills and self-confidence to achieve intimacy with adults. This lack of intimacy skills compounded with emotional loneliness can result in sexual offenders seeking emotional intimacy through sex, even if they have to coerce another person to participate.

Emotional loneliness is said to lead to hostile attitudes and interpersonally aggressive behaviour (Diamant and Windholz 1981). From this standpoint, the need for attachment and intimacy with another in order to fulfil a human need enables our understanding of some of the early unmet psychological, emotional and social needs of sex offenders (Ainsworth 1989; Ainsworth and Bowlby, 1991; Alexander 1992; Bowlby 1969, 1973, 1980; Hartup 1986).

The lack of emotional closeness fused with the drive for sex, plus the obscured cognisance that this need may remain unfulfilled, can lead to the offender's increasing sexual deviancy, as the offender tries to attain emotional intimacy through sexual contact (Blaske *et al.* 1989; Hazelwood and Warren 1989; Kahn and Chambers 1991; Levant and Bass 1991; Lisak and Roth 1990; Shaver and Hazen 1988; Tingle *et al.* 1986; Ward *et al.* 1997).

Sexual offenders experience high rates of physical and sexual abuse (Fagan and Wexler 1988; Kahn and Chambers 1991; Milner and Robertson 1990; Prentky *et al.* 1989; Ryan and Lane 1991; Seghorn, Prentky and Boucher 1987; Seidman *et al.* 1994) and are more likely to experience loss of caregivers (Ryan and Lane 1991). The assumption is that their internal working models reflect these cumulative early experiences with relationships and lead to problematic interpersonal expectations, goals and strategies.

A CASE FOR TREATMENT

Current evidence available supports the effectiveness of some treatment interventions provided for sex offenders in reducing re-offending rates (Hall 1995; Lotke 2000; McGrath 1994; Marshall and Barbaree 1990b; Prentky and Burgess 1990; Scheela 1997). Becker, Cunningham-Rather and Kaplan (1986) assert that the recidivism rate for untreated sex offenders is about 60 per cent within three years of release from custody, while the recidivism rate of treated sex offenders from the same institution is about 20 per cent.

It appears that not only are the majority of sex offenders treatable, but there is more than one way to treat them effectively. Also, the treatment of sex offenders compared with incarceration is cost-effective (Abel, Becker and Skinner 1983; Becker *et al.* 1986; Marshall 1989; Prentky and Burgess 1990; Scheela 1997; Sinclair 1992). Further, Lotke (2000) asserts that by dealing with whatever psychological, social or emotional harm sexual offenders have had in the past is one way of reducing the harm they inflict on others and society, which helps to break the intergenerational cycle of abuse.

Evidence base for treatment interventions

Clinical work with sex offenders has included a range of approaches from psycho-therapy, biomedical and psychiatric, to more recent cognitive-behavioural therapies with individuals or in groups. The treatment involves a variety of profes-sional disciplines focusing on many variables such as personal, social, cognitive, sexual, and predisposing and precipitating factors within the offender's lifestyle that impacts on their behaviour (Marshall, Barbaree and Fernandez 1995, Ward, Hudson and Marshall 1995b). Further, some sexual offenders pose a continuing serious threat to society and need treatment interventions to be provided within settings that reflect the degree of risk they pose.

Cognitive behaviour therapy has been evidenced as the most effective approach to the treatment of sex offenders in parallel with other forms of treatment (Beech, Fisher and Beckett 1998; Hall 1995; Marshall *et al.* 1991). An advantage of interventions with a cognitive-behavioural angle is that they allow practitioners to have at their disposal a range of intervention methods, many of them with proven efficacy aimed at specific functional problems that reduce rates of re-offending (Beech *et al.* 1998; Marshall *et al.* 1991; Marshall, Hudson and Ward 1992). This enables practitioners to construct programmes for particular groups of offenders and to tailor programmes, where resources allow, to the needs of the individual offender. Most cognitive-behavioural programmes for sexual offenders have at their core a range of interventions aimed at modifying three main sets of problems common to sexual offenders: deviant sexuality, social competence, and attitudinal and cognitive distortions (Epps 1996).

Nurses working in forensic environments with sexual offenders provide numerous interventions as nurse therapist or co-therapist, and alongside other members of the multidisciplinary team. Many interventions have been suggested (Adams 1995; Argyle 1975; Cameron 1996; Enright 1989; Marshall and Barbaree 1990b; Miller 1983; Miller, Hubble and Duncan 1996; Schwartz and Masters 1983; Scottish Intercollegiate Guidelines Network 1998; Sgroi 1982; Wilkinson and Canter 1986). These include:

- o anger management
- o cognitive behaviour therapy
- o social competence skills training
- o counselling
- o solution-focused therapy
- o reality orientation
- o compliance therapy

- family therapy
- problem-solving
- stress and anxiety management techniques
- physical exercises and relaxation exercises
- sex education
- health promotion/education
- diversional therapy
- motivational interviewing
- parenting skills
- positive role modelling
- psychosocial therapies.

The interventions listed above are not exhaustive and can be used in combination to help sex offenders re-learn how to control and modify their behaviour, depending on the individual sex offender's specific needs and the type and combination of interventions utilised. The nature of nursing interventions within secure environments require nurses to work with other professional disciplines and agencies, such as the criminal justice system, to address the needs of sexual offenders. As forensic nurses working with sex offenders, we can contribute greatly to their reintegration into society, provided we deal with their lack of social competence and enable them to develop the necessary skills for social interaction to fulfil their human needs appropriately. At this point it is worth mentioning how sex offenders, such as paedophiles and chronic violent sex offenders, are treated and the difficulties encountered. For more information on this particular group of sex offenders, readers are directed to the works of Enright (1989), Fisher (1994), Glasser (1990), Hollin and Howells (1991), Langevin and Lang (1985) and Spencer (1999).

CASE ILLUSTRATION

Simon is a 28-year-old married college domestic worker admitted from the local prison as a convicted prisoner under section 71 of the Mental Health (Scotland) Act 1984 to the local mental health secure facility for assessment and treatment. He, on occasions, engaged in lewd and libidinous activities in public places, mostly where women and children were gathered, and secretly masturbates while fantasising sexually about the women and children without their awareness.

Simon is one of three siblings and described the family as 'not being that close'. His father was a long-distance lorry driver and was away from home for quite lengthy periods, while his mother was known to abuse alcohol and apparently did not pay much attention to parenting the family. By the age of nine years, Simon had a long history of social and behaviour problems, having spent some time in various children's homes following the divorce of his parents. He describes himself as not being his parents' favourite; his relationship with his father was described as always tense, lacking in emotional closeness, and communication was almost absent. On occasions, he was physically assaulted by his father when his father was drunk. He did not have many friends.

Simon attended mainstream schools and described himself as bottom of the class. He left at age 16 with no qualifications. Simon mentioned that an uncle he looked up to as a father figure introduced him to alcohol and pornographic material, and he sometimes took part in play sessions with his uncle and friends of his uncle. He had brief relationships with girls but described these as mostly superficial. He married his present wife when he was 26 years old (a previous marriage had ended in divorce). Simon maintains that the marriage was not working as he could not communicate his sexual fantasises to his wife and there had been sexual difficulties in the marriage. Simon mentioned that a family friend sexually abused him on several occasions when he was eight years old while his dad was away on long work trips. Recently, he was convicted of gross indecent sexual assault towards under-age girls. His wife was unsuspecting of his deviant sexual behaviour, and she later divorced Simon following public disclosure of his sexual offences.

While in the prison facility he began to exhibit increasingly strange behaviour, such as shouting obscene phrases, also saying things like 'I was only having fun with them', relating to the two under-age girls he had been sexually indecent towards. It was at this point that a consultant forensic psychiatrist was called to assess his mental state, which resulted in him being admitted to the local mental health secure facility for assessment and treatment.

On admission, Simon presented as an overweight, stocky young man, dishevelled in appearance, with shoulder-length hair tied in a ponytail and with tattoos on his arms and neck. He appeared shy and displayed poor social skills, tending to avoid conversation and wanting to withdraw from others socially. While on the ward, Simon reported that he did not need to be in hospital or to be given treatment. Simon stated that he was not ill but just having a bit of fun, and admitted to abusing alcohol. His indecent sexual offences happened while heavily under the influence of alcohol (see the studies by Coid (1982, 1986) and Phillips (2000) on the relationship between substance misuse and criminal offending). On assessment by the multidisciplinary team, involving both medical and nursing staff, ICD–10 diagnoses of bipolar affective disorder and voyeurism (World Health Organization

1992) were made. Initial assessment, and subsequent functional analysis, of information collated at the assessment interview highlighted several key issues, some which may have contributed to Simon's offending behaviour, and which were amenable to intervention. These are summarised below. This is followed by discussion of the intervention approaches implemented:

o alcohol abuse

o non-compliance

o poor social skills

o lack of victim empathy

o transient adjustment problems

o socially unacceptable sexual behaviour

o expressing sexuality with cognitive distortions

o disregard for others in masturbating publicly

o distortions in perception

o excess body weight

o lack of constructive use of time.

It is important to see Simon as worthy of treatment and not in terms of his offending behaviour (Scheela 1997). The above key variables are not to be viewed as separate entities as they link with each other, consequently affecting Simon to become a risk to the community as evidenced in his sexual behaviour and mental state. The reason why such a structured framework is required is to enable nursing staff and Simon to target all the necessary components that were precipitants of Simons's situation.

Alcohol abuse
Simon admits to using alcohol from an early age as a means of coping in social situations and other times of stress, but will not describe himself as a heavy drinker.

Nursing intervention
Motivational interviewing/counselling/CBT compliance therapy:

o Motivational interviewing was used to enable Simon to identify and accept that he has a problem and that he wants to do something about it.

o Referred to nurse specialist in alcohol-misuse treatment to help him make the link between his alcohol intake and his current situation.

o Simon was involved in a series of clinically structured sessions on an individual basis and sometimes in groups.

o Simon signed an agreement to practise abstinence from alcohol while in hospital.

o To help Simon achieve this goal, he was randomly breathalysed for alcohol consumption following granted unescorted passes from the ward while in hospital and deemed mentally stable.

o Ensured compliance by Antabuse medication prescribed to aid abstention from alcohol consumption.

Objectives

o Simon will reduce his use of alcohol.

o Simon's awareness of the dangers of alcohol misuse and its relationship to his offending behaviour and health will increase.

o After therapy sessions offered by the nurse specialist in alcohol misuse, Simon should be able to incorporate his new-found knowledge into his personal lifestyle and either abstain from alcohol or have more control over his consumption.

o Simon will use his new effective coping skills acquired to manage his problem with alcohol.

Non-compliance

Simon is non-compliant with Lithium medication treatment for bipolar affective disorder. He has distorted perception and a lack of insight, as evidenced in his belief that he does not need hospitalisation and treatment. He thinks he is not ill, was just having fun, and fails to acknowledge the effects of his behaviour on others.

Nursing intervention
Compliance therapy/solution-focused therapy/health education/sex education/reality orientation/psychosocial intervention therapy:

o establish good therapeutic relationship with Simon to help him examine his psychosocial problems

- concentrate on his concerns; examine his cognitive constructs of reality and insight in order to understand his problem and present situation
- educate about his inappropriate sexual behaviour as well as issues, factors and situations that provoke him to offend
- encourage Simon to keep a log of his feelings and how he copes with these, and for Simon and the nurse to review and discuss his progress and new issues that may have emerged
- provide relevant information on his mental illness, drug treatment plan and related issues
- discourage from stopping medication and treatment as agreed
- help to examine distorted perception of his behaviour and impact on himself and others
- monitor refusal to partake in any agreed plan of treatment to prevent possible relapse
- share relevant evidence from research about treatment effectiveness with Simon to help him see the benefits of having treatment, as this will form the basis of his motivation to comply with agreed treatment needs as planned
- provide opportunities for Simon to discuss thoughts and feelings about his illness and his views on the future.

Objectives

- Simon will know about his treatment programmes and what is expected of him.
- Simon's knowledge and understanding of treatment will help him prevent future offence relapse.
- Simon will be aware of the consequences for him of failure to receive treatment.
- Simon will have validation of his experiences.
- Simon will be able to make informed decisions about his care and treatment.
- Lithium serum levels for Simon will be well controlled.
- Simon will continue to comply with his treatment programme.
- Relapse will be reduced.

Poor social skills

Simon has poor social competence, as evidenced in his shyness, social withdrawal from others, poor conversational skills, poor assertive skills and poor social skills.

Nursing intervention

Social competence skills training/role modelling/solution-focused therapy:

- o establish warm and trusting rapport with Simon
- o create a positive and supportive atmosphere to work in
- o assess what general social skills Simon is lacking as well as the ones he is good at
- o agree with Simon on a strategy to improve these, either one-to-one or in groups
- o use experiential learning approaches to teach Simon appropriate ways of developing and improving his identified social skills deficits, such as role-modelling
- o involve in activities where the opportunity exists to initiate, maintain and conclude conversation with others, initially with support, then tailing off the support as he gains confidence
- o teach assertive skills
- o involve Simon in wider social activities within his environment to prevent social isolation and withdrawal, providing the opportunity to learn by example how to converse, when to self-disclose, learn how to maintain eye contact, maintain body boundaries and give and receive compliments
- o offer wider opportunities to practise social skills learned
- o give Simon feedback on progress, and reward with praise and discuss areas that he needs to still work on; practise social reinforcement
- o focus on what Simon can achieve rather than on weaknesses, but have awareness of weaknesses.

Objectives

- o Simon will show ability to converse with others in his environment.
- o Simon will be more assertive, and accurately identify and express his feelings in more socially acceptable ways.

○ Simon will be able to make his own requests, cope with refusal, refuse a request from others and show appreciation in offering apologies.

○ He will deal with his feelings and situations in a more socially acceptable manner.

○ Simon will have adequate problem-solving skills to allow him to follow through his treatment plan.

○ Social skills acquired will allow Simon the opportunity to reduce constant passivity, which could lead to a relapse.

Lack of victim empathy

This is evidenced in Simon's distorted perception of the impact of his sexual behaviour on others, and in his comments made about his sexual acts towards two under-age girls.

Nursing intervention
Solution-focused therapy/motivational interviewing/problem-solving skills/ cognitive behaviour therapy:

○ help Simon to learn, understand and appreciate the effects of his sexual behaviour on women, children and society

○ help Simon to explore what it is like for the victim; encourage taking perspective of the victim as an ongoing process

○ educate on the law regarding sexual relationships with children and vulnerable people.

Objectives

○ Simon will accept responsibility for his actions and realise that he has choice over his behaviour.

○ Simon will have respect for women and children and perceive them positively rather than as objects for feeding his sexual fantasies.

○ Simon will have an increased awareness of the impact of his sexual behaviours on others and be able to do something about it.

○ Simon will be able to use his acquired social skills to show compassion for his victims and be able to offer an apology.

○ He will appreciate and have awareness of his victims' suffering.

Transient adjustment problems

Transient and situational adjustment anxiety arises from Simon's reaction to present changes in his circumstances. Simon feels a sense of loss owing to his recent divorce. The social consequences of public disclosure, loss of his job, and the stigma attached of being labelled a sex offender all create situations that need adjusting to.

Nursing intervention
Stress and anxiety management techniques/solution-focused therapy/counselling/psychosocial therapies/diversional therapy:

- o build a trusting relationship with Simon

- o set time aside weekly to allow Simon the opportunity to talk about his fears regarding public disclosure of his sexual offence, marital breakdown, divorce and what he hopes for in the future – this will help Simon to explore what options are open to him to help reduce his anxiety

- o help Simon identify difficulties in his present life and fears associated with present life changes and stress

- o help to build on previous coping strategies and to develop new strategies to combat anxiety and stress

- o offer a variety of relaxation techniques

- o encourage him to focus on the positive things he has achieved to develop a success identity instead of a failure identity.

Objectives

- o Simon will exhibit adaptive coping strategies incorporating newly acquired social skills to solve his problems with anxiety while in the hospital and to deal with life changes outside the hospital setting on discharge.

- o He will be able to tolerate moderate anxiety and manage it.

Socially unacceptable sexual behaviour

Simon's inappropriate sexual behaviour is evidenced in his fantasies over children and women in public places, sexual indecency with under-age girls, and masturbating in public without regard to the feelings of others. Simon's cognitive and perceptual processes are distorted in this area.

Nursing intervention
Cognitive behaviour therapy/solution-focused therapy/sex education/social skills training/reality orientation:

o be receptive and understanding to Simon's situation and be tactful in attitude and approach

o assess current level of cognitive and perceptual distortions through obtaining a comprehensive sexual history; be objective and show sensitivity in actions

o explore and discuss with Simon sexual behaviours that are socially unacceptable and those that are socially acceptable

o give reasons for this in order to educate Simon about sexual offences and their impact on society and on him as an individual

o challenge Simon about his beliefs on inappropriate sexual relationships and sexual behaviour

o prevent feelings of isolation, hopelessness and embarrassment

o use direct questioning approach to promote reality orientation to his sexual behaviour, focusing on Simon's feelings and beliefs regarding his deviant sexual behaviour and his feelings and beliefs regarding the victims' reactions

o help Simon to acknowledge that he has a problem and wants to do something about it

o help him to identify his offence cycle and to prepare his relapse prevention plan to help him monitor when he feels vulnerable and likely to offend

o provide sex education by exploring issues of sexual relationships and intimacy to dispel any myths and misconceptions he has; focus on human sexuality, sexual values and sex roles.

Objectives

o Simon will have developed self-control strategies to avoid re-offending.

o He will have understanding of sexual behaviours that are socially unacceptable and carry a legal censure.

o He will show respect to the autonomy and rights of others and their body boundaries.

Excess body weight

Simon decided to do something about his excess body weight when told by medical staff that failure to act will affect his physical health.

Nursing intervention
Health promotion/health education/physical exercises/nutrition/dietary intake education/counselling:

- o discuss with Simon his food intake regarding likes and dislikes
- o establish an agreed plan and target weight to achieve
- o provide access to dietician and exercise therapist
- o offer encouragement with dietary choices
- o provide access to gym facilities as appropriate, utilising input from trained nurse fitness instructors to help Simon achieve his goal
- o educate Simon on the benefits of eating well and the advantages of taking regular physical exercise, and the disadvantages in failing to pursue this.

Objectives

- o Simon will have achieved his target weight for height and age.
- o He will have improved self-confidence.
- o He will improve his physical and mental well-being.
- o The possibility of developing illnesses and diseases related to being overweight will reduce.
- o Simon will adopt healthy living and lifestyle.

Lack of constructive use of time

Simon lacks structure to his day. He does not use his free time constructively and spends a lot of time alone, which can lead to high-risk stimulus situations.

Nursing intervention
Diversional/recreational therapy:

- o help Simon to seek leisure and recreational pursuits of interest and support to participate in these

- o encourage an interest in exercising and incorporating this into his weekly activities

- o utilise the skills of nurse trained fitness instructor and physiotherapy staff to guide with physical exercises

- o encourage participation in activities on the ward, and outside the hospital if allowed

- o encourage new interests and hobbies.

Objectives

- o Simon will have a more structured day to his life and use his free time constructively for his own benefits.

- o Opportunities to establish contact in social situations using social skills will arise, and new insight into his problems will be gained.

- o Simon will be involved in some form of work to use his time gainfully.

The outcome for Simon

The belief was that improvement in these areas would contribute to reduce Simon's risk of re-offending, which is at the core of the intervention approaches mentioned. His use of alcohol was given priority alongside his bipolar affective disorder, as his offence occurred while under the influence of alcohol.

After a period of just over 30 months in the secure facility, having completed the period of his sentence, Simon was considered as no longer requiring hospital-based care. It was decided to consider discharge to a forensic outreach hostel in the community, which has 24-hour cover from a multidisciplinary team comprising mental health nurses, a forensic psychiatrist, social workers and pharmacy staff. This community hostel is geared towards providing care and treatment for mentally disordered offenders with the view of moving them on when appropriate. A case review meeting was set up including all the professional disciplines that had input into Simon's care and a representative from the community hostel where he was relocated. This involved the nursing staff, psychiatrist, psychologist, social worker, pharmacist and forensic outreach staff from the hostel. At this meeting, Simon's case review was presented, examining past and present risk assessments performed on Simon based on the HCR–20 scheme developed by Webster and Eaves (1995). This allowed informed clinical decisions to be made regarding his future care in the community, identifying risk factors and how these will be managed in the light of Simon's sexual behaviour and alcohol misuse. A Care Programme Approach meeting (Clinical Resource Audit Group

1997; Drew and King 1995) took place where Simon and the relevant multidisciplinary team members met to set out the specifics of risk-management issues as identified at the case review meeting.

A key worker, a social worker with training in mental health and an interest in working with sex offenders, was identified and assigned to Simon's case. The Care Programme Approach meeting helped clarify individual roles and responsibilities within the programme and support arrangements that Simon will require to prevent him from relapsing and re-offending (Clinical Risk Audit Group 1997; Drew and King 1995). It was decided to review the Care Programme Approach process at three-monthly intervals to monitor Simon's progress, and to check if any necessary changes were required to ease the anxiety that Simon would experience in relocating to the forensic outreach community hostel. His transition was achieved in a graduated manner, whereby Simon was granted passes from the hospital from Friday to Sunday to the forensic outreach community hostel, returning to the hospital on Monday for review. Following six consecutive weekend passes from the hospital and successful reviews, Simon was discharged under section 74 of the Mental Health Act (Scotland) 1984 to the forensic outreach hostel in the community.

FUTURE DIRECTIONS WITH NURSING INTERVENTIONS FOR SEX OFFENDERS

In the past, the most widely held belief about sex offenders was that they were not worthy of treatment, but should be punished and locked away to protect society (Scheela 1997). Locking sex offenders away without attempting to offer them any form of intervention is not the solution to the problem. It seems that providing protection for society can be offered by teaching sex offenders to learn self-control, to modify their behaviour and to seek socially acceptable ways to meet their essential needs.

Most treatment seems to follow a medical model that sees the offender as a sick person whose deviant behaviour is a form of illness brought about by some pathological condition with a diagnosis. Despite the good intentions of the medical model, we are faced with a paradox – whilst the goal of treatment may be on controlling impulses and behaviour, the very nature of the medical model informs the offender that his behaviour is something that happened to him from the outside, and thus he is not totally responsible for his actions (Stanton 1992). The point is that when sex offenders are made to believe that their behaviour is some kind of disease that has no cure, and worst of all that they are powerless to do anything about their condition, they may rightly question the purpose and value of any treatment programme offered. While it is difficult for society to afford any compassion to the sexual offender, Stanton (1992) maintains that there is no behaviour known to humankind of which any of us is incapable, and that we can only relinquish our judgement of others by realising the potential for great evil as well as for great good that exists in us. In contrast to the medical model, the goal for treatment must be not only to help the offender manage and control his behaviour but also actually to change his behaviour to something that better meets his needs (Stanton 1992). Thus, as forensic nurses working with sex offenders, we need to look at and consider alternative ways of achieving successful long-term results, working in collaboration with other agencies by combining traditional and contemporary approaches to fulfil this challenge.

Reality therapy and control theory are alternative approaches cited in the literature in addition to current practice (Stanton 1992). Reality therapy and control theory see deviant behaviour as a sign of weakness, not sickness (Glasser 1975) and offer phenomenological approaches that focus on values, beliefs, goals, purposes, meaning in life, and the person's freedom to choose and be responsible for what he makes of himself (Corey 1986).

According to Glasser (1998), the basis of reality therapy is helping the sex offender fulfil his essential needs. These essential needs are the need to love and be loved, and the need to feel worthwhile to themselves and others. When sex offenders break the law in their attempt to fulfil these needs, they have contravened the rules of society and the reality of the world around them. It is only when the offender recognises that reality exists, and that he must fulfil his essential needs within the framework of reality, that treatment can begin.

The treatment goals in reality therapy include helping the offender to learn new ways of fulfilling essential needs; confronting denial; developing responsibility, which is a central premise in the application; involvement in therapy; and emphasis on the present and on morality. The essence of this framework is the fact that the offender is viewed as a person who needs love and self-worth (Glasser 1975). This assertion is further supported by Stanton (1992), who maintained that unless a caring, supportive relationship is woven into treatment programmes, sex offenders are reinforced in their beliefs that they are unworthy as humans.

Also, treating only the deviant behaviour of sex offenders is incomplete. In the same vein, a holistic approach must be used with the offender, taking into account his total behaviour – his acting, thinking and feeling – along with the spiritual dimension. The spiritual factor and beliefs should not be ignored in the overall scheme of sex offender treatment as evidenced in a study by Ellerby and Ellerby (1998). Further support comes from Stanton (1992), who states that he has worked with clients who took the initiative and introduced the spiritual dimension in treatment and found it to be a powerful resource in helping them achieve the desired changes in the course of their treatment.

The greatest challenge for forensic nurses working with sex offenders is enabling them to become socially competent individuals who can be reintegrated into society without attacking, degrading or condemning them as inhuman. This can be achieved through the creation of care settings that encourage positive behaviour, which promotes and enhances change, rather than care settings that dwell on negative behaviours. Typically, treatment of sex offenders has tended to focus less on the therapeutic relationship and more on confrontation. This presents us with a unique challenge since the evidence shows that many sex offenders have been victimised themselves (Carter *et al.* 1987; Groth 1979a, 1979b; Lotke 2000).

Adopting the concepts of reality therapy and control theory through the therapeutic relationship framework should be embraced, as the evidence shows that these are critical and effective means of treatment both with adolescents and with adult sex offenders generally (Henry and Cashwell 1998). The appeal of the reality therapy approach is that it helps in the facilitation of personal responsibility, and requires the nurse to become involved with the offender, so that the offender can begin to face reality and see how his sexual behaviour is unrealistic; and it stresses responsibility, involvement and morality. These three components have proved effective in the treatment of adult sex offenders and adolescents (Henry and Cashwell 1998). In the light of the available evidence of the effectiveness of reality therapy in providing interventions for sex offenders, it appears to offer a responsible and reasonable approach to helping sex offenders find acceptable ways of meeting their essential needs.

Nonetheless, it has to be said that not all sex offenders are like Simon in our case study. The type of intervention that each sex offender will require depends on their particular circumstance, as sex offenders are not a homogeneous group. Risk assessment and relapse prevention programmes should be tailored with the specific identified needs of each individual sex offender in mind. Chronic and violent sexual offenders pose a real challenge to forensic nurses. Forensic nurses not only have to help these people find acceptable ways to meet their essential needs, but they also have to deal with the complex feelings that may be induced, as frequently forensic nurses have to listen to descriptions of distasteful acts committed by such sex offenders. This can lead to at times powerful feelings of revulsion and anger; and if staff are not supported, it is possible for these strong induced feelings to impede the progress of therapy, and left unrecognised will give rise to significant stress at a personal level (Gournay and Carson 2000; Heron 1977). It is important for the multidisciplinary team to provide a supportive context where these evoked feelings are recognised, acknowledged and understood, and help is provided. These feelings may be based on personal biases or a reactivation of uncomfortable unpleasant scenarios in the nurses' life experiences. Thus, clinical supervision is part of the helping process in working with sex offenders (Addo 1997).

This calls for giving consideration to the preparation and supervision of staff providing care and treatment interventions for sex offenders. Forensic nurses who want to work with sex offenders should develop the requisite knowledge, skills, and self-awareness in order to be effective in dealing with this challenging population and clinical issue. There is a need to develop ethical knowledgeable individuals working in partnership with other agencies who share a common concern for society and those they care for. We need to develop advanced specialist practitioner roles within forensic nursing as the clinical, educator and counselling roles of the forensic nurse become the mainstay in the treatment of sex offenders and related issues.

As forensic nurses working with sex offenders, we need to educate other clinicians and the community in the incidence and prevention of sexual victimisation. We need to develop both advanced practice skills for identifying risk factors and specific offence relapse approaches (based on research evidence) to inform the individual assessment of each sex offender's requirements and to formulate comprehensive care packages to meet treatment goals.

This chapter has presented an overview of sexual offending, nursing interventions and related issues. Sexual offence treatment is a complex social phenomenon and requires a sophisticated unified collaborative approach between a wide range of agencies and professionals in tackling the problem. There is a need to combine both traditional and contemporary approaches to tackling the treatment of sexual offenders, as evidenced in the study of Ellerby and Ellerby (1998).

Society cannot be protected without motivating sex offenders to change and modify their social behaviour through rehabilitation. Involving the public in this process will help break down some of the barriers that prevent the advancement of interventions sex offenders require to reintegrate into the community. The provision of interventions for sex offenders represents a substantial challenge. More applied research is needed into the successes and failures of specific interventions that are used to inform future practice.

ACKNOWLEDGEMENTS

I am grateful to the staff of the The Blair Unit, Royal Cornhill Hospital, Mick Collins, Dr Phil Woods, Alyson Kettles and George Skinner for their detailed comments and help in developing this chapter. Thanks must also go to Stuart McKenzie for his help in clarifying and developing ideas for the chapter.

CHAPTER 12

Socially Constructed Narrative Interventions

A Foundation for Therapeutic Alliances

Stephan D. Kirby and Dennis Cross

INTRODUCTION

Forensic nursing raises many dilemmas with which the forensic nurse must wrestle on a daily basis, none more problematic than having respect for patients, who could be deemed not to deserve it, and the formation of personal relationships with difficult, manipulative, psychotic and dangerous patients. Whilst there may be continuing debates over the precise role of the forensic nurse, there is a general consensus that at the heart of the forensic nursing task is the desire to care for patients in all their fullness and to enable them to attain and maintain the maximum possible quality of life (Tarbuck 1994b). Consequently, according to Swinton and Boyd (2000), the ethical principle of respect for patients is fundamental to the forensic nursing task, in that it suggests that forensic nurses should retain respect for mentally disordered offenders, irrespective of their capacities, capabilities, social status, offences, behaviour or values. This places all human being as equals, and assigns them equivalent rights and responsibilities based on the assumption that as 'persons' they have a degree of worth that transcends that of other creatures and objects within the world.

Acknowledgement of this human equality is fundamental to recognising that each person must be accorded equal and fair care and treatment according to their individual needs and requirements. This must be without prejudice or favour, regardless of behaviour, actions, race, sexuality, gender, criminality, mental disorder or any other areas that could be used as discriminatory.

This principle calls on forensic nurses at all times to ensure that their patients are treated as people with relational, spiritual and material needs befitting of such a

187

status (Swinton and Boyd 2000). Forensic nurses care for vulnerable people who may be thought disordered, may have relationship difficulties or may be emotionally fragile; and despite frequent encounters with violence, 'inhuman' behaviour and deviance, forensic nursing remains a fundamentally relational enterprise. It has to do with people relating to other people, and through that relationship bringing some form of healing or relief from psychological or physical disorder (Swinton and Boyd 2000).

Contemporary health care provision is a dynamic process, which should be, and is, continuously evolving in order to remain responsive to the needs of individuals and groups within a changing society and care arena. This is directly mirrored within society in its views towards both forensic nurses and their patient group. This is regularly fuelled by the media feeding frenzy during and following high-profile inquiries. However, as we are all too aware, we are, contrary to popular belief, nurses first and (involuntary) agents of social control second. Forensic nurses clearly operate within such a dichotomy, which is created by their conflicting paternalistic custodial role and their roles as agents of therapeutic change (Watson and Kirby 2000). Irrespective of specialism, all nurses have a responsibility within their role for maintaining patient safety and adapting the physical care environment to enhance the promotion of patient health (mental and physical). This is obviously an integral part of the therapeutic process.

Nursing has traditionally been delivered within systems and processes that generally highlight the role of the nurse in managing the therapeutic environment. The collaborative nature of present-day forensic health and social care expects and demands a care arena where alliances between patients and health and social care professionals are seen to be the cornerstones of the treatment process. Watson and Kirby (2000) clarified this notion further by stating that this is not only to promote a culture of patient empowerment where the patient takes more responsibility for their life and their actions, but also to support and facilitate greater client engagement with their condition. Professionals within care teams need to see patients in relation to their social and personal realities and address the needs presented accordingly. The therapeutic alliance is a useful and potentially powerful vehicle within which individual responsibility is promoted and monitored. This emphasis on individual empowerment must remain one of the fundamental principles of nursing care, as it lies at the heart of the caring process. Nurses help patients to identify how they might take greater charge of their lives and all their related experiences.

It is the intention of this chapter to explore further the notion of therapeutic alliances and propose some guidance as to how this can be beneficial to both the nurse as well as the patient within the forensic health and social care setting. The authors, therefore, wish to suggest that any therapeutic alliance within mental health nursing consists of five conceptual and theoretically based phases (see p.192) which should be acknowledged and explored by the nurse and the patient together. This continuum is distinguished by the dynamic mutual learning that supports and guides both parties within the alliance – the patient helps the nurse to understand (in their own use of words) how they conceptualise, rationalise, explain and cope with their mental health problems (e.g. hearing voices, depression, anger/aggression problems, behavioural problems, sexual dysfunction), and the nurse learns from the patient's experiences, both positive and negative. This will allow them to enter into treatment strategies which are meaningful and contextual and promote deeper learning through their individuality and focus. This would be represented by an alliance where the decision-making and 'therapeutic and professional power' would swing pendulum-like from one individual to the other, constantly changing as the focus and nature of the therapy changes. The authors would also like to propose that central to this approach is the use of discourse and reflexivity as a therapeutic medium. Discourse is described as conversation with others as well as a social process (Rorty 1979). We may choose to engage in a discourse, or conversation, about the present, past or future. What discourse we choose depends upon what our patients 'bring to us' in terms of life experiences. Reflexivity is described as the 'capacity of any system of signification to turn back upon itself, to make its own object by referring to itself' (Ruby 1982, p.2). It is through reflexivity that we make ourselves an object of our own observations. By being reflexive the patient is able to 'step aside' from the discourse/conversation they were initially engaged in and view it from another perspective, their preferred reality (Lax 1992).

WHAT DO WE MEAN BY A THERAPEUTIC ALLIANCE?

The therapeutic alliance or working alliance is probably best encountered as a concept in psychoanalytical theory (Greenson 1967; Sterba 1934; Zetzel 1956).

> The therapeutic alliance is the powerful joining of forces which energises and supports the long, difficult and frequently painful work of life changing (psycho)therapy. The conception of the therapist here is not of a disinterested observer but of a fully alive human companion for the client. (Bugental 1987, p.49)

The terms *therapeutic alliance, working alliance* or *helping alliance* have been used by Foreman and Marmar (1985) to describe the necessary relationship that must exist between a nurse and a patient for positive therapeutic change to take place. They go on to expand upon this by stating that the therapeutic alliance is the ability of the nurse and the patient to work together in a realistic, collaborative relationship based on mutual respect, liking, trust and commitment to the work of treatment. This alliance is the product of the patient and nurse's combined and unified conscious determination and ability to work together on the troublesome aspects of the patient's internal and external worlds: their relationships with others and other aspects of life; the multiple realities caused by both an illness and an offending personality profile. Part of the patient's personal growth process involves an increased awareness and acceptance of their own problems, so that problem-solving can occur. It is proposed that successful therapy cannot take place without such an alliance, which is equivalent to a working relationship in any team effort outside the therapeutic setting.

Nurses (and other mental health professionals) must be committed to the development of individual and collaborative therapeutic alliances with patients to prepare them to self-manage their problems, achieve and maintain optimum independent functioning and reintegrate into social life in the community (where appropriate). Mental health nursing has been in the shadows of the medical establishment where care is often viewed as something we do *to* and *for* people, rather than *with* people. This paternalistic view infantilises people and keeps them in a state of dependency (Barker 1990). Therefore, this approach to forensic mental health nursing care has arisen from a (perceived) need to control mentally ill people.

Interpersonal relations represent the proper focus of nursing, and a nurse's therapeutic strength lies in the ability to enhance a patient beyond the restoration of rationality towards life-enhancing growth – that is, empowerment. Paternalism should be a graduated response and take the least restrictive form (Chan 1998). Health care professionals, especially nurses, cannot empower patients, rather the patient empowers the professionals. The only way professionals can be of real service to the patient is to learn from the patient's experiences and facilitate a dynamic learning process whereby the professionals learn what to do with the patient, *from* the patient (Barker 1995).

The questions nurses must ask themselves include: 'Can I permit myself to enter into the private world(s) of this patient, explore their feelings without judging them [which is especially relevant in the case of serious and heinous offences] and in some significant and honest way, respond in a manner that lets them know that I have listened and that I want to provide whatever assistance or comfort I can?' 'Can I see this person as unique in his/her reaction to illness?' 'Can I see what is different, and the same, about this person so that any insight or assistance I may give is the most useful to this patient?' (Safran, McMain and Crocker 1990).

The attitude of the nurse towards both the patient and the formation and success of the alliance are of paramount importance and central to their work, as are the therapeutic techniques employed. At all times, nurses must have an awareness of their first duty, which is not to harm the patient – either directly or indirectly, by omission or neglect. Nothing should override the patient's best interest or the nurse's common sense. The nurse must be convinced of the effectiveness of what they are doing. This can be provided through the use of an empirically sound and research-based approach to care within the therapeutic alliance. If the principal motivation is to help the patient, then freedom from therapeutic ideology and dogmatism and flexibility in the range and variety of techniques is essential.

Therefore, the therapeutic alliance is just one element of an integrated psychological approach to forensic health and social care. It is assumed that appropriate caring for the mentally ill cannot occur in the absence of a therapeutic alliance or relationship. The therapeutic alliance is, according to Bordin (1979), the best predictor of therapeutic outcomes, as the alliance successfully measures and accounts for a reasonably good proportion of therapy outcomes. The issue, however, of how the practical application of interventions within a therapeutic alliance in nursing is developed is, as yet, unknown: What interventions are more suited to this approach? How does/will the theoretical underpinnings influence and inform the choice and practical application of the interventions? What psychoeducation, competency-based, strategies are required?

Notwithstanding the fact that the notion of therapeutic alliances is a fundamental concept within the field of psychoanalysis and psychodynamic counselling, it would be advantageous if we adopt the principles and guidance of relationship formation in our everyday nursing life. Numerous articles (e.g. Dickes 1975; Fulton 1997; Repper, Ford and Cooke 1994; Speedy 1999; Sullivan 1998) have been written describing the necessary conditions and practitioner behaviours that promote a therapeutic alliance, and hence problem-solving behaviours. It seems reasonable to believe that the profession of nursing can learn much about building a therapeutic, alliance-based, relationship with the patient from over 50 years of research on this topic in psychology.

The authors consider that by working collaboratively in a therapeutic alliance with patients (and other carers) it is possible to develop an alternative, theoretically based, approach to care delivery. This is grounded in the sharing of life experiences through narrative approaches (to know madness we have to get inside the experience); the sharing of decision-making and problem-solving techniques; and the construction and sharing of a mutual language and discourse that supports (mutual) empowerment. While there is recognition of the expertise of patients as direct consumers, this expertise has only been partially exploited. Their obvious expertise in 'madness' has barely been explored. The dynamics of the therapeutic alliance could benefit from further demystification of professional expertise in the face of madness. Campbell (1998) considers that respect for the insights of 'mad persons' would not only be courteous, it would be useful.

A CONTINUUM FOR THERAPEUTIC ALLIANCES

Earlier, we referred to our proposal for a therapeutic alliance continuum based on five phases. This was designed to support and empirically underpin therapeutic care strategies that could be utilised to engage those patients who may have had some or many (unsuccessful) therapeutic experiences. These may be patients who have become untrusting of the care environment because of previous unsuccessful, or painful, strategies. They may expect that the treatment programme being offered will be comparable to any negative experiences in the past. Instead, the authors hope that patients will find somebody (the nurse) who may be willing to use any number of therapeutic strategies with them in order for them to believe that the changes can be made. The foundation work for this is the creation of a dynamic mutual learning environment, which will allow the patients' experiences to be shared and understood within the context of mutual growth.

This alliance for mental health care is depicted by a continuum from the patient's first contact with the nurse, to a state of improved self-management, and increased levels of autonomy and engagement appropriate to their environment and level of functioning. In order to achieve progression along this continuum the authors propose the following phases (this is further described in Kirby 2001):

o *survival* – maintaining existence and surviving risk associated within critical times of acute mental distress

o *recovery* – developing an increasing level of functioning to allow the patient to take more involvement in and responsibility for their own mental health care

o *growth* – a time of increasing self-knowledge, greater social awareness and understanding relating to the patient's mental health problems

o *reconstruction* – a time of personal change, where the patient finds new ways to live and cope more effectively with their mental health problems through the development of new interpersonal skills and problem-solving approaches

o *reintegration* – the final phase, when the patient is able to demonstrate their full potential relating to self-management skills and optimum levels and methods of empowerment to safeguard their mental health and rejoin their social world.

Each of these phases and the care continuum are underpinned by predominant philosophical perspectives. These run concurrently with the continuum and influence the conceptual thinking behind the construct formation and therapeutic strategy design.

The first perspective reflects the biomedical or task-centred model of care with its emphasis on maintaining professional, therapeutic power and decision-making.

There is still an important place for the biomedical model within current mental health nursing care delivery, as it can be used to provide scientific and medical knowledge to help those who are severely mentally ill to improve their 'wellness' or at least to become functional in a social context (Parkes 1997).

The second perspective is the phenomenological existentialist model of care, which helps people to strive towards growth and fulfilment. The primary purpose of this stage is to help patients to know better how to move on (Clarke 1999). Within such a framework of care, individuals have the philosophical device by which they can validate their experiences within the social world. The person (patient) and world (clinical environment) are said to co-constitute one another (Braud and Anderson 1998). One has no meaning when it is regarded as independent of the other. The patient becomes an active agent who makes choices within a given external situation.

The third philosophical perspective is firmly embedded in social constructionism (McNamee and Gergen 1992). This could be construed as the deconstruction and clinically applied reconstruction of the biopsychosocial model (Geller 1995; Gordon 1990; Shannon 1989; Vasile et al. 1987). McNamee and Gergen (1992) consider that theories of therapy are rapidly moving towards a more hermeneutic and interpretative position. They go on to say that over the last several decades, developments in the systemic therapies (e.g. family therapy, cognitive behaviour therapy, narrative therapy, psychosocial interventions) have attempted to develop a conceptual framework that bypassed the earlier empiricism of theories of therapy. This view emphasises that the individuals' 'meanings of being-in-the-world' are created, constructed and experienced by individuals during their interactions and conversations with one another. This third perspective leans heavily on the view that human action takes place in a reality of understanding that is created through social construction and dialogue. From this position, individuals live, and understand their living, through socially constructed realities that give meaning and organisation to their experience in a world of human language and discourse.

Adopting a postmodern, narrative, social-constructionist world-view offers useful ideas about how power, knowledge and 'truth' are negotiated. It is important to have a brief overview of four ideas that relate to this world-view influencing the construction of any therapeutic practices (Freedman and Combs 1996):

o Realities are socially constructed.

o Realities are constituted through language.

o Realities are organised and maintained through narrative.

o There are no essential truths.

Inherent within this therapeutic alliance continuum is a theme that connects the phases and influences and theoretically informs the development of therapeutic interventions – the narrative therapeutic approach. Figure 12.1 summarises the therapeutic alliance model discussed.

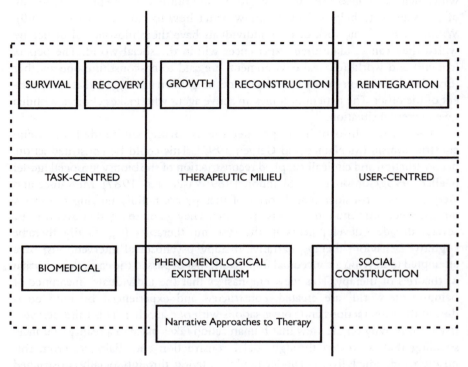

Figure 12.1 A therapeutic alliance continuum

NARRATIVE THERAPEUTIC APPROACHES

The development of narrative therapy is credited to Michael White and David Epston. Its central idea is that 'the person is never the problem, the problem is the problem' (White and Epston 1990, p.36). This was reinforced some years later when Barker (1995) stated that one of the key tenets of nursing must be the belief that 'people are not the problem, the problem is the problem'. By adopting this view we allow patients to distance themselves from their problems, thereby allowing them to work objectively within the therapeutic alliance. A problem is something you have, not something you are. You don't have to change your nature. You have to fight the influence of the problem on your life.

All our patients have a tale to tell. They are tales of survival – survival from the most overwhelming of mental and physical conditions; trouble and trauma; separation, loss or bereavement; shame or guilt; violence and aggression; jealousy or envy. Some tales, if not most, are worthy of carrying an 'X certificate'. The important point to remember is that they are *their* stories and these narratives are the entry point into therapeutic interventions. It is through the re-telling of these narratives and focusing on the problems that we can help to find an alternative and more meaningful way to live. We simply need to learn to listen.

One of the interesting practical aspects of narrative therapy is what it suggests about listening. Unlike the Rogerian therapist, whose active listening is intended to reflect back the client's story like a mirror without distortion, the narrative therapist looks for hidden meanings, spaces or gaps and evidence of conflicting stories. This process of listening for what is *not* said, is known as deconstruction. The narrative therapist, or nurse, is actively involved from the outset in delving into the meanings of the patient's life. In narrative work the process of deconstruction is not done to disprove the construction, for example self-esteem or mental illness, nor to say that this particular construction is wrong and ought to be replaced by another one which is right or correct. Rather, deconstruction is done in order to be able to notice the effects of the construction on the person's identity so that sufficient space will open up for the person to be able to decide if he or she prefers that construction or not. Anything which has been constructed can be deconstructed.

The therapeutic and beneficial nature of narrative therapy is described at length by McNamee and Gergen (1992), Freedman and Combs (1996), Dwivedi (1997) and Josselson and Lieblich (1999); while narrative interaction, the sharing of personal stories, is offered by Canales (1997) as a therapeutic form of communication. This recognises and respects that the knowledge and authority of mental health patients can be achieved through narrative encounters. Through such encounters, nurses can begin to understand the context of patients' lives and learn what is meaningful for them from their perspective.

The primary focus of a narrative approach is the expression of patients' experiences of life. It is through interpretation of these expressions that patients can give meaning to their experiences of the world. These interpretative acts make people's experiences of life sensible, to themselves and to others. In all considerations of people's expressions of life, meaning and experience are inseparable.

White and Epston (1990) state that narrative therapy is based on the idea that the lives and the relationships of persons are shaped by:

o the knowledges and stories that people negotiate and engage in to give meaning to their experiences o certain practices of self and of relationship that make up ways of life associated with these knowledges and stories.

A narrative approach to therapy assists people to resolve problems by:

o enabling them to separate their lives and relationships from these knowledges and stories that they judge to be impoverishing

o assisting them to challenge the ways of life that they find subjugating

o encouraging people to re-author their own lives according to alternative and preferred stories of identity, and according to preferred ways of life – preferred realities.

Personal narratives are characterised by their focus on the individual experience of specific events and are, in this sense, accounts of the unique. The process of therapy based on this stance is what Anderson and Goolishian (1992) call a therapeutic conversation. This refers to an endeavour in which there is a mutual search for understanding and exploration through dialogue. Therapy, and hence the therapeutic conversation, entails an 'in there together' process. The emphasis is not to produce change but to open space for conversation. In this hermeneutic view, change in therapy is represented by the dialogical creation of new narratives, new life stories and preferred realities, through mutual exploration of the patient's understanding and experience. Thus, the process of interpretation becomes collaborative and a dynamic learning process (Anderson and Goolishian 1992). In this context, hermeneutic refers to the interpretation of conversation, with the conversation being the central metaphor for therapy. This is reinforced and authenticated by reflection and reflexivity.

Narrative interactions are offered by the authors as being not only a first step towards the development of a therapeutic alliance, but also an integral part of the therapeutic process. Although narratives can provide forensic nurses with a deeper understanding of the lives of their patients, we must be mindful of the fact that these stories reveal only a partial meaning of their (in some cases multiple) realities. Narrative is an attempt at describing the immensely complex world of human interaction (Canales 1997) and, therefore, must be viewed within the constantly changing, ever-evolving cultural context in which nurses and patients exist.

The nurse contributes the alternative knowledge base (for example, in this context, socially constructed narrative approaches) to the therapeutic alliance, while the patient and nurse agree the alternative, though beneficial, therapeutic skills and strategies within the therapeutic alliance continuum. The common denominator throughout the care-delivery strategy to assist and develop the mutual dynamic learning regime is the recurring and ongoing use of socially constructed narrative therapeutic interventions which the nurse and patient return to regularly to help them evaluate and plan.

Case study: Polly's tale

Polly was 24 years old when she was admitted to the medium secure unit. She came directly from Crown Court (under section 3 of the Mental Health Act (England and Wales) 1983) where she had been charged with attempted murder.

On admission, she admitted to hearing voices of a derogatory nature, and was isolated and aloof, preferring to offer a 'macho' presentation by wearing male clothes, big boots, having her hair cut short and adopting a swagger in her gait and aggressive posturing. Despite this 'hard case' image, however, the only violent behaviour exhibited was directed towards herself. She exhibited low self-esteem and a poor, if not negative, self-image as she preferred to adopt this defensive façade. During this admission, numerous therapeutic approaches were initiated in an attempt to address the underlying causes of her 'voice hearing' and (what appeared to be) associated self-harming behaviour. Psychological, nursing and medical assessments all agreed that her negative self-image and damaged self-esteem all appeared to culminate from childhood experiences of sexual and physical abuse.

As we got to know her better, it became very apparent that Polly had had an abusive and chaotic life, resulting in her having poor coping skills. Polly had self-harmed for the majority of her life, indeed it was her main coping strategy; it was something she was not prepared to relinquish readily, and we should not be expecting her to do so! For her, self-harm is functional and meaningful and therefore serves an important purpose. She self-harms in response to her 'derogatory voices', which emerged in response to external stressful situations and stimuli.

Following (or perhaps despite) intensive work by the clinical team and Polly, her section 3 admission lapsed and (supported by a Mental Health Review Tribunal) was not renewed, and she was allowed to discharge herself. But 16 weeks later she came to the medium secure unit demanding admission, claiming that if she was not admitted she felt or knew that she would 'kill a man' as her previous 'bad thoughts' about males and 'derogatory voices' had returned. She proved her determination by producing, upon enquiry, a 12-inch kitchen knife, which was strapped to her leg. It was felt by the clinical team that, because of her history, readmission was the most prudent move at that time.

Following readmission, her self-harming behaviour escalated dramatically to, at times, quite dangerous levels. She was performing acts of self-harm on a daily basis (sometimes two or three times a day if nursing staff were not increasingly stringent with their observations). The severity of these acts was also increasing as was her desperation to perform them; so much so that she had now scarred and disfigured her throat and face (which had always been 'taboo' areas) and damaged beyond repair a number of tendons in both hands.

The plan to use a narrative-focused intervention package within the context of a therapeutic alliance was initially jeopardised by Polly's approach towards treatment. She perceived herself to be detained in a hostile environment by hostile people. It was, therefore, understandable that the process of forming a therapeutic alliance with Polly was not only essential but would also take time.

The narrative therapy process began by Polly describing her dominant story. If life were a novel, the dominant story would be the main plot. This is one story of her life, but it is the one which has been ultimately influential in defining who she is today.

> She described how she was adopted into a family at six months old, with her 'brother' also being adopted by their parents when he was a toddler. She describes her mother as being a kind woman, though she described her father as a tyrannical man who ruled the house with a 'rod of iron in one hand and the Bible in the other'.
>
> From about the age of eight she started to have problems at home and at school. This presented as unruly, disruptive behaviour and a marked lack of respect for authority figures. Throughout these years, she had attended the local church with her parents as a matter of duty. When this behaviour became too much for her parents to handle and the school were on the verge of referring her to an educational psychologist, the Church decided it was time to act. As a result of her non-conforming and anti-establishment behaviour (by this time she was about 11 years old) she claimed that the Church decided to 'exorcise her of her Devils'. By the age of 13 or 14, both her father and the Church 'washed their collective hands' of her, branding her an 'evil person'.
>
> She claimed that following the initial incidents with the Church her brother started to abuse her physically and sexually on a regular basis, which invariably culminated in him 'cutting her anus' with a razor blade. Over the years, he 'passed this responsibility' to her. This appears to have been the starting point of her self-harming behaviour. Throughout her adolescence, Polly began abusing solvents, alcohol and soft drugs, and by the age of 16 had a local reputation for being a 'hard case', a 'trouble maker' and a 'disturbed and disturbing young lady'. Numerous arrests, convictions and spells in penal institutions followed. It was during one of her spells in a penal institution that she remembered hearing the 'voices' for the first time and this appeared to be the trigger to her regular self-harming.

As the sessions progressed Polly came to recognise and acknowledge that the cause of her self-harming behaviour was a reaction to the instructions given by her 'voices' Though what were the cause of the voices? It became essential to explore with her the significance of the 'voices' to her. It was, however, apparent that these 'voices' were how she described her ruminative thought processes – another maladaptive by-product of her early life experiences.

> When she was 18, Polly formed a relationship with an older, divorced man, whom she had met during her last stay in the local psychiatric services. He was, according to Polly, a 'control freak'. She stated that he made *every* decision in the relationship, making it difficult for her to 'even breathe without permission'. This resulted in an escalation in her self-harming behaviour and general antisocial behaviour, and a total destruction of her self-esteem and self-image.
>
> One night, in the depths of desperation, she decided to end this relationship. Reports detail how she, in essence, attempted to poison him by putting paracetamol in his drink and then, when she felt that this had not worked, stabbed him three times. He subsequently recovered from this attack. She was arrested and charged after handing herself into the police, and was found guilty of attempted murder.

By the telling of her dominant story Polly was able to see how this was 'problem-saturated'. Polly's saturating problems were:

o unresolved issues around being adopted – i.e. the quandary created by wanting to find her natural mother and the fear that she 'may be just like me'

o a disruptive and disturbed childhood

o being 'exorcised' by her family's Church

o being (effectively) disowned by both her father and the Church

o being branded an 'evil person' (at the age of 14)

o the sexual and physical abuse by her brother

o being 'introduced' to self-harming behaviour by her brother

o abuse of solvents, alcohol and soft drugs, and gaining a local reputation for being a 'hard case', a 'trouble maker' and a 'disturbed and disturbing young lady' (all by the age of 16)

o acquiring a criminal record

o hearing 'derogatory voices'

o overwhelming and constantly growing feelings of low self-esteem and failure and the erosion of a positive self-image

- o the ongoing conflict between the desire not to self-harm against the fact that this was the only way she knew to relieve inner tension caused by the derogatory voices

- o an overwhelming fear of abandonment linked to feelings of worthlessness

- o the relationship with her victim

- o her index offence.

To say that Polly's dominant story is problem-saturated is a very different thing than to say Polly has a lot of problems. For her to say 'I have a lot of problems' is to identify those problems as being either in her possession or somehow within her. To place the problems within her dominant story, and as actually saturating that story, is to identify a very different notion of where these problems are situated. Rather than being defining of her identity, then, the problems can be seen as having a powerful effect on the story that most prominently constitutes her life. This allows for a much more powerful set of options to be available to her in dealing with those problems.

She was able to see how such a dominant story became pervasive and influential in determining her life and that it became difficult to notice anything that did not fit in with that story. In Polly's case, as she was living a story of a 'self-harmer and victim', she did not consider it important or appropriate to see herself as a survivor with more to offer herself and others than destructive self-harming behaviour. By the narrative process, she opened up narrative space sufficiently to explore an alternative story. At first, this alternative story was not clear to Polly as her dominant story was a powerful definition of herself. In narrative work, identity is seen as being constantly formed and re-formed through experiences with others, and through our understanding of what is expected of us by the dominant culture in which we live. In our interactions with others, one story is often underlined, emphasised, noticed, told and re-told more than others. If the story that is told most often happens to be a story that is full of problems (problem-saturated), as in Polly's case, then it would be very difficult for Polly not to have that story strongly defining her identity. Polly reinforced this self-definition by self-deprecating statements like 'I am a failure', 'I am un-likeable', 'I always have been abandoned – and always will be'. These were further reinforced by her 'derogatory voices'.

Polly's dominant story had been developed and reinforced over most of her life; therefore, her alternative story was very thin and poorly defined, and needed to be thickened. In order to achieve this, it was necessary to call in an expert who could help Polly interpret certain events of her life, in particular the sexual abuse. This was a case for a clinical psychologist to join the therapeutic process. As her alternative story became thicker and richer, then it became more prominent in defining her life and clarifying an identity of who she is as a person. Polly was determined that she would take control of her life and not let the 'voices' and self-harm continue to control her.

To Polly, the most important aspect of the therapeutic approach, one which to her was a revelation, was when she and her story were accepted at face value without judgement. This is known as 'not knowing' (Anderson and Goolishian 1992; Freedman and Combs 1996). This position requires the nurse or therapist to adopt a position that entails a general attitude or stance in which their actions communicate a genuine curiosity. That is, their actions and attitudes express a need to know more about what has been said, rather than convey preconceived opinions and prejudices about Polly, her voices and self-harming behaviour, or expectations that she must change. In 'not knowing', the nurse must adopt an interpretative stance that relies on the continuing analysis of experience as it is occurring in context. By using this approach, Polly is not prejudged by her actions, there is no negation of her as an individual – she is not a 'self-harmer', a 'dangerous person' or a 'criminal'. She simply is who she is – Polly, a human individual.

To help reinforce her preferred story of herself as a survivor (as opposed to a victim), Polly was encouraged to think of examples of times she had survived in other difficult situations in her life. These examples, in order to constitute a true plot, would need to be linked by common themes that tied these events together and by doing so thickening her alternative (now preferred) life story. She engaged in a process that required her to tell and re-tell these alternative, preferred stories and events and listen to others re-tell these stories in ways that acknowledged, affirmed and supported her in her new chosen role as a survivor. Her main objective in constructing her preferred reality was to be known as a survivor of abuse – not an eternal victim. It was the victim reality that had created the self-punitive and destructive Polly – the survivor now had hope and a reason to feel proud.

The authors need to point out though that this is a very simplified version of 'Polly's tale'. There were regular traumatic incidents where her 'voices' and self-harming behaviour increased as a response to the memories that the telling and re-telling invoked, and regress was more common than progress. But as the sessions progressed and she became more confident and comfortable with her narrative (dominant and preferred), she successfully 'thickened' the plot. By telling and re-telling (at her own pace) she drew out the problematic areas of her life. Whenever someone in our life listens to our story (the telling) and is affected in some way by it, and then shares with us the effect on him or her of hearing this story (a re-telling), we will be affected. That story will be strengthened. The plot of that story will be thickened through the telling and re-telling, and possibly re-telling of the re-telling, and on and on until these preferred plots become thickened enough to where they will take a dominant place in our life. For Polly, the journey along the continuum was not a simple, progressive affair. There were, especially in the early days, regular revisits to previous stages of the continuum to allow her to strengthen the therapeutic effect – to consolidate some of the learning and coping strategies. Though as she became more attuned to and comfortable with her new 'life story', then these revisits became less frequent and for shorter periods.

Narrative interventions are very challenging because of the nature of the life stories the practitioners will encounter. They will require high-quality clinical supervision throughout their application to practice. As practitioners come into contact with patients who are damaged or dangerous, vulnerable or manipulative, and who may have carried out, or are victims of, horrific offences, they will need expertise and appropriate support to help them to deal with the kind of material that this approach may uncover. Narrative therapy cannot and should not be carried out in isolation; it is, as stated earlier, one (albeit, in this case, major) element of an integrated psychological approach to care.

The authors hope that the reader could also see the links to the continuum of therapeutic alliance as Polly's tale unfolded – how she came to the medium secure unit in a state of 'survival' and how, through the use of a narrative approach to care, she managed to 'recover' sufficiently to start taking some degree of responsibility for her behaviour. As the dominant story unfolded and developed through the telling and re-telling, she was able to grow by gaining, acknowledging and accepting an increasing self-knowledge, and a greater understanding of her mental health problems. 'Reconstruction' occurred as she started to reconstruct her preferred life story – survivor not victim. By accepting this premise and all the benefits and new opportunities that this brought to her life, she went through a major (though at times traumatic) time of personal change, where she discovered new ways to live and cope more effectively by developing new interpersonal skills and problem-solving approaches. The final phase, 'reintegration', was a cause for celebration as she felt that she was ready and able to join society – with the obvious and necessary safeguards, safety nets and contingency plans (which, incidentally, have not been required to date). She felt ready to use her newly found self-management skills as she was enjoying and benefiting from a degree of empowerment and self-management that she had never experienced before.

CONCLUSIONS

The evolution of this chapter, and its proposed continuum of therapeutic alliance, arose from the expressed needs of users, health care professionals and from issues derived from contemporary mental health care research (e.g. Barker 1990, 1995; Barker, Reynolds and Stevenson 1997; Campbell 1998; Coleman 1998; Martin

1992; Romme 1996, 1998; Romme and Escher 1993; Sullivan 1998; Thomas 1997).

Through exploration of the theoretical underpinnings of the continuum, the patient's ability to understand their experiences and an increase, through exploration and enlightenment, in their self-management skills will occur to their fullest potential. In terms of the timing for this continuum, Fee (2000) states that it is important to present ways in which mental illness can be 'removed from its objective status' and 'reintroduced into the language of relationship and recognition'.

Personal understanding of the nature of the problem-creating experience may take its place alongside biological explanations of issues such as hearing voices, but it is a prerequisite for successful self-management and coping. Therefore, it is critical that mental health nurses and other professionals develop a greater understanding of alternative knowledge bases that explore representations of self and other, the individual and the social and cultural environment in which they all exist.

Patients and user groups are concerned that nurses are being taught the wrong skills and are becoming less, rather than more, conversant with the day-to-day practical and spiritual concerns of service users. They are insistent that no one is listening to them. Wherever mental health nursing is taking place, it is essential that nurses are sensitive to the barriers and constraints that obstruct reciprocal communication and discourse and the differences between having power, even beneficial power, over a subordinate and sharing power with a partner. In a service with an 'asylum mentality', the greatest power that mental health nurses hold is the power of denial (Campbell 1998).

Stories reflect the multiple identities and shifting realities of the storyteller (patient) and the listener (nurse). Thus, according to Canales (1997), we can never fully know the stories of others or ourselves. Within such a shifting framework, how is it possible for nurses ever really to know their clients? Through narrative approaches to interactions, nurses and patients, as listeners and tellers, can 'build a world richer than either could make alone' (Delgado 1989, p.2439). Building on their differences, nurses and patients can develop a therapeutic alliance grounded in the client's strengths, abilities and attributes and realised within the context of a dynamic learning environment. Narrative interactions offer nurses an opportunity to share in their patients' lives and intervene in ways that respect, rather than denigrate, their patients' differences.

This narrative-based therapeutic alliance is but one part of an integrated psychological approach to providing care for mental health patients, and we strongly recommend that they are carried out in the context of a multidisciplinary team approach. Similarly, training in the necessary intervention strategies – particularly narrative-focused interventions – is imperative. As the proposed therapeutic alliance will be very challenging owing to the nature of the patients involved, nurses must ensure that high-quality and appropriate clinical and academic supervision is available and utilised throughout the practical application of any intervention strategies.

FUTURE DEVELOPMENTS

The continuum/framework for therapeutic alliance was developed in the firm belief of the value of nursing as an enduring social construct. The authors feel strongly that the use of more qualitative and hermeneutic approaches to care are imperative, as well as fundamental, to the creation of effective therapeutic alliances with our patients. In our desire to develop our nursing care approaches we need to acknowledge and adopt the premise that we need to embrace change.

Many nurses are, traditionally, encouraged to believe that in order to become effective in mental health care, they need to develop 'new' skills and learn 'new' therapeutic models. The continuum of therapeutic alliances, being underpinned as it is by social construction, promotes the premise that nursing is effective when the person (patient or staff member) begins to experience growth and development – a dynamic, mutual, learning process. The continuum offers nurses the security of a philosophically underpinned 'model of practice' that provides some boundaries for their practice while maintaining the freedom and flexibility to develop, ethical and inclusive, effective and knowledgeable, flexible and collaborative processes of nursing interventions that will become the future focus of their practice.

The authors wish to point out that the utilisation of the continuum for therapeutic alliance and (in this instance) narrative therapy as therapeutic vehicles are still in their infancy (though we would be more than happy to hear of examples of similar projects and approaches to care within our readers' workplaces). We accept that this is not 'rocket science', nor are we the first to propose such person-focused approaches to mental health nursing. We do feel, however, that the future of collaborative nursing care with patients within secure settings is through the use of therapeutic alliances and more interpersonally focused care strategies. As nurses, we need to embrace the benefits that can be gained from utilising alternative knowledge bases. The authors are convinced that, as one strategy within an integrated psychological approach, narrative therapy is ideal and appropriate for investing in our patients' future well-being and growth. We hope that this approach (or at least the underpinning principles and concepts) can be considered for exploration and adoption, and utilised in a range of care settings across the spectrum of forensic (as well as general) mental health and social care settings.

The authors are under no illusion – nor do they wish to portray – that this approach is an easy option to take. On the contrary, it can be (and is) expensive in time and investment in staff; it can be (and is), even with the necessary support mechanisms in place, traumatic for the staff member as well as the patient. Utilising a narrative therapy approach to enhance the therapeutic alliance will ensure that the approach provided is not only robust and empirically sound but is transparent and collaborative. As already stated, investment in both staff and patients is essential in terms of formalised training and appropriate support for staff, so too is the development of effective, complementary and individual competency-based psychoeducation programmes for the patient, which will ensure an ethical, inclusive and knowledgeable process of care.

In closing, Fee (2000) considers that this is an important and encouraging time to reconnect the pathological to the rapidly shifting, material, cultural and psychosocial realms of life, and likewise to alter our theoretical and methodological frameworks for a better understanding of such connections.

CHAPTER 13

Spiritual Care in Forensic Nursing

Spiritual Interventions and Future Directions for Care

John Swinton

INTRODUCTION

As one reflects upon the nursing literature, it quickly becomes clear that the idea of holism and person-centred care planning sits at the heart of a good deal of contemporary thinking and theorising (Department of Health 1993b). Likewise, the importance of a holistic approach is emphasised within the guidelines for the professional nursing bodies. For example, the UKCC's Code of Professional Conduct (1992a) instructs nurses that they must 'recognise and respect the uniqueness and dignity of each patient and client, and respond to their need for care'. At least in its ideal form, nursing seeks to care for patients in all of their dimensions: body, mind and spirit. However, in practice, there is a significant gap between what nurses might desire to do in theory, and what they actually do in practice. While holism remains the ideal, in practice this frequently means catering for the physical and psychological needs of patients, to the exclusion of the spiritual (Oldnall 1996). Consequently, spiritual care is often poor, infrequent or non-existent (Boutell and Bozett 1987; Carson 1989; Granstrom 1995; Oldnall 1996; Taylor, Amenta and Highfield 1995). The reasons for this are complex. Some of the main difficulties encountered by nurses wishing to include the spiritual dimension within their practice are as follows:

- Nurses do not receive adequate education about the fourth domain of holistic care owing to the narrow outlook imposed on them by the nurse theorists, educationists and society (Oldnall 1996).

- Spiritual care is seen as the realm of hospital chaplains/religious agents (Ross 1994).

○ Spiritual care is influenced by narrow conceptualisations of spirituality (Granstrom 1995).

○ Nurses may have problems with patient assessment – the nurse may, for example, diagnose anxiety as purely psychological and plan care accordingly when, in fact, the patient may be suffering from spiritual distress. Care from a purely psychological perspective may therefore be inappropriate (Oldnall 1996).

○ There may be an inability to distinguish between spiritual and religious concerns and care (Harrington 1995).

○ Nurses may lack self-spiritual awareness (Pullen, Tuck and Mix 1996).

○ There may be a fear of imposing personal beliefs on the client (Taylor *et al.* 1995).

○ There may be fear of incompetence, uncertainty about personal spiritual and religious beliefs/values and uneasiness with the circumstances which bring spiritual needs to the surface (Oldnall 1996; Swinton 2001; Taylor *et al.* 1995).

○ There is some evidence that nurses believe that spirituality does not lie within the domain of nursing (Carson 1989).

○ Lack of time, a focus on physical needs and low nurse–patient ratios may also interfere with provision of spiritual care (Boutell and Bozett 1987; Highfield 1992; Piles 1990; Sodestrom and Martinson 1987).

This chapter will concentrate on the ways in which forensic nursing care and intervention need to be grounded in the spirituality of the person being cared for. This chapter will argue that as well as effective learning on an emotional and cognitive level, there is also a need for professional competence in spiritual functioning.

WHAT IS SPIRITUALITY?

It is not possible here to go into a detailed explanation of what spirituality is and how it relates to mental health in general. (Readers wishing to explore this area more fully as it relates to mental health care in general and forensic nursing in particular should see Swinton 2000, 2001.) Nevertheless, there are some important aspects of spirituality that must be highlighted at this point. For current purposes a definition of spirituality will be used that the author has developed elsewhere:

> ...spirituality refers to: *that aspect of human existence that gives it its 'humanness'*. It concerns the structures of significance which give meaning and direction to a person's life and helps them deal with the vicissitudes of existence. As such it includes such vital dimensions as the quest for *meaning, purpose, self-transcending*

knowledge, meaningful relationships, love and *commitment,* as well as the sense of the Holy amongst us. A person's spirituality is that part of them which drives them on towards their particular goals, be they temporal or transcendent. (Swinton 2000, p.115)

This definition includes, but is not defined by, religion. As such, it incorporates such things as the search for meaning and transcendence, hope, meaningful relationships, value, love and commitment (Goldberg 1998; Martsolf and Mickley 1998). These are basic human needs. They are experiences and feelings which provide a context for human living that moves beyond the materialistic and mechanistic into dimensions transcending purely biological explanations. These feelings and experiences are present in all human beings. For some, they will be expressed in formal religious language and through adherence to recognised religious traditions. For others, these common experiences will be expressed in different ways and through different avenues, such as the quest for meaning, hope and purpose and the search for meaningful relationships. Most importantly, the previous definition suggests that human beings are more than the sum of their parts. There are aspects to being human and living humanly that cannot be encapsulated within standard paradigms of theory and research, which are consequently often omitted from nursing assessment and planning that is often based on such assumptions.

SPIRITUALITY AND HUMAN WELL-BEING

There is a good deal of evidence to suggest a positive correlation between spirituality and human well-being. This literature has been well summarised elsewhere (Koenig 1997; Larson and Larson 1994; Larson *et al.* 1992; Larson, Swyers and McCullough 1997; Swinton and Kettles 2001). It is possible to extrapolate four central themes that encapsulate something of the ways in which the literature suggests spirituality functions in the process of mental health development and maintenance:

- o interpretative framework

- o emotional support

- o source of coping strategies

- o sense of community.

Interpretative framework

Spirituality provides a powerful interpretative framework within which a person can make sense of their experiences. It offers an interpretative lens through which people view and make sense of their world and their experiences within it. It provides the signs, symbols, hopes, explanations and expectations that give a person's life its meaning and direction.

Emotional support

Spirituality enables a person to develop a sense of relational connection with God, self and others. A person's spirituality can be a vital source of social and emotional support. This is particularly important when a person is isolated from primary sources of value – spouse, family, friends, etc. – as occurs when they are incarcerated.

Source of coping strategies

A person's spirituality helps them to develop ways of coping that are often unavailable from other established therapeutic sources. The spiritual dimension offers an added resource for reframing and coping with trauma, confusion and potentially negative experiences. A person's spirituality can be a powerful base for the positive reframing of situations and experiences.

Sense of community

A person's spirituality binds them symbolically and actually to a specific form of community, the nature of which can have a profound impact upon their attempts to cope constructively with the experience of mental health problems. This is particularly relevant for those people whose spirituality is located within a religious tradition. Here, either symbolically or actually, a person's spirituality ties them into a community and a common story, which offers not only social support but also symbolic and ritualistic avenues through which a person can express their inner needs and desires. Now of course, within a forensic nursing setting, it may be impossible for a person actually to join a spiritual community outside the hospital context. However, it remains possible for them to be linked with a community, either through the chaplain or through hospital visitation.

INTRODUCING SPIRITUALITY INTO FORENSIC NURSING PRACTICE

If spirituality is to be accepted as a significant aspect of the forensic nursing process, it will be helpful for forensic nurses to be able to find ways of incorporating this dimension of their patients' experiences into their daily practices. One way in which this can be done is through the use of the nursing process. Ross suggests that:

An individual entering hospital will do so with particular spiritual needs. Whether or not these needs are met may determine the speed and extent of their recovery and the level of spiritual well-being and quality of life they experience. It is important, therefore, that they receive the necessary help to meet their spiritual needs. (Ross 1994, p.441)

Ross proposes that the nursing process presents a helpful framework and an effective 'mechanism to deliver systematic individualised spiritual care' (see also Govier 2000). By incorporating spirituality into the nursing process, forensic nurses can begin to explore the practicalities of introducing spiritual interventions. The essential structure of the nursing process is presented in Table 13.1.

Table 13.1 The nursing process	
Stage of nursing process	*Knowledge required*
Assessment	What are spiritual needs, and how can they be recognised?
Planning and Intervention	What types of intervention could be applied to meet these needs?
Evaluation	What criteria might we use to determine whether or not a patient's spiritual needs have been met?

For the purposes of this chapter, the nursing process will provide a useful structure which will enable us to explore what spiritual care might mean in practical terms. It will also allow us to explore other conceptual frameworks and in so doing help develop a possible model for the implementation of spiritual care.

ASSESSMENT

Here the objective is for the nurse to recognise and assess the spiritual state of the patient and to identify their spiritual needs. This will, *inter alia*, involve exploring such things as spiritual and religious orientation, specific belief structures, and the particular ways in which a patient's belief system functions in framing and interpreting their illness experiences.

The assessment stage of the process is designed to enable the forensic nurse to gain a deeper insight into the spiritual experience of the patient and to care more fully and empathetically. In many ways, this is the most important stage of the process, both for the nurse and for the patient. It is also the most difficult. It has been noted that nurses in general and mental health nurses in particular, are not equipped educationally or in terms of their personal spirituality, to recognise and cope with the spiritual dimensions of patients' experiences (Oldnall 1996).

Because nurses are not trained to function within this area, the tendency is to draw spiritual problems into the psychological or psychoanalytical framework within which they are more comfortable. Consequently, the real meaning of a person's spiritual experience is often overlooked and under-utilised within the therapeutic process. As HRH the Prince of Wales (1991, p.763) correctly observed in his address to the Royal College of Psychiatrists, 'we ask patients to which religion they ascribe, but we neglect the much more important question of "what does your religion and your faith mean to you?"' In order to care for the spiritual needs of mentally disordered offenders, it is necessary not only to acknowledge a religious or spiritual belief, but also to be able to assess its *meaning* for the individual and to *understand* the ways in which such belief structures function within a person's life.

To this end, the process of assessment requires a framework within which nurses can be enabled to begin to explore questions such as these. Such a framework is supplied by Stoll (1979), who offers a simple yet effective model for the development of 'spiritual questions' that can help orient nurses to the area of the meaning of spiritual issues. Stoll suggests that in order to attend effectively to the meaning dimensions of a person's spiritual experience, nurses need to focus on four main areas:

o the person's concept of God or deity

o the person's source of strength and hope

o the significance of religious practices and rituals to the person

o the person's perceived relationship between their personal beliefs and state of health.

Stoll's model might be criticised for being too focused on specifically religious forms of spirituality. Nevertheless, it is possible to adapt it to include the wider dimensions of spirituality highlighted above.

The person's concept of God or deity

Polner (1989) has pointed out the therapeutic role that people's images of God or divine figures can play within their general social support networks. Polner's research suggests that people relate to divine images in ways not dissimilar to the way they relate to 'real people'. Consequently, a person's divine images are incorporated into their general system of social support and can function as a powerful source of self-valuing, reframing and coping, particularly in times of stress. This being so, the task of the forensic nurse is to begin to explore what kind of God-concept, if any, a person might have and to examine just how powerful the role of such an image might be in the way the patient views their situation, and themselves within it. By focusing on the nature of a person's divine/spiritual images, it is possible to develop some significant questions concerning the nature and function of a person's spirituality and spiritual experiences:

o Does the person have a God concept?

o How does it function in their lives?

o From where does a person gain strength to cope with their experiences?

o What do religious practices mean to the individual?

o How do they interact with the person's illness experience?

o Do they have a positive or a negative influence on the progress of their condition?

By constructively utilising a framework of questions such as this, the forensic nurse can be enabled to enter into a patient's meaning systems and accurately assess the place and role of their beliefs within the overall care plan.

The person's source of strength and hope

Here the nurse reflects on what it is that gives this person's life meaning and purpose and where they draw their strength and hope from. For those who are religiously oriented, this might mean engaging with a specific religious tradition, and exploring the ways in which the rites, symbols and concepts enable the development of strength and hope. For example, in a recent study by Swinton (2001) into enduring depression, it was discovered that, at least for some, it was very important that their illness should be understood as something that was being *done to them* by a divine being for a purpose which lay beyond their immediate experience. On the surface, the idea of a divine being inflicting serious mental illness appears to be pathological. However, when the researcher entered into the world-view of the sufferer, it became clear that this was in fact a powerful coping mechanism that injected meaning and purpose into an apparently meaningless and hopeless situation. By attributing their illness to a divine being, they were enabled to hold on to the idea that there was meaning beyond their immediate suffering and that the pain and confusion they were experiencing had a purpose within a divine plan. As such, their current pain was viewed as a preliminary to their ultimate release from their current pain. Of course, certain belief structures may well be the pathological results of a person's illness. Nevertheless, if the nurse misses this vital meaning dimension of the patient's experience, or omits to ask these vital questions, they risk misinterpreting what is actually going on and missing something vital to the person-as-person. (The question of how to determine between pathological and non-pathological expressions of spirituality is complex. Readers wishing to reflect on this more fully should see Swinton 2001.)

For those who do not adhere to a specific religious tradition, the search for the source of strength and hope may mean exploring what it is that provides patients' lives with vision, meaning and purpose. For some, this may be a set of non-religious beliefs about life, themselves, happiness, and so forth. Here the nurse's task is to excavate these belief structures and to seek to determine what difference, if any, they might make to the patient and to the caring process. For others, and probably for most patients, their primary source of strength and hope will involve some kind of search for meaningful relationships. In a sense, this quest for meaningful relationships, at a temporal and a transcendent level, lies at the heart of spirituality and spiritual care. A person's spirituality may be expressed in a vertical relationship with the transcendent/God or whatever supreme values guide the person's life. It may also be expressed horizontally in relationships with self, others and the environment (Carson 1989). These attempts at meaningful relationships may be distorted and confused by illness, but they are ever present and nurses need to be aware of them and able to assess their meaning and importance for the caring process. Even people with enduring mental illness and certain personality disorders, who are often assumed to be unfeeling and in some senses 'arelational', in fact retain a desire to relate and be related to (Gilligan 2000).

For some patients, their religion or spirituality may make no real difference to their lives. For others, their faith may be fundamental to the ways in which they view the world and make sense of their experiences. It is not necessary that nurses become experts in the intricacies of all of the world's religions or all of the complexities of people's personal spiritual belief structures. What is required, however, is that nurses are sensitised to the possible significance of these areas and are prepared to learn and assess what the patient's religious and spiritual beliefs mean for the individual patient. Only in this way can the possibility of genuinely informed choices and person-centred, holistic care be assured.

The significance of religious practices and rituals to the person

Addressing this question enables the nurse to explore the meaning of religious practices and to explore how they might be best utilised within the therapeutic process. Questions that might be asked here would include:

- o Does this person pray?

- o If so, what effect does this have on their behaviour, attitude, emotional state, and so forth?

- o Does this person read from the scriptures of one of the world's religions?

- o If so, how do they use the text? For example: Do they identify with characters in a healthy or an unhealthy way? Do they find peace and renewed vision? Does reading the scripture cause agitation, fear, nervousness, concern, and so forth?

- o Does the patient attend chapel?

- o If so, how important is this to their life?

Questions such as these can be designed to explore the ways in which religious beliefs, rites and rituals function in constructing the patient's experiences and enabling them to cope with their life experiences.

The person's perceived relationship between their personal beliefs and state of health

Here the nurse explores questions of how the patient views the relationship between their illness and their particular belief systems. As has been mentioned, this can be a difficult area to assess. Often there can be a conflict between the way in which the nurse interprets the patient's belief systems and the ways in which they actually function in the patient's life. As was highlighted previously, apparently pathological beliefs can in fact be powerful sources for re-framing and coping with illness experiences. The task of the nurse is to be able to listen to the voice of the patient in a way that does not presuppose the pathological nature of their expressed beliefs, but respects it as a valid experience that may well have significant therapeutic meaning. The nurse must be able both to *listen* and to *hear* the full meaning of what patients express in their conversations.

Using a structure such as Stoll's (1979) as a framework for developing appropriate assessment questions and approaches can enable carers to assess such things as religious orientation, the personal meanings of spirituality, the relationship of the individual to a wider spiritual community, the relationship of their belief structures to their religious tradition, and how best this dimension of the patient's experience can be highlighted and cared for effectively. Stoll's framework, therefore, provides a way of exploring the deeper regions of a person's spiritual life.

PLANNING AND INTERVENTION

The next stage of the nursing process is planning and intervention. This stage involves the planning and implementation of appropriate forms of intervention that may be required to meet the spiritual needs identified in stage one. Planning requires developing an understanding of the patient's meaning systems, exploring the types of questions highlighted previously, and using those data to develop the most appropriate forms of spiritual intervention.

The term 'spiritual intervention' refers to the specific strategies employed by nurses to meet a patient's identified spiritual needs. Spiritual interventions are the outcome of the thoughtful, reflective process that has been outlined in the previous sections. They are used to help promote patients' religious and spiritual growth and well-being, thereby helping them to cope more effectively and to overcome their problems (Richards and Bergin 1997). There is now a good deal of empirical evidence that spiritual practices promote physical and emotional healing (Miller 2000; Richards and Bergin 1997; Worthington 1998). Spiritual interventions are often presented as if they were specific techniques that are learned in the same way as one might develop competencies in therapy, pharmacology or any other dimension of mental health care. However, in this author's opinion, this is a mistaken emphasis. While spiritual intervention may indeed relate to specific forms of practice, as will become clear, they have more to do with what the nurse *is* and how she views the world than with things that she may or may not *do*.

Like every other aspect of care, the introduction of spirituality and specific spiritual interventions demands care and sensitivity to the particular needs of the individual. A spiritually oriented attitude may be desirable in the care of all patients, but specifically spiritual interventions may not be appropriate for everyone. Indeed, under certain circumstances they may in fact be harmful and intrusive, serving to abuse or disempower patients rather than increase their well-being. For example, Richards and Bergin (1997) inform that direct spiritual interventions may be contraindicated when:

o patients make it clear they do not wish to participate in them

o patients are delusional or psychotic

o spiritual issues are not relevant to the patients' presenting problems.

Spiritual interventions should always be person-centred and should fully respect the wishes and desires of patients at all times. Unlike certain other forms of treatment, spiritual interventions can never be compulsory! Nurses should always carefully describe whatever spiritual interventions they wish to use and obtain the patient's consent before implementing them. They should also be careful to work within their patient's value systems and belief structures and not impose their own spiritual beliefs. This is an important point. Forensic nurses are in a position of tremendous power over patients and the potential for abuse at the spiritual level is as high as it is at the physical, emotional and sexual levels. The task of the nurse is spiritual nurturance and not proselytisation.

Nurses need not be religious or spiritually oriented themselves in order to use most spiritual interventions. Although some spiritual interventions may require that the nurse believes in God and in the influence of the transcendent (e.g. praying for patients), most do not. If forensic nurses are willing to expand their sensitivity and skills into the spiritual domain, it is possible for them to encourage and enable patients to engage in spiritual practices. Several recent books are available to assist carers who would like more information about how they can effectively incorporate spiritual perspectives and interventions into their practices (e.g. Miller 2000; Richards and Bergin 1997; Shafranske 1996). What *is* required is that spirituality is placed on the nursing agenda and that nurses are aware and equipped to deal with this dimension of patient care.

SPIRITUAL INTERVENTIONS

For the purposes of this chapter five areas of spiritual care and intervention will be focused on:

1. therapeutic communication
2. therapeutic understanding and love
3. religious interventions
4. seeking spiritual direction
5. referral.

Points one and two relate primarily to the type of attitude that nurses need to adopt if they are to be spiritual carers. Points three, four and five highlight some specific forms of intervention that can be adopted and incorporated within caring strategies.

Therapeutic communication

Learning the language of spirituality

Nolan and Crawford (1997) highlight the need for contemporary health care practitioners to develop a 'rhetoric of spirituality'; that is, a revised form of language that does not focus simply on the technological and pathological aspects of mentally disordered people, but seeks to speak to and from the previously hidden spiritual dimensions of the person. This is a useful suggestion. Forensic nurses need to begin to feel comfortable using words such as *love, hope, value* and *meaning* as they relate to the experiences of the patients in their care. This will mean learning a 'second language' that can be used alongside the technical-legal-psychiatric (frequently illness-focused) language that often guides forensic nursing theory, practice and research. If forensic nurses are to become competent within the area of spirituality and spiritual care, they must begin to learn and feel at home with the language of spirituality, and start to notice and respond to the hidden dimensions of those to whom to offer care. This being so, therapeutic communication, when developed within a spiritual context, has to do with changing the forms of language forensic nurses use in response to their encounters with patients' spiritual experiences and with enabling patients' spiritual needs not only to be listened to, but also to be heard. As a beginning point, this will mean creating a space in the therapeutic process within which the types of questions highlighted previously in the assessment phase of the nursing process can be asked, reflected on and worked through.

Creating a space for spirituality
One acknowledged barrier to spiritual care is the nurse's fear of imposing his or her own views on a patient (Pullen *et al.* 1996). This, of course, is a valid concern. As has been mentioned, forensic nurses are in a position of considerable power and influence over patients in their care. It would be wholly inappropriate for them to attempt to force their views on what is a particularly vulnerable patient population. And yet, there is evidence that a significant number of patients might welcome the direct introduction of spiritual issues into their daily care (Charters 1999; Fitchett, Burton and Sivan 1997). Ironically, it could be that by not having spiritual issues on our caring agendas, we may be forcing patients to adopt a professional, materialist world-view that is alien to them. In other words, we may be unconsciously proselytising patients into materialist forms of care and belief structure that are inadequate for their felt needs. Therapeutic communication requires the forensic nurse to 'create spiritual spaces' within which it is possible to assess and explore issues relating to the spiritual dimensions of patients' experiences. In so doing, the nurse opens up the possibility of holistic care that meets the real needs of patients.

Therapeutic understanding and love

Therapeutic understanding relates to the forensic nurse's ability to recognise and respond to the hidden dimensions of patients' experiences. In order for this to happen, forensic nurses need to become aware both of their own spirituality and of the specific barriers preventing them from viewing their patients as full human beings with a spiritual dimension that needs to be cared for. If forensic nurses have never had the chance to reflect on their own spirituality and what it may or may not mean to them, it will be very difficult for them to recognise and deal effectively and empathetically with the spiritual needs of patients. This is particularly so in a forensic context within which violence, deception and disorder can often define the roles of both nurses and patients as somewhat less than human.

The problem of evil

Within such a context, there is a danger that forensic nurses will simply write off patients as evil and hopeless, with subsequent serious implications for nursing care. An example of this difficulty is found in Mercer, Mason and Richman's (1999) research into discourses around evil within forensic nursing. They suggest that, within a forensic nursing context, the allocation of the label 'evil' can have significant implications for nurse–patient relationships. Mercer *et al.* note that the term *evil* is quite regularly used within the 'lay' nursing discourse (i.e. the day-to-day language used by nurses as opposed to the professional language of psychiatry or law). Whilst they found that there was a good deal of tolerance for people who were 'classically' mentally ill (i.e. psychotic, even if they had committed acts of extreme violence), those with a diagnosis of psychopathy tended to be labelled as evil, and in significant ways written off as fully human persons. This split between lay and professional discourses meant that there was a significant dichotomy between the ways in which patients were viewed 'officially' and in the attitudes that nurses had towards them 'on the ground'.

What Mercer *et al.* found was a clash of discourses and a fundamental confusion over precisely what patients are, why they are the way they are, and how best they might be cared for. The allocation of the label 'evil' in the lay nursing discourse, signifies and reflects a movement away from viewing patients as full human beings with very specific nursing needs, toward an understanding that encapsulates them linguistically as less than human. Such a discourse of dehumanisation not only degrades the patient, it also forces the nurse into a position where the danger of inhumane practices becomes a real possibility.

Bearing all of this in mind, unless nurses are tuned in to the possibility of the existence and significance of a spiritual dimension (i.e. something that identifies even the most apparently inhuman offender as fully human), it will be very difficult for them to offer the type of spiritual care that patients may require and indeed be looking for. 'Therapeutic understanding' attempts to move beyond the level of gut feelings and understandable repulsion at particular acts, and reclaim the humanity of the person with whom we are faced.

A loving attitude

Here we need to think about what it might mean to reintroduce the language of love to forensic nursing practice. A loving attitude towards patients is the most fundamental spiritual intervention, and one which underpins every other spiritual practice. Nurses need to recognise and adopt this. But what is a loving attitude? A loving attitude is a way of approaching and understanding patients that begins with the fact that they are broken human beings who may well desire to experience love, but may never have had the opportunity to do so (Gilligan 2000). Even within the context of violence and aggression, a loving attitude seeks to hold on to a positive, empathetic view of the patient-as-a-person and in so doing attempts to minimise violence (physical, psychological and linguistic), as it manifests intself in both carer and cared for. In this way the humanity and the spirituality of both carer and cared for is maintained and the possibility of meaningful holism is achieved.

Religious interventions

Prayer

There is evidence that people who pray do feel better, both physically and emotionally (Dossey 1996). Prayer seems to help patients relax, feel less isolated and more hopeful, accepting, and optimistic (Dossey 1993; Koenig 1997). There is evidence to suggest that prayer and meditation can effectively be incorporated into anger management training (Ingram), adding a new and vital dimension which is omitted from many standard programmes. Prayer can be a powerful resource to assist religious (and some non-religious) patients in their coping, healing and growth. While it can be directly attached to a formal system of religion, there is evidence suggesting that prayer as a general human response to particular experiences can be beneficial (Dossey 1996). In terms of the nurse's facilitation of prayer, it is not necessary for them to share the patient's beliefs. It is, however, necessary for them to acknowledge that this may be important to certain patients, and to create an atmosphere and adequate space (psychological and physical) for the person to be enabled to develop and utilise this aspect of their spirituality.

Meditation

Meditation and contemplation require a trusting, passive attitude of release, surrender of control, active focusing of thoughts, awareness of task, and relaxation of muscles (Martin and Carlson 1988). Meditation enables a person to transcend the immediacy of their situation and discover a degree of serenity, even in the midst of psychological disturbance. Meditation is a learned skill to which it is possible to apply some basic principles from behaviour therapy. Martin and Booth (2000) put it thus:

> Principles of behaviour management are directly applicable in strengthening spiritual practices. *Goal setting* is one important aspect of effective behaviour change. Setting appropriate goals and systematically tracking and monitoring

them may be equally critical to the acquisition of spiritual behavior and its maintenance within lifestyle patterns. For example, prayer and meditation goals could be specified in terms of frequency, duration, time and place, and type, all of which make it possible to define progress towards goals. (p.163)

Other forms of behaviour modification can be adapted. 'Shaping', for example, can be used in prayer and meditation. One might:

Begin from a first approximation (e.g. two minutes of prayer) towards the person's target goal (e.g. perhaps an hour of prayer or meditation at the start of each day). First steps are best kept simple, brief and highly achievable. This may be followed by gradual progressive increases towards the behavioral goals (e.g. adding one minute per day or five minutes per week). (Martin and Booth 2000, p.164)

Other behavioural techniques, such as contingency management, stimulus control, positive reinforcement, chaining and social modelling can be utilised to enable the enhancement of spirituality. In this way, it is possible to enable patients to develop a technique of meditation and an ability to relax through this process in a way that is practical, manageable and understandable according to acceptable behavioural techniques.

Encouraging forgiveness

Much has been written recently about the importance of forgiveness in healing and therapy (Worthington 1998). Research has indicated that it is one of the most frequently used spiritual interventions in psychotherapy (Richards and Bergin 1997). The most profound healing and peace occur when patients are able to forgive themselves and others. Personal bitterness, resentment or unforgiveness are often cited as being particularly destructive to physical, mental and spiritual health (Ornish 1998). Unforgiveness is a state of fragmentation and destroyed relationships. Forgiveness is closely associated with love and connectedness, two fundamental pillars of spirituality. Some patients have particular difficulty with self-forgiveness; feelings of shame and spiritual unworthiness cause them to believe they cannot or do not deserve to be forgiven. This being so, the enabling of forgiveness of self, others and God, is an important aspect of spiritual care.

Psychologically, it has been suggested that forgiveness can promote positive changes in affective well-being and physical and mental health. It can help restore a sense of personal power and enable reconciliation between the offended and offender (Bergin 1988). McCullough and Worthington (1994a, 1994b) suggest that by choosing forgiveness, people increase their options and are given the freedom to grow. When seeking forgiveness, people take responsibility for their wrongdoings, and in so doing make it easier for those that have hurt to heal

(Richards and Bergin 1997). Thus, forgiveness can be a significant source of empowerment for patients who may be struggling with issues of guilt, failure or lack of self-acceptance.

Many of the world's religions have built-in mechanisms for enabling forgiveness, penance and self-acceptance. Most of the great Western religious traditions include teachings about the love and mercy of God. This being so, when it seems relevant, such teachings should be emphasised to patients in order to help them understand the healing process of self-forgiveness, a process that includes responsibility and accountability but not self-punishment. For those with an intrinsic religiosity (that is, a form of religion foundational to their being and to the way in which they view the world), it is possible for forensic nurses, working in conjunction with the religious adviser, to work through and resolve issues of guilt, forgiveness and an inability to accept oneself or others.

However, encouraging forgiveness is a form of spiritual intervention that can be carried out without any necessary reference to religion. Techniques such as re-framing (Richards and Bergin 1997), counselling, and behavioural and cognitive approaches (Miller 2000) have all been applied to the religious and non-religious dimensions of forgiveness, with promising results. While the scientific study of forgiveness has not yet been applied to a forensic nursing context, it is an area that has the potential to be fruitful, and, in this researcher's opinion, should be placed high on the research agenda.

Seeking spiritual direction

It may be helpful to encourage patients to seek guidance and direction from their religious and spiritual leaders, such as their priest, minister, pastor, guru, rabbi, or bishop. When the patient and religious adviser/leader have had a trusting relationship since before psychological treatment began, it is often helpful for such patients to experience the leader's caring and support during their treatment. Because of the authority of their role, religious leaders can sometimes influence patients to stay in treatment or comply with therapeutic recommendations (Scott Richards *et al.* 1998). Spiritual advisers/leaders can provide meaningful spiritual and emotional guidance and comfort to clients and staff, as well as assist in correcting faulty and dysfunctional religious beliefs. They can provide information to help with patient assessment and give nurses an invaluable insight into patients' functioning outside of the treatment context. If the patient's in-patient treatment comes to an end, religious leaders can assist in relapse prevention by enabling social networks and providing social and emotional support within the patient's religious or spiritual community.

Referral

In her study of nurses' attitudes to spirituality, Linda Ross (1994) discovered that 60 per cent of the nurses she interviewed saw referral as a primary mode of spiritual care. The fact that so many nurses felt that referral was the most appropriate response to expressions of spritual need, may indicate a lack of confidence among nurses rather than an effective, measured spiritual strategy. Nevertheless it is vital that nurses recognise when it is time for them to refer the patient on to someone who has specific expertise within the more complex dimensions of spiritual care and who can offer an expertise which is not available to most forensic nurses. The most common agent of referral, with regard to spiritual matters, is the hospital chaplain. As it has been suggested, spiritual care is the responsibility of each and every forensic nurse. That responsibility must not be shirked or taken lightly. However, the chaplain is trained and able to offer specialised forms of spiritual care beyond the capabilities of the majority of nursing staff. This being so, there is no shame in referring. In fact it is often far and away the best thing for both client and nurse. What is required is a constructive dialogue between chaplaincy and nursing, within which avenues and communicational conduits can be opened up and the possibility of shared spiritual care developed as a genuine therapeutic possibility. Of course it is not only the chaplain to whom patients may be referred. Other agencies would include:

o religious advisers

o other health professions, e.g. social worker, occupational therapist, etc.

o family/significant others

o group support

o friends or faith community members/others from outside the system.

Whomever the person is referred to, it is vital that the nurse remains involved with the spiritual caring process in order that whatever therapeutic benefits that can be gained from referral are noticed, understood and carried on in the day-to-day life of the patient.

EVALUATION

The final aspect of the nursing process is evaluation. The evaluation of the person's spiritual care is an ongoing process within which those hidden dimensions of their experiences are brought to the forefront of the multidisciplinary team's thinking, and current ways of caring are revised, reviewed and focused into a truly holistic model of care. Evaluation is also important in that it prevents the harming or abusing of patients. Like all forms of therapeutic intervention, spiritual interventions can be dangerous if used abusively or insensitively. Particularly when experimenting with this form of intervention for the first time, it is important constantly to be examining and re-evaluating whether this way of caring is genuinely bringing health, wholeness and peace to individuals. In order to do this, spiritual issues must become an acknowledged and accepted aspect of the forensic nurse's professional discourse. It must form part of team discussions, reports, assessments, and so forth. In other words, as well as speaking in the language of pathology, law and security, forensic nurses need to incorporate the language of spirituality into their day-to-day caring and evaluating strategies. In this way, the integrity of the patient's personhood will be ensured and the possibility of genuinely person-centred spiritual care opened up and worked out.

CONCLUSION AND RECOMMENDATIONS

It has become clear that spirituality and spiritual interventions hold much potential for improved professional practice within forensic nursing. The understandings and suggestions put forward in this chapter have pointed towards ways in which forensic nurses can take seriously the idea of holism and develop strategies and understandings that can genuinely care for mentally disordered offenders in the fullness of their beings, and at the same time enable nurses to hold on to the humanness of their patients. In concluding, it will be helpful to make three recommendations:

1. There is a serious lack of research focusing directly on the forensic nursing context and the ways in which spirituality works itself out there. There is therefore an urgent need for a research agenda that will address this significant gap in theory and practice.

2. There is a significant educational gap in nurse training. Nurses are well versed in psychology and biology, but seriously under-educated in the third dimension of the human person: spirituality. Consequently, when it comes to the practice of caring, nurses are under-confident in this area and, in fact, simply often fail to address it. There is therefore an important educational agenda that needs to be thought through and worked out. Forensic nurses need to be educated and trained to recognise and deal with the spiritual dimensions of their patients, and indeed within themselves. There is plenty of literature, some of which has been touched on in this chapter, showing the physical and psychological benefits of spirituality for patient care. This literature needs to be incorporated into forensic nurse training and continuing education in order that nurses can be enabled to develop the knowledge and confidence to

care effectively in this dimension. Until that happens, holism will remain a theoretical nicety that is fundamentally missing from practice.

3.   Forensic nurses must look beyond their current psychological and physical paradigms of intervention, and venture into new and challenging areas of care which incorporate, but are not defined by, the psychological paradigm. Of course, it is possible simply to draw spirituality into the psychological world-view and pretend that that is all there is to it. That could be one danger in using the kind of behavioural approach highlighted earlier. However, if forensic nurses are genuinely committed to caring for *persons* rather than *cases*, they must begin at least to open themselves up to the possibility that, even in the worst offender, there may be another dimension that, as holistic carers, it is their responsibility to recognise, explore and care for in as effective a way as possible. This is no mean task! However, if the integrity and humanity of both carer and cared-for is to be sustained even in the midst of the most troubled storms, it is a pathway that needs to be reflected on and worked through.

Forensic nurses have a critical task as spiritual healers – as injectors of meaning, hope and purpose into the lives of a population who are often starved of all three. This chapter has offered some pointers towards ways in which this could be done. If this chapter has contributed to the movement from fragmentation towards holism within forensic nursing practice, it will have served its purpose.

CHAPTER 14

Nursing Interventions and Future Directions in Community Care for Mentally Disordered Offenders

Helen Edment

INTRODUCTION

In the last 30 years, recognition of the need for effective and efficient forensic community care has been significantly highlighted owing to several community care tragedies involving mentally disordered offenders (Reith 1998a). Numerous recommendations were the product of the investigations that naturally followed each one of these tragedies, which have resulted in the adoption of such interventions as the Care Programme Approach (Department of Health 1990), supervision registers (National Health Service Management Executive 1994c), and supervised discharge (Department of Health 1995) as recommended by the Reed Report (Department of Health and Home Office 1992). The Reed Report remains the most recognised and acknowledged review of health and social services for mentally disordered offenders that has affected service development for this group. Most mentally disordered offenders will find themselves the subject of these interventions, thereby enabling forensic mental health professionals to monitor them closely, and administer treatment quickly and effectively in the event of relapse.

The literature pertaining to forensic nursing remains, regrettably, short on the ground compared with the volumes published for general psychiatry. What follows will provide a description of interventions employed in community forensic care to prevent and treat repercussions from traumatic incidents. Specific focus will be on the carer, the victim, the perpetrator and their family, and the role of the multidisciplinary team in addressing their multifarious needs. The effects of traumatic incidents on these individuals and their families will also be examined by exploring some of the complex issues around the relationship between the perpetrator and the victim. There will be exploration of the effects of traumatic incidents on staff in the context of a forensic setting, and of the intervention strategies deployed in a traumatised population in the context of care and support of staff working within a forensic environment.

INTERVENTIONS EMPLOYED IN COMMUNITY FORENSIC CARE TO PREVENT AND TREAT REPERCUSSIONS FROM TRAUMATIC INCIDENTS

Most mentally disordered offenders, in addition to being the subject of one or more of the interventions previously mentioned (Care Programme Approach, supervision register or supervised discharge) will also have had a contingency plan devised for them in the event of a traumatic or violent incident occurring. Such contingency plans will be tailored to individual needs and may contain provision for short-term readmission, if considered by the forensic team to be necessary. It is a natural consequence that those traumatic or violent incidents occurring in the community also impact on staff within in-patient services (during a period of readmission), and of course, on community staff, carers, victims, relatives and the wider community. Currently, contingency plans are becoming increasingly necessary, with an increasing number of community forensic teams providing an 'out-of-hours' service (Coffey 1998).

Coffey (1998) also advocates those individual contingency plans be supplemented by telephone support as a means of supervising mentally disordered offenders. This may alleviate both the need for high-volume staffing and the number of home visits to forensic patients out of normal working hours. Telephone support is undoubtedly important to carers and families of mentally disordered offenders, who should be aware that a mental health professional, with whom they are familiar and whom they trust, is accessible to them 24 hours of each day to deliver advice and direction when needed.

An assertive outreach model is a prerequisite of any forensic community service, and attains particular significance whenever forensic community staff have cause for concern about patient presentation. This form of care delivery has been described as the 'aggressive application of the case management model of care' (Coffey and Chaloner 2000). Any conscientious community mental health professional will be aware of their patients' background and mental and physical problems, and will also know family, friends and general lifestyle. Forensic mental health professionals are expected to take this approach one step further by adequately carrying out an up-to-date risk assessment for each of their client group (Bingley 1997). Woods (2001) describes good practice issues and discusses several aspects of risk assessment and management, both from the individual perspective and the forensic service perspective. Exploration in some depth is made here of the risk assessment tools that exist, and the importance of a risk management plan following assessment is stressed. These assist in determining the level or nature of risk and facilitate focus on the responses required to deal with potential or anticipated risks, thereby allowing for effective monitoring and progress made by implementation of the plan. Woods (2001) describes this risk management process as 'dynamic risk assessment'.

It is submitted that the caseload of forensic community staff should invariably be significantly smaller than that of their generic counterparts. This is on the basis that assertive follow-up can be time consuming and stressful, with forensic staff often carrying out joint visits to their client. The submission is supported where it is perceived that there may be more than the predicted amount of risk present, or if it is considered that an objective opinion or alternative viewpoint may be required.

Regularly, the erratic behaviour and lifestyle of forensic patients create difficulties for forensic community staff in their monitoring role. It is important, therefore, that a good relationship built on trust is developed between family and carers in order to enlist assistance in the monitoring process. Traumatic incidents resulting from the behaviour of mentally disordered offenders may have a profound impact on their families and carers. Again, a quality relationship fostered by forensic mental health professionals provides help and support through stressful and trying times. Family and friends often feel threatened by the very person they care for, and the forensic mental health team can help them work through their feelings and provide vital information on the likelihood of re-offending. Such assistance should also foster the improvement of relationships by facilitating communication between the offender and their family/carer, and by providing information on the individual's mental illness. Often, a bond can be established over a period of time preceding discharge, allowing all parties to feel comfortable with each other. The reintegration of mentally disordered offenders into the community during the last several decades has shown both that the vast majority do not re-offend and that they pose no more serious a threat than members of the general public (Wright and Stockford 1999). It is worthy of comment however that when any member of this group does commit an offence, the media attention generated is prominent to say the least.

In 1996 the Health Education Authority carried out a study of press coverage of mental health issues for that year. The findings (reported in NACRO 1998) included:

o Almost 46 per cent of all press coverage of mental health issues was about crime, harm to others and self-harm – with 54 per cent of tabloid coverage devoted to these issues and almost 43 per cent coverage in the broadsheets.

o Both broadsheets and tabloids made a clear link between mental disturbance, criminality and violence – stories making such a link were generally given greater prominence than more positive pieces.

o Forty per cent of daily tabloid articles and 45 per cent of Sunday tabloid articles about mental health contained stigmatising words like 'nutter' and 'loony'.

It is hardly surprising, therefore, that the anxieties, fears and concerns of communities are heightened when mentally disordered offenders are settled in their midst. Likewise, families and carers feel that both themselves and their charges are stigmatised and unwanted often within the very community they were brought up in. Such circumstances become exacerbated when relapse occurs. One of the NACRO (1998) recommendations was for assertive outreach to be available for vulnerable individuals in the community, designed to ensure that they receive the care they need, and for urgent action to be taken if their condition worsens or they lose touch with the relevant services.

Awareness of this practice must be made clear to offenders and their families and carers prior to their discharge into the community. The conditions and restrictions they are subjected to may be a daunting prospect for many offenders, but when relapse occurs and readmission becomes necessary, even for a short while, the overriding emotion experienced by families, carers and the wider community tends to be one of relief.

Court and prison liaison/diversion services which aim to identify, and thereafter divert, mentally disordered offenders away from criminal justice services are being increasingly developed by forensic teams across the country. In 1999, there were in excess of 100 schemes at various stages of development across the UK (Hillis 1999). The Reed Report (Department of Health and Home Office 1991) addressed the issue of closer working between agencies such as health and social services, and the police and the prosecution services to avoid unnecessary prosecution of mentally disordered offenders. An extension of this list of agencies would include housing and voluntary agencies, thereby making multi-agency working all-encompassing. It follows that whilst forensic mental health professionals are working within the areas of courts and prisons, they are well placed to track mentally disordered offenders from court to prison, to hospital and to the community. A safety net is thereby provided to tackle re-offending. The offender can be quickly reunited with familiar services or introduced to such other services as they may need upon liberation or discharge.

Control and restraint training will be discussed in more detail later. It is worth mentioning here, however, that practitioners in the community usually work alone or in pairs when dealing directly with patients. Consequently, they will not have the resource of a three-person team to deal with a patient who becomes violent.

Nonetheless, they should have been trained in basic breakaway techniques to provide them with the knowledge of how to extricate themselves from potentially difficult situations.

Cognitive behaviour therapy will be described in more depth in a later section, but it should be noted here that there is an increasing prevalence of forensic community workers being trained in this therapy, a therapy which was formerly mainly the domain of psychologists.

Diversion/work therapy may be employed to occupy patients and foster within them a feeling of worth. As with the taking of medication, ritualistic behaviour can be established to ensure attendance at places of work or day centres. It has been demonstrated that forensic patients can function perfectly well within local communities when their mental health is stable, provided the appropriate support is forthcoming. Employment is difficult to obtain for anyone with a major mental illness, but when this is compounded by a history of offending it is even more elusive. One type of resource going some way towards filling this gap is forensic-specific day services, which provide an array of activities and work opportunities tailored to the needs of their attenders. They also provide a much needed area of contact that can be utilised by professionals involved in the individual's care. Mention should be made here that this has to be carefully balanced as clinical procedures, such as depot clinics, if not handled carefully can damage the therapeutic milieu of the day services.

Exercise is popular with a large percentage of mentally disordered offenders in the community. This can be used to relieve frustrations, increase and maintain fitness and occupy time productively. Courses can also be accessed which provide certificates at the end, instilling a sense of achievement.

Relapse prevention and neuroleptic medication are probably the two areas where forensic community workers enjoy the most tangible control. Relapse prevention can be achieved through thorough risk assessment, which identifies early warning signs of relapse, and through provision of a contingency plan. With a view to stabilising the patient, the plan may provide for an immediate short readmission to in-patient services. Medication alteration is an area that can usually be addressed in the community. On occasion, however, a short readmission, as in the commencement of Clozapine therapy, may be appropriate. Compliance with medication is a major feature of community forensic psychiatry, with research suggesting that up to 50 per cent of patients do not fully comply with the terms of their prescription (Sackett and Snow 1979). It is a well-recognised fact that non-compliance is a principal risk indicator of violence to self or to others. Methods and techniques used to improve compliance are usually those of involving patients in decisions regarding their medication, providing information on medication, educating patients and their relatives/carers on the signs of relapse and establishing rituals in the taking of medication (Howlett 1998).

ROLE OF THE FORENSIC TEAM IN ADDRESSING THE NEEDS OF CARERS, VICTIMS, PERPETRATORS AND THEIR FAMILIES

Upon discharge to the community, forensic patients are more likely than not to be returned to their areas of origin. The Reed Committee (Department of Health and Home Office 1992) indeed recommended that 'patients should be cared for as near as possible to their own homes or families if they have them' (p.68). A common departure from this practice is where the index offence has been committed within the area of origin and it is not considered prudent or safe for either the victim or the offender to return there. The multidisciplinary team have a duty to ensure that no victim is placed in a position where they may have to confront their aggressor. Exceptions to this practice may be permitted in circumstances where the victim is a family member who still wishes contact with, or indeed expresses a wish to care for, the perpetrator.

Any forensic professional delivering care to the mentally disordered offender in the community will generally come into close contact with friends and relatives. Community staff must ensure that family members, or friends in close contact with the mentally disordered offender, have almost as much knowledge as the offender does of their mental illness, medication and individual early warning signs of relapse. The issue in this instance is one of education delivered in uncomplicated and understandable language. Ambiguity and uncertainty are to be avoided, but due care should always be employed to ensure that confidentiality is not breached. Ideally, such a level of understanding in relatives or friends and a good knowledge of community staff who will be involved in the care, should be achieved prior to the offender's discharge. It is as important for forensic community staff to create and develop a therapeutic relationship with the carers, as it is to do so with the offender. Trust is a significant indicator as to whether signs of relapse are reported.

The not insubstantial burden of care placed on families who care for a psychotic patient is well documented (Gibbons *et al.* 1984, Kuipers, Leff and Lam 1992). The personal consequences of caring for these individuals over an extended period of time may often have a detrimental effect on the carer's own mental health (Fadden, Bebbington and Kuipers 1987). Carers, therefore, should also be observed to ascertain whether they themselves are under stress. Alleviation should be provided where possible. Any problems in coping experienced by the carer should be addressed by the multidisciplinary team, who should be best placed to increase support. There may be a tendency for relatives to harbour fears of stigma, anxiety, intolerance, and an apprehension of the future. Such emotions emanate from the knowledge that they may have many years of caring for the offender ahead of them. Often, as a result, they present as defensive and unco-operative with staff. Early resolution may be very difficult to attain. One programme currently operating in Victoria, Australia, aims to provide assertive outreach support to both families of clients who have a psychiatric disability with a forensic history, and to the clients themselves. This support is provided on the basis that patients with a major mental illness are prone to stress-related breakdown. Needs are addressed in a community setting and psychoeducation, emotional support and practical assistance are utilised. Results have shown a diminution of anxiety levels in both families and clients, and in addition relapse and re-offending rates have been reduced (James 1996).

COMPLEX ISSUES AROUND THE RELATIONSHIP BETWEEN PERPETRATOR AND VICTIM

A significant number of violent and homicidal incidents perpetrated by mentally disordered offenders are against a relative, often the perpetrator's mother (Reith 1998b). Hafner and Boker (1982) noted that 60 per cent of violent incidents perpetrated by mentally disordered offenders were against close family members and only 9 per cent involved a stranger. The reason given for this was that the family member becomes incorporated into the offender's delusions as a villain who will harm or cheat them. Conflict usually escalates over a period of time until it culminates in an attack. Obviously, this can create a barrier to the offender, once stabilised, being returned to the family bosom. If relationships are to be maintained or rebuilt, then there will be the need for education delivered by the appropriate forensic staff to both perpetrator and victim and, maybe, for family therapy or counselling. On numerous occasions, relationships are so badly damaged that whole families can withdraw their support leaving the offender to continue their life with no further contact.

When the victim is a staff member who works closely with the offender, then relationships can be difficult to re-establish. If the attack takes place in the community, the likely outcome will be readmission. The staff member may be reluctant to visit the offender again after their discharge in case the attack is repeated, even if there have been attempts made to rebuild the relationship whilst the offender is an in-patient. There may also be resentment harboured by the offender as they may blame the staff member for their readmission to hospital and the subsequent constraints imposed upon them. In the event of this type of occurrence, it may be more prudent to change the community staff who will attend in future.

Other victims may be friends of the offender. A breakdown in relationships here can be detrimental to the maintenance of the offender's social support network, as other friends will possibly melt away if they perceive themselves to be at risk of an attack also. This could lead to social isolation and loneliness for the offender.

POST-TRAUMATIC STRESS DISORDER

Traumatic incidents can affect everyone, mentally disordered offenders included. What follows here is an account of the results of a traumatic incident on a member of the public. This man did not initially suffer from a major mental illness but became a mentally disordered offender owing to the trauma he experienced. He committed his offence as a result of poor coping skills in dealing with his trauma.

Within any community forensic team, it is important to have a wide variety of skills and the skill which will be addressed here is that of cognitive behaviour therapy training and how it can be used in a traumatised individual.

Case study

Fergus was a 42-year-old man referred to forensic community mental health nurses whilst in prison. The initial referral stated that he was suffering from 'anxiety' and 'suicidal ideation'. He was due for liberation in approximately three months' time and would be returning to live with his parents in his home village in Scotland. Upon initial assessment, Fergus was unco-operative stating that he did not want to see a psychiatric nurse. The following day, Fergus was admitted to the hospital wing of the prison after a suicide attempt where he tried to hang himself in his cell. Whilst in the hospital wing, he was visited daily by the community mental health nurse, and a tentative relationship was established.

After his return to the prison hall, the community nurse maintained daily contact, sometimes in the hall, sometimes at a workplace within the joinery department. Fergus increasingly became forthcoming about the events of his past. He explaining that he had been a fireman until two years previously when he had been 'pensioned off'. He attributed this to his inability to perform his duties. He also spoke about his family and described close and cohesive relationships. Both parents were alive. Fergus had one brother and one sister. The siblings were relatively close in age. His sister was married and had two sons. His brother was the youngest of the three siblings and had a live-in girlfriend with whom the family got on well. Fergus divulged that, approximately one year previously, he had seriously assaulted his brother-in-law causing a rift in the family. Fergus's parents had supported him throughout the period of his subsequent prosecution and imprisonment and were keen to have him home. During his period of incarceration, Fergus's brother and his girlfriend visited regularly. In contrast, his sister refused to speak to him as did his brother-in-law. They also denied him contact with their two sons.

During the first attempt to explore his anxiety, Fergus was unable to articulate what he perceived to be the cause. He continually referred to his job as a fireman but could or would not elaborate on his inability to continue with this employment. Finally, Fergus confided that he had witnessed two children being burned to death in a fire. He had been unable to reach them. Fergus referred to repeated flashback experiences of the events. He felt that he did not deserve to live when the children had died. He stated that the date and time of these events were indelibly printed on his memory and that he had a suicide plan he intended to implement once liberated. Prison staff confirmed that Fergus had never divulged any of these feelings to them. They had, however, treated him for the apparent depression from which he suffered, with antidepressant medication.

The forensic nurse who assessed Fergus had recently completed her diploma in cognitive behaviour therapy. She considered that with the consent of the prison health centre manager and the visiting psychologist, she would be capable of treating him. The nurse therapist then delivered treatment over the course of the remainder of Fergus's time in prison, employing a combination of cognitive behaviour therapy techniques. During this time, a support network within Fergus's home community was established consisting of a psychiatrist, a psychologist and a community psychiatric nurse. The intention was to ensure that an effective package of care would be provided for him upon discharge. The community psychiatric nurse from his home town also visited Fergus on five occasions prior to his liberation again to ensure that an operative relationship was established and also to liaise with the forensic nurse therapist on the matters of his history, presenting symptoms and treatment already delivered.

One year on, Fergus is coping well with his mental health problems aided by the supports enlisted and has not re-offended.

Post-traumatic stress disorder is treated by many different methods

Cognitive behaviour therapy, incorporating treatment techniques such as systematic desensitisation, exposure, stress inoculation training, assertiveness training, cognitive processing therapy, relaxation training, biofeedback, or indeed a combination of these methods is becoming increasingly popular. To date, well-controlled trials provide strong evidence that exposure is the most effective (Rothbaum et al. 2000).

Pharmacotherapy, utilising medication such as selective serotonin reuptake inhibitors, monoamine oxidase inhibitors, tricyclic antidepressants, antiadrenergic agents, anticonvulsants, benzodiazepines, other serotonergic agents and antipsychotics, has enjoyed varying degrees of success with best evidence supporting the use of selective serotonin reuptake inhibitors as first-line drugs in this condition (Friedman et al. 2000).

Eye movement desensitisation and reprocessing (EMDR) is a treatment where the patient is required to track the clinician's moving finger in front of their eyes whilst remembering a disturbing image, an associated negative cognition and bodily sensations associated with a traumatic memory. EMDR has been found to be efficacious based on a review of seven published randomised controlled studies (Chemtob *et al.* 2000).

Group therapy is delivered in 'covering' or 'uncovering' formats. This refers to whether traumatic experiences are addressed directly or not. One 'covering' type is supportive group therapy, which makes members aware of current coping. The two 'uncovering' types are: (1) psychodynamic groups, which aim to instil an understanding of reactions to trauma and to help address continuing issues; and (2) cognitive behavioural group therapy, which emphasises cognitive restructuring in relation to members' experiences. Recent evidence has shown that this therapy is potentially effective but doesn't favour one type over the others (Foy *et al.* 2000).

Psychodynamic therapy requires a therapeutic relationship between patient and therapist and explores fears, fantasies, wishes and defences triggered by the trauma, thereby attempting to reinstate normal mechanisms of adaptation. Investigations into the success of this treatment with post-traumatic stress disorder are currently very limited (Kudler, Blank and Krupnick 2000).

In-patient treatment usually occurs in crisis situations where the patient may become a danger to self or others. The patient is usually subjected to numerous therapeutic interventions. Owing to the complexity of treatment programmes, there is little research to demonstrate a success rate (Courtois and Bloom 2000).

Psychosocial rehabilitation is recommended for use in traumatised adults. It includes techniques such as case management, vocational rehabilitation, health education and psychoeducational techniques, self-care/independent living skills training, supported housing, family skills training and social skills training. The benefits of these psychosocial techniques have been illustrated in clinical observations and naturalistic studies (Penk and Flannery 2000).

Hypnosis is dependent upon the receptiveness or otherwise of the patient to hypnotic suggestion. It can be used in three ways: (1) to enhance the patient/therapist relationship, to promote relaxation and to strengthen the patient; (2) to address traumatic memories and suggest resolutions; and (3) to achieve adaptive coping responses. Most evidence to support the use of hypnosis in post-traumatic conditions is based upon studies of service provision and case studies (Cardena *et al.* 2000).

Marital and family therapy is employed either to support family members who care for an individual suffering from post-traumatic stress disorder or to treat family disruption. Little empirical investigation of this therapy is available. Data on the efficacy of this therapy encompasses clinical descriptions from a single clinician or clinic (Riggs 2000).

Creative therapies such as art, music, drama and poetry are used in psychotherapy, counselling, special education or rehabilitation. Evidence for the efficacy of these therapies in treating post-traumatic stress disorder is insufficient to allow meaningful conclusions.

All of the therapies mentioned require, for their application, the appropriate qualifications and should not be undertaken other than by properly trained and experienced practitioners (Foa, Keane and Friedman 2000).

INTERVENTIONS USED TO CARE FOR AND SUPPORT STAFF IN FORENSIC ENVIRONMENTS

Effects of traumatic incidents on staff can manifest themselves in a variety of ways. The spectrum ranges from disappointment to post-traumatic stress disorder. The nature and severity of the incident coupled with the individual sensitivity of the staff member will dictate the level of effect and impact. One area where impact is amply demonstrated is the incidence of staff sickness. Gournay and Carson (2000) state that forensic staff who have been assaulted have sickness rates two times higher than that of their non-assaulted colleagues. They also estimate that in one study they carried out within two special hospitals, 16 per cent of staff drank more than 21 units of alcohol per week and that 11 per cent of staff suggested that alcohol helped them cope better with job pressures.

It is commonly supposed that levels of stress are greater in staff working in forensic services than in general psychiatry. The reasons proffered for this supposition include a greater potential for violence from forensic patients, a prison culture within forensic wards, escape attempts and hostage-taking attempts. There is limited literature exploring this theory, and that which does exist tends to relate to general psychiatry. It tends to cite issues such as inadequate staffing, work overload, interpersonal conflict with other professionals and dealing with patients' families as the most frequently noted stressors for staff (Numerof and Abrams 1984). One further area, which is rarely addressed when occupational stress in nursing staff in general is researched, is the particular effect of stress on forensic community mental health nurses. One study carried out on this subject measured occupational stress in all the forensic community mental health nurses in England and Wales who were attached to medium secure units at that time (Coffey 1999). Results of the study showed that 44.3 per cent of these nurses were experiencing high burn-out in relation to emotional exhaustion, although having to deal with violent patients did not feature in the top ten stressors. Dealing with suicidal patients, however, did. These figures appear to disprove the idea that violence is the principal threat in forensic services. It seems, however, that it is not the actual violence but the supposed threat of violence that creates the stress. For this reason, staff in forensic services require a high level of support.

Staffing levels are invariably and perhaps inevitably a bone of contention within any area of mental health care. Restricted or minimum staffing numbers cannot always cover clinical activity. Staff are, therefore, reliant upon a manager responsible for a budget to approve overtime to accommodate that activity. A study conducted in 1995, which compared stressors in ward-based staff and community-based staff, showed that in ward staff the number one stressor was 'inadequate staffing to cover in potentially dangerous situations' (Carson *et al.* 1995). Within forensic services, both staffing levels and staff quality are of paramount importance for achieving and preserving equilibrium and for de-escalating volatile situations. From a community perspective, staffing numbers are crucial to ensure that caseloads are not unduly burdensome and that community staff are able to allocate time to make joint visits to patients where it is considered necessary.

It is crucial for the staff selection process to ensure that an individual both truly wishes to practise in this specialist area and possesses the skills and attributes that will foster personal and professional development. Dale (2001) provided a potential framework of nine competencies for staff working in forensic environments:

o self-awareness

o perception of role

o ability to communicate

o empathetic approach to patients

o negotiation of relationship boundaries

o reality-based risk taking

o achievement/motivation

o sense of humour

o ability to seek support.

Induction of staff should be thorough with no staff member being expected to carry out specific duties until they have attained the competence to do so. Expectations should be made clear at the outset, and the staff member should be comfortable with these expectations.

Jennings (2001) describes the principles of clinical supervision as 'assisting patients and clients to receive high quality, safe care in a rapidly changing care environment'. The UKCC (1995) position statement on clinical supervision states '…clinical supervision is necessary in clinical practice to enable practitioners to establish, maintain and promote standards and innovation in practice in the interests of patients and clients' (p.3). Clinical supervision in the area of forensic psychiatry is utilised to ensure that staff have the opportunity to review their practice regularly and to gain an understanding of alternative solutions to, and methods of dealing with, varying situations. Moreover, in the aftermath of a traumatic incident, clinical supervision can encourage exploration of the triggers to the incident and the appropriate methods employed to handle it.

Critical incident review/debriefing is an important tool to be employed following a traumatic occurrence. It gives staff the opportunity to explore their reactions to the incident and to reassure themselves that they performed in an appropriate manner. There are always lessons to be learned. Contingency plans can also be devised for dealing with similar incidents in the future. Errors made can be identified and preventive measures agreed. Special attention should be given to the mental and physical condition of staff in the immediate aftermath of a traumatic incident. Thereby, long-term effects may be avoided. Staff should have the opportunity to discuss the incident and express any feelings and emotions which may have been evoked. There should always be provision made for staff to access counselling if necessary.

Peer support within the forensic setting is vital to allow staff to vent their feelings to their counterparts. Although this may be seen as a function of clinical supervision, comfort is often to be obtained in comparing practice with peers. It allows staff to perceive that there is no significant divergence in their performance from that of their colleagues. By contrast, clinical supervision normally involves interaction with a superior. Peer support also assists in the building of relationships with colleagues and serves to reinforce the ready availability of support upon the occurrence of violent or traumatic incidents.

Personal development plans are instrumental in ensuring that all staff receive training and development in areas related to their practice. One specific area requiring particular attention is that of control and restraint training. Although controversial to some, with the growing awareness of violence towards health service employees, control and restraint training is becoming more popular in all areas where patient contact features. The very title of this form of training, to people who have not previously participated in it, involves notions of a custodial setting where staff practise physical restraint and forced medication. Professional control and restraint training, however, instils confidence in staff in their ability to deal with physically aggressive patients. Physical control should only be employed when all other methods of intervention have been attempted and found unsuccessful (Bates, McCourt and Tarbuck 1997; Royal College of Nursing 1992).

Security reviews are a further important feature of forensic nursing designed to minimise the incidence of security transgressions. In any forensic service, risk assessment is of paramount importance, and numerous tools are available to guide staff through this process. Patients are assessed on their individual needs and circumstances and should be subject only to commensurate measures of security or supervision. This can be a difficult balance to achieve within the in-patient domain, as the security requirements of that environment invariably dictate fairly onerous constraints upon the patients resident there. Achieving a balance is especially dependent upon the interpersonal skills of staff and their management of contentious issues (e.g. a patient's resentment of perceived discrimination in the application of security measures towards their peers). Upon the occurrence of a traumatic incident, staff need to be confident in the reviewing of security arrangements and be prepared to alter them more or less immediately to prevent escalation or recurrence of the problem. Thereafter, and soon, a full critical incident review must be undertaken.

FUTURE DIRECTIONS IN COMMUNITY CARE FOR MENTALLY DISORDERED OFFENDERS

The future of forensic mental health care seems assured owing to the high media and public profile of mentally disordered offenders, the demand for high and medium secure care provision, and the requirement for close monitoring and supervision within the community. Literature pertaining to this speciality is beginning to flourish in response to demand. Additionally, legislation seeking to promote and regulate services for this challenging patient group appears steadily to be finding its way on to the statute books.

Forensic psychiatrists and forensic community nurses are now increasingly involved in diversion and liaison schemes within courts, police stations and prisons, as recommended by Hudson, James and Harlow (1995). One problem regularly faced by forensic services in the diversion of people from the criminal justice system is the apparent scarcity of appropriate services to care for them. It is only by the establishment of such services, and the development of the skills and confidence in the staff therein engaged, that there would be the creation of sufficient capacity to care appropriately for these individuals.

As with many other services in the public sector, finance in community forensic care is a major consideration. Policy proposals for the treatment and care of mentally disordered offenders, published by the National Health Service Confederation and Sainsbury Centre for Mental Health (1997), recommends that 'health authorities and trusts should be encouraged to think innovatively and creatively about the funds available, and to work with a wide range of agencies to ensure that the full range of care is offered' (p.13). Integration of forensic services with general mental health services is planned for the future and the commissioning of medium and high security services, formerly the responsibility of the High Security Psychiatric Service Commissioning Board, are now within the remit of local health authorities. This transfer of responsibility is intended to facilitate the smooth transition of patients through the appropriate levels of security (National Health Service Management Executive 1999).

Review of mental health laws (Department of Health 1999c) will ensure that future mental health legislation will provide an effective regulatory framework to govern the circumstances of mentally ill offenders, who pose a danger to themselves or others, and who seek to live in the community.

CONCLUSION

Dealing with the consequences of traumatic incidents is part and parcel of the day-to-day work of forensic staff, whether the person affected is the perpetrator, the victim, a family member or a friend of the offender. Specialised skills are often required to cope adequately with individual needs, and attention must be paid to ensuring a wide range of skills are acquired by forensic teams. It must be remembered, however, that the process of identifying, addressing and resolving the fallout of a traumatic incident can be a trauma in itself, and staff will need copious support in carrying out these duties, whether it be within in-patient services or the community. The effects of trauma should never be underestimated, and whether or not a person verbalises about the trauma they have suffered, measures must always be taken to provide as much support as possible.

CHAPTER 15

Forensic Nursing Interventions and Future Directions for Forensic Mental Health Practice

Phil Woods, Mick Collins and Alyson M. Kettles

INTRODUCTION

A text such as this has as many omissions as it does inclusions. We, as editors, are aware that the choice of nursing interventions that have been included can only represent a small proportion of the developing armoury for the increasing group of nurses who are adopting a forensic label or have some responsibility for forensic issues. For example, dialectical behavioural therapy, self-harm focus, and treatments for drugs and alcohol, learning disabilities and arson are not included as distinct interventions (nor are they intended to be an exhaustive list). Many of these are becoming individual specialities within forensic nursing and are likely to become or already have become forensic nurse consultant options. Each could form the subject of a whole book. For example, forensic learning disability nursing is becoming a very distinct and specialist area, particularly within high security. We have tried to concentrate on interventions that are more readily available to the general practising forensic nurse with different levels of expertise, rather than those that require intensive and long-term training. Substance misuse is another good example: many patients who have contact with forensic services have some documented history of substance misuse, which can form a part of problematic functioning or dangerous behaviour. Mary Addo describes such problems as part of a complex series of care delivery in a clinical vignette in Chapter 11. However, substance misuse and other therapies require specialist training of the kind that is described in Chapter 10 by Paul Rogers and Kevin Gournay.

One distinct and fundamental question that arises from this text is 'Is there a national knowledge base for forensic nursing from which we are developing our interventions?' If we were to take a rather sceptical view from the evidence that has unfolded from previous chapters, it is difficult to suggest that there is. However, this is dependent upon where such evidence is to be placed in the hierarchy of accepted best evidence. While what has been written may be low down within such a hierarchy in theoretical terms, there is a problem in judging such humanistic enterprise in these terms, although we do need to develop such 'higher' hierarchical evidence where possible. There is then much to be gained from the text to suggest where we should be heading as a profession, and some strong foundations to develop from.

Drawing upon the humanistic side of the debate that we have begun to expound, we still have a belief that the essence of forensic nursing is in the essential foundations of the nurse–patient relationship. This is the vehicle through which all other interventions proceed, and the effectiveness of this relationship would seem to have a proportional link. This is an extremely hard concept to evidence in totality, when building such relationships is dependent on a combination of personality, experience and interpersonal dexterity, none of which are easily measurable attributes. We must be careful that the quest for, and the application of, acceptable forms of evidence do not take precedence over a successful nurse–patient relationship and favour technical and theoretical descriptions instead of a symbiotic relationship between these two factors.

Stephan Kirby and Dennis Cross in Chapter 12 describe some of the essential qualities of forensic nursing. They state that 'despite frequent encounters with violence, "inhuman" behaviour and deviance, forensic nursing remains a fundamentally relational enterprise'. This emphasises the humanistic element we have just described. How this is done is not always well defined. The issues of severe criminality and deviance alluded to above have to a degree been skirted in this text in deference to clinical examples, which are relatively 'safe' in forensic terms. The 'sex offender' who exposes himself in public can be very different in terms of required nursing interventions in comparison with a child rapist and murderer. This latter kind of offending behaviour can evoke very different emotions among different nurses. Carol Watson in Chapter 3 takes up elements of this challenge in identifying the need to develop competencies for forensic nurses and in the developing agenda for recognition and high-quality support and supervision.

Anne Aiyegbusi in Chapter 9 further describes some of the areas we have referred to. She describes the complexities of forensic nursing and the difficulties and emotions that can accompany the care of patients. While this chapter is reserved for nurses working with women, many of the issues could equally be transferred to other areas of forensic nursing. One emerging area must be to investigate whether separation is practised when nurses are engaged in therapeutic relationships with patients who have committed offences that nurses find emotionally stressful, or with patients who continually engage in stress-provoking behaviours.

Penny Schafer describes in some detail one aspect of such difficult behaviours in Chapter 4. By separation we are asking whether forensic nurses are able to compartmentalise differing aspects of the patient in order that they can provide excellent care. Forensic nurses are clearly able to work with such difficult issues on a therapeutic basis within an effective nurse–patient relationship. Maybe it is a professional taboo to discuss this because we fear that it will show weakness to our colleagues or even ourselves, or that we are abandoning the Rogerian principle of unconditional positive regard. However, we can see from the range of interventions described in this text that there is an increasing expectation for nurses to address offending behaviour as part of their care programmes. This will inevitably require both an in-depth knowledge of offending behaviour and the need to confront such behaviour directly as part of a rehabilitative process that manages risk and reduces dangerousness. The emotional discomfort that this can produce and implications for support and supervision should not be underestimated.

Managing dangerous behaviour necessitates the utilisation of security. While the concept of security has been mentioned, little has been said about its therapeutic application. Generally, forensic nurses carry out security procedures at differing levels of practice within a carefully built and effective nurse–patient relationship. There is still much debate about how security and therapy are theoretically diametrically opposed to one another to the point where in some cases security procedures are carried out by non-nursing staff. However, the two can be combined effectively into the additional and very unique concept of *relational security* (Collins 2000). This is where the nursing knowledge of and relationship with the patient and their particular risk factors interact to ensure that the patient is kept in the least restrictive regime possible, and can operate to their full potential. Relational security is a factor unique to forensic nurses who have responsibility for security procedures, and can be regarded as an intervention in its own right. It is an underrated and seldom investigated area. Security is a complex area made up of procedures, physical elements and relationships. One author of this chapter (Collins) has recently been investigating how to split these areas into measurable categories which highlight the complex decision-making processes and amalgamation of unique skills that forensic nurses use. He believes that forensic nurses ignore this area at their peril, and that it is generally ignored because it brings out the (often) overemphasised custodial focus that critics are all too quick to throw at the profession. There is a danger that ignoring the skills associated with the application of security procedures will result in patients being subject to a level of security designed for the worst-case scenario with little or no variation related to individual need.

THEMES EMERGING FROM THIS TEXT

The themes emerging from this text can only be viewed as varied. Firstly, forensic nurses are moving towards professional recognition, and generation of a slowly building but encouraging evidence base. There is a continuing trend of the application of generic mental health concepts straight into forensic mental health care, which some of the authors have tried to unravel (for example, John Gibbon in Chapter 2 and Carol Watson in Chapter 3).

All the authors have begun to describe what makes forensic nurses different from their general mental health nursing counterparts, and at the same time describe the enormous crossover in similar core skills. It is how these skills are applied in the forensic context that is important. If this text serves to pave the way for future research, then the editors and the authors will be extremely satisfied.

What also emerges is the huge variation in the field of forensic nursing in terms of the range of environments that can be included. Herein lies one of the difficulties with such a book as this: the application of the interventions may be subject to different predominant factors within the different environments. For example, high, medium and low security are now all established facets of forensic care.

The chapter authors have begun to unearth some intriguing and politically sensitive subjects. For example Paul Rogers and Kevin Gournay in Chapter 10 introduce us to the concept of post-traumatic stress disorder among the perpetrators of violent acts. This, while unusual, certainly warrants some further investigation. Two of the editors of this text have experienced this in the clinical setting when working with some patients who have committed terribly violent acts. These acts have been perpetrated while the patient was suffering acute symptoms of mental disorder, and upon entering a period of stability either through medication or other therapies, have become profoundly depressed or exhibited symptoms associated with post-traumatic stress disorder. This phenomenon has generally arisen upon realising the enormity of what they have done. This was certainly touched upon by Cordess (2000) when he described such a situation.

Each chapter author sums up the particular difficulties of applying their chosen interventions within the forensic environment and the value of integrated and whole approaches. John Swinton in Chapter 13 serves to remind forensic nurses yet again of the intrinsic humanness of forensic nursing and the associated unique attributes of each and every one of us. He emphasises the concept of the whole person and seeing beyond what may be either a set of undesirable behaviours, horrific offence or both. He introduces the very apt concept of forgiveness, and forces forensic nurses to rethink their practice and the differing interpretations of spirituality and how important these are to the individual.

Other themes that can be seen emerging include the ways in which forensic nurses are maintaining their core skills and building on them with advanced therapeutic practice, the many ways in which interventions can be used to the benefit of the patient and the methodical nature of each of the interventions as well as the precursors for each intervention to work.

This book represents the healthy striving of professionals to do more for those under their care. While elements undoubtedly have been missed, and probably always will be in texts of this kind, the further we travel on the journey of understanding and evidence generation the more we realise that we still have further to travel, and more importantly that we have the potential to do so.

DEVELOPING THE FORENSIC NURSING EVIDENCE BASE

The Mental Health National Service Framework (Department of Health 1999a) clearly lays out what levels of evidence should be used to determine which interventions should be used for quality patient care. The Scottish Executive Health Department (2001) has also clearly identified nursing in secure environments for the first time as an action area. This means that, also for the first time, a set of core forensic nursing competencies has been published by the National Board for Nursing, Midwifery and Health Visiting for Scotland (NBS 2001) and that these competencies can be used as the basis for research and for outcome measurement. If forensic mental health nurses are to develop their unique evidence base, consideration needs to be given to researching the effectiveness of the interventions they utilise. In the current climate, where only best evidence will do, it is no longer acceptable practice to publish the effectiveness of care with no systematic research to support this. Without such systematic review, evidence provided can only be viewed at best as the author's opinion.

This, however, is not to say that forensic nurses should be moving towards only using interventions that have been shown to be effective through randomised controlled trials. Consideration should be given to utilising more pragmatic yet well-designed research approaches. For example: (1) multiple interrupted baseline measures (with patients acting as their own controls); (2) single- or multiple-case studies utilising before and after measures with long-term follow-up; or (3) observational studies with a battery of before-and-after measures with long-term follow-up.

In essence, the way the evidence-based practice develops depends on how the forensic service sees the role of forensic nursing practice. Does this involve all forensic nurses drawing on an advanced knowledge base, using best available evidence, standardised assessments, positive risk taking, offence-focused work, and so on; or is this relying on one or two clinical nurse specialists or nurse consultants using their advanced clinical skills in a narrowly focused way?

The authors of this chapter suggest that in order for forensic nursing practice to develop its own clear evidence base this has to involve interrogating current practice, adding an advanced knowledge base, synthesising and evaluating – so that practice will be teased and steered to only that which is evidence-based. This would encourage nurses to challenge their existing practice and encourage positive risk-taking, but more importantly would ensure their practice was outcome-driven.

Forensic nursing needs to develop its evidence in relation to the day-to-day management of patients to compensate for very specific specialist intervention from other members of the multidisciplinary team. But the mistake should not be made in assuming that this is any less valuable. Fundamentally, this would develop the knowledge base around just how forensic nurses intervene and meet the individual needs of the patients under their care. Indeed, it would help to ensure that care was simplistic yet effective, maximising benefits, thus improving quality. All this would help to develop practice in a meaningful and sustainable way to define forensic nursing and its role, skills and competencies.

However, even if forensic nurses manage to achieve (or should we say develop?) their unique evidence base, they need to bear a crucial thought in mind – treatment fidelity. For the true effect of a particular treatment to be known, independent assessments of treatment fidelity are required. For example, it is not adequate to train nurses to deliver interventions by providing support and guidance through supervision alone: independent assessments through audiotape recordings, diaries or videos are required.

Finally, through current governmental mental health initiatives and guidelines, the challenge has been set forensic mental health nurses to develop evidence to support what exactly they do, which means that the care they provide is effective. The chapter authors of this book have helped to move this challenge forward, but there is still much to do.

References

Abel, G.G., Becker, J.V. and Skinner, L.J. (1983) 'Treatment of violent sex offenders.' In L. Roth (ed) *Clinical Treatment of the Violent Person. Crime and Delinquency Issues.* Rockville: National Institute of Mental Health.

Adams, L. (1995) 'How exercise can help people with mental health problems.' *Nursing Times 91*, 36, 37–39.

Addo, M. (1997) *Clinical supervision: 'We don't want to stand alone'. Views from the front-line.* Unpublished MEd Thesis. Available at Queen Mother Library, University of Aberdeen.

Adshead, G. (1994) 'Damage: Trauma and violence in a sample of women referred to a forensic service.' *Behavioral Sciences and the Law 12*, 235–249.

Adshead, G. (1997) 'Written on the body: Deliberate self-harm and violence.' In E.V. Welldone and C. Van Velsen (eds) *A Practical Guide to Forensic Psychotherapy.* London: Jessica Kingsley Publishers.

Adshead, G. (1998) 'Psychiatric staff as attachment figures: Understanding management problems in psychiatric services in the light of attachment theory.' *British Journal of Psychiatry 172*, 64–69.

Adshead, G. and Morris, F. (1995) 'Another time, another place.' *Health Service Journal*, 9 February, 24–26.

Ainsworth, M.D.S. (1989) 'Attachments beyond infancy.' *American Psychologist 44*, 709–716.

Ainsworth, M.D.S. and Bowlby, J. (1991) 'An ethological approach to personality development.' *American Psychologist 48*, 333–341.

Alexander, P.C. (1992) 'Application of attachment theory to the study of sexual abuse.' *Journal of Consulting and Clinical Psychology 60*, 185–195.

Allen, J. (1997) 'Assessing and managing risk of violence in the mentally disordered.' *Journal of Psychiatric and Mental Health Nursing 4*, 369–378.

Allison, D.B, Fontaine, K.R., Heo, M., Mentore, J.L., Cappelleri, J.C., Chandler, L.P., Weiden, P.J. and Cheskin, L.J. (1999) 'The distribution of body mass index among individuals with and without schizophrenia.' *Journal of Clinical Psychiatry 60*, 215–220.

Alty, A. and Mason, T. (1994) *Seclusion and Mental Health: A Break with the Past.* London: Chapman and Hall.

American Psychiatric Association (1994) *Diagnostic and Statistical Manual of Mental Disorder (4th ed).* Washington: APA.

Anderson, H. and Goolishian, H. (1992) 'The client is the expert: A not knowing approach to therapy.' In S. McNamee and K.J. Gergen (eds) *Therapy as Social Construction.* London: Sage.

Appleby, L., Shaw, J. and Amos, T. (1997) 'The national confidential inquiry into suicide and homicide by people with a mental illness.' *British Journal of Psychiatry 170*, 101–102.

Argyle, M. (1975) *Bodily Communications*. London: Methuen.

Ash, J. (1996) 'Is theory enough?' *Psychiatric Care 3*, 5, 177–180.

Awad, G., Saunders, E. and Levene, J. (1984) 'A clinical study of sexual abuse.' *International Journal of Offender Therapy and Comparative Criminology 28*, 105–115.

Baker, A.W. and Duncan, S.P. (1985) 'Child sexual abuse: A study of prevalence in Great Britain.' *Child Abuse and Neglect 9*, 457–467.

Barker, P.J. (1990) 'The philosophy of psychiatric nursing.' *Nursing Standard 5*, 12, 28–33.

Barker, P.J. (1995) *Healing Lives, Mending Minds*. University of Newcastle: Professorial Inaugural Lecture.

Barker, P.J., Reynolds, W. and Stevenson, C. (1997) 'The human science basis of psychiatric nursing: Theory and practice.' *Journal of Advanced Nursing 25*, 660–667.

Barnes, M. (1996) 'Challenging the culture: Representing the rights of women in special hospitals.' In M. Hemingway (ed) *Special Women? The Experience of Women in the Special Hospital System*. Aldershot: Avebury.

Barr, H. (1999) *Review of the Evidence to Support Interprofessional Learning*. Report commissioned by UKCC from the Centre for the Advancement of Interprofessional Education. London: UKCC.

Barrowclough, C. and Tarrier, N. (1992) *Families of Schizophrenic Patients: A Cognitive Behaviour Intervention*. London: Chapman and Hall.

Barrowclough, C. and Tarrier, N. (1994) 'Interventions with families.' In M. Birchwood and N. Tarrier (eds) *Psychological Management of Schizophrenia*. Chichester: Wiley.

Bartemeier, L.H., Kubie, L.S., Menninger, K.A., Romano, J. and Whithorn, J.C. (1946) 'Combat exhaustion.' *Journal of Nervous and Mental Disease 104*, 358–389.

Bass, E. and Davis, L. (1988) *The Courage to Heal: A Guide for Women Survivors of Child Sexual Abuse*. New York: Harper and Row.

Bassett C. (1993) 'Nurse teachers' attitudes to research: A phenomenological study.' *Journal of Advanced Nursing 19*, 1–8.

Bates, A., McCourt, M. and Tarbuck, P. (1997) *Care of the Aggressive Individual*. London: Royal College of Nursing.

Baumeister, R.F. and Leary, M.R. (1995) 'The need to belong: Desire for interpersonal attachments as a fundamental human motivation.' *Psychological Bulletin 117*, 497–529.

Beattie, A. (1987) 'Making a curriculum work.' In P. Allen and M. Jolley (eds) *The Curriculum in Nursing Education*. London: Croom Helm.

Becker, J.V., Cunningham-Rather, J. and Kaplan, M.S. (1986) 'The adolescent sexual perpetrator: Demographics, criminal history, victims, sexual behaviour and recommendations for reducing future offences.' *Journal of Interpersonal Violence 1*, 4, 431–445.

Becker, M.H. (ed) (1974) 'The health belief model and personal health behaviour.' *Health Education Monographs 2*, 324–508.

Beech. A., Fisher. D. and Beckett, R. (1998) *An Evaluation of the Prison Sex Offender Treatment Programme*. Home Office report. London: HMSO.

Belfrage, H., Fransson, G. and Strand, S. (2000) 'Prediction of violence using the HCR–20: A prospective study in two maximum-security correctional institutions.' *Journal of Forensic Psychiatry 11*, 1, 167–175.

Bell, R. and Cooney, M. (1993) 'Sporting chances … Gains made in mental and physical well-being through exercise.' *Nursing Times 89*, 43, 62–63.

Bentall, R.P. (1992) 'Reconstructing psychopathology.' *The Psychologist 5*, 61–66.

Bentall, R.P., Kaney, S. and Dewey, M.E. (1991) 'Paranoia and social reasoning: An attributional theory analysis.' *British Journal of Clinical Psychology 30*, 13–23.

Bentall, R.P., Kinderman, P. and Kaney, S. (1994) 'Cognitive process and delusional beliefs: Attributions and the self.' *Behaviour Research and Therapy 32*, 331–341.

Bergin, A.E. (1988) 'Three contributions of a spiritual perspective to counselling psychotherapy, and behavior change.' *Counseling and Values 32*, 21–33.

Berlin, F.S. and Malin, H.M. (1991) 'Media distortion of the public's perception of recidivism and psychiatric rehabilitation.' *American Journal of Psychiatry 148*, 11, 1572–1576.

Bernard, G. (2000) 'Criminal violence associated with borderline and non-borderline cases: Characteristics of the acting-out process.'
Available online: http://www.csc-scc.gc.ca/text/rsrch/regional/summary9811e.shtml

Berren, M.R., Hill, K.R., Merikle, E., Gonzalez, N. and Santiato, J. (1994) 'Serious mental illness and mortality rates.' *Hospital and Community Psychiatry 45*, 6, 604–605.

Bingley, W. (1997) 'Assessing dangerousness: Protecting the interests of patients.' *British Journal of Psychiatry 170*, 32, 28–29.

Bird, S. (1997) 'Is exercise really good for us?' *Biologist 44*, 5, 465–468.

Bland, J., Mezey, G. and Dolan, B. (1999) 'Special women, special needs: A descriptive study of female special hospital patients.' *Journal of Forensic Psychiatry 10*, 1, 34–45.

Blanes, T. (1994) 'Review of anxiety disorders.' *Psychological Review 12*, 56–68.

Blaske, D.M., Borduin, C.M., Henggeler, S. and Mann, B. (1989) 'Individual, family and peer characteristics of adolescent sexual offenders and assaultive offenders.' *Developmental Psychology 25*, 846–855.

Boland, F.J., Burrill, R., Duwyn, M. and Karp, J. (1998) 'Fetal alcohol syndrome: Implications for correctional service.'
Available online: http: //ww.csc-scc.gc.ca/text/rsrch/reports/r71/r71eshtml

Bordin, E.S. (1979) 'The generalisibility of the psychoanalytic concept of the working alliance.' *Psychotherapy: Theory, Research and Practice 16*, 252–260.

Boutell, K.A. and Bozett, F.W. (1987) 'Nurses' assessment of patients' spirituality: Continuing education implications.' *Journal of Continuing Education in Nursing 21*, 172–176.

Bowlby, J. (1969) *Attachment and Loss: Attachment (vol.1).* New York: Basic Books.

Bowlby, J. (1973) *Attachment and Loss: Separation (vol.2).* New York: Basic Books.

Bowlby, J. (1980) *Attachment and Loss: Loss, Sadness and Depression (vol.3).* New York: Basic Books.

Bowlby, J. (1988) *A Secure Base: Clinical Applications of Attachment Theory.* London: Routledge.

Braud, W. and Anderson, R. (1998) *Transpersonal Research Methods for the Social Science.* California: Sage.

Brazire, S. (2000) *Psychotropic Drugs Directory.* Wiltshire: Quay Books.

Bridges, N.A. (1995) 'Managing erotic and loving feelings in therapeutic relationship: A model course.' *Journal of Psychotherapy Practice and Research 4*, 4, 329–339.

Briere, J. and Runtz, M. (1987) 'Post sexual abuse trauma. Data and implications for clinical practice.' *Journal of Interpersonal Violence 2*, 367–379.

Brooker, C., Falloon, I., Butterworth, A., Goldberg, D., Graham-Hole, V. and Hillier, V. (1994) 'The outcome of training community psychiatric nurses to deliver psychosocial intervention.' *British Journal of Psychiatry 165*, 222–230.

Brown, G.W., Birley, J.L. and Wing, J.K. (1972) 'Influences of family life on the course of schizophrenic disorders: A replication.' *British Journal of Psychiatry 121*, 562, 241–258.

Brown, G.W., Manch, E.M., Carstairs, W. *et al.* (1962) 'Influence of family on the course of schizophrenic illness.' *British Journal of Preventative Social Medicine 16*, 55–68.

Bugental, J. (1987) *The Art of the Psychotherapist.* New York: Norton.

Bumby, K.M. and Marshall, W.L. (1994) 'Loneliness and intimacy deficits among incarcerated rapists and child molesters.' Paper presented at the 13th Annual Research and Treatment Conference of the Association for the Treatment of Sexual Abusers, San Francisco.

Burbach, F.R. (1997) 'The efficacy of physical activity interventions within mental health services: Anxiety and depression.' *Journal of Mental Health 6*, 6, 543–566.

Burgess, A.W. and Holmstorm, L.L. (1974) 'Rape trauma syndrome.' *American Journal of Psychiatry 131*, 981–986.

Cadbury, A. (1992) *Report of the Committee on the Financial Aspects of Corporate Governance.* London: Gee and Co.

Cahill, C.D., Stuart, G.W., Laraia, M.T. and Arana, G.W. (1991) 'Inpatient management of violent behaviour: Nursing prevention and intervention.' *Issues in Mental Health Nursing 12*, 239–252.

Cameron, C. (1996) 'Patient compliance: Recognition of the factors involved and suggestions for promoting compliance with therapeutic regimes.' *Journal of Advanced Nursing 24*, 244–250.

Campbell, I. (2001) 'National obesity forum: Combating overweight in primary care.' *Scottish Nurse 5*, 7, 30.

Campbell, P. (1998) 'Listening to clients.' In P. Barker and B. Davison (eds) *Psychiatric Nursing: Ethical Strife.* London: Arnold.

Canales, M. (1997) 'Narrative interaction: Creating a space for therapeutic communication.' *Issues in Mental Health Nursing 18*, 477–494.

Cardena, E., Maldonado, J., Van der Hart, O. and Spiegel, D. (2000) 'Hypnosis.' *Journal of Traumatic Stress 13*, 4, 580–584.

Cardin, V.A., McGill, C.W. and Falloon, I.R.H. (1986) 'An economic analysis: Costs, benefits and effectiveness.' In I.R.H. Falloon (ed) *Family Management of Schizophrenia.* Baltimore: Johns Hopkins University Press.

Carson, J., Leary, J., DeVilliers, N., Fagin, L. and Radmall, J. (1995) 'Stress in mental health nurses: Comparison of ward and community staff.' *British Journal of Nursing 4*, 579–582.

Carson, V.B. (1989) *Spiritual Dimensions of Nursing Practice.* Philadelphia: Saunders.

Carter, D.L., Prentky, R.A., Knight, R., Vanderveer, P.L. and Boucher, R.J. (1987) 'Use of pornography in the criminal and developmental histories of sex offenders.' *Journal of Interpersonal Violence 2*, 196–211.

Centre for Disease Control and Protection (1997) 'Violence as a public health problem.' American Association of Colleges of Nursing.
Available online: http: /www.aacn.nche.edu/Publications/position/violence.htm

Chadwick, P.D.J. and Birchwood, M.J. (1994) 'The omnipotence of voices: A cognitive approach to auditory hallucinations.' *British Journal of Psychiatry 165*, 190–201.

Chadwick, P.D.J., Birchwood, M.J. and Trower, P. (1996) *Cognitive Therapy for Delusions, Voices and Paranoia.* Chichester: Wiley.

Chadwick, P.D.J. and Lowe, C.F. (1990) 'Measurement and modification of delusional beliefs.' *Journal of Consulting and Clinical Psychology 58*, 225–232.

Chamove, A.S. (1986) 'Short-term effects of activity on behaviour of chronic schizophrenic patients.' *British Journal of Clinical Psychology 25*, 125–133.

Chan, P, (1998) 'Paternalistic intervention in mental health care.' *Nursing Times 94*, 36, 52–53.

Chandley, M. (2000) 'Time and confinement: Towards a common sense or socio-temporality in a special hospital.' *British Journal of Forensic Practice 2*, 2, 30–37.

Charters, P.J. (1999) 'The religious and spiritual needs of mental health clients.' *Nursing Standard 13*, 26, 34–36.

Chemtob, C.M., Tolin, D.F., van der Kolk, B.A. and Pitman, R.K. (2000) 'Eye movement desensitization and reprocessing.' *Journal of Traumatic Stress 13*, 4, 569–570.

Chirboga, D.A. and Bailey, J. (1986) 'Stress and burnout among critical and medical surgical nurses: A comparative study.' *Critical Care Quarterly 9*, 84–92.

Chiswick, D. (1993) 'Forensic psychiatry.' In R.E. Kendall and A.K. Zealley (eds) *Companion to Psychiatric Studies*. Edinburgh: Churchill Livingstone.

Cioffi, J. (1997) 'Heuristics, servants to intuition, in clinical decision making.' *Journal of Advanced Nursing 26*, 203–208.

Clarke, L. (1999) *Challenging Ideas in Psychiatric Nursing*. London: Routledge.

Clayton, P. (2000) 'Cognitive analytic therapy: For learning disability and firesetting.' In D. Mercer, T. Mason, M. McKeown and G. McCann (eds) *Forensic Mental Health Care: A Case Study Approach*. Edinburgh: Churchill Livingstone.

Clinical Resource Audit Group (1997) *The Future Role of Psychiatric Nursing in the Community. A Good Practice Statement.* CRAG Working Group on Mental Illness. Edinburgh: Scottish Executive.

Coffey, M. (1998) 'Provision of out-of-hours support to a forensic population: Strategies and research potential.' *Journal of Psychiatric Mental Health Nursing 5*, 5, 367–375.

Coffey, M. (1999) 'Stress and burnout in forensic community mental health nurses: An investigation of its causes and effects.' *Journal of Psychiatric Mental Health Nursing 6*, 6, 433–443.

Coffey, M. and Chaloner, C. (2000) *Forensic Mental Health Nursing: Current Approaches*. London: Blackwell Science.

Coid, J. (1982) 'Alcoholism and violence.' *Journal of Drug and Alcohol Dependence 9*, 449, 1–3.

Coid, J. (1986) 'Alcohol, rape and sexual assault. Socio-culture factors in alcohol related aggression.' In P.F. Brain (ed) *Alcohol and Aggression*. London: Croom Helm.

Coid, J. (1993) 'An affective syndrome in psychopaths with borderline personality disorder.' *British Journal of Psychiatry 162*, 641–650.

Coid, J., Kahtan, N., Gault, S. and Jarman, B. (1999) 'Patients with personality disorder admitted to secure forensic psychiatry services.' *British Journal of Psychiatry 175*, 528–536.

Coleman, R. (1998) *Politics of the Mad House*. Runcorn: Handsell Publishing.

Collingwood, T.R. and Willer, L. (1971) 'The effects of physical training upon self-concept and body attitudes.' *Journal of Consulting and Clinical Psychology 27*, 411–412.

Collins, M. (2000) 'The practitioner new to the role of forensic psychiatric nurse in the UK.' In D.K. Robinson and A.M. Kettles (eds) *Forensic Nursing and Multidisciplinary Care of the Mentally Disordered Offender*. London: Jessica Kingsley Publishers.

Cooper, N.A. and Clum, G.A. (1989) 'Imaginal flooding as a supplementary treatment for PTSD in combat veterans. A controlled study.' *Behaviour Therapy 20*, 381–391.

Cordess, C. (2000) 'A forensic psychiatry perspective.' In D.K. Robinson and A.M. Kettles (eds) *Forensic Nursing and Multidisciplinary Care of the Mentally Disordered Offender*. London: Jessica Kingsley Publishers.

Corey, G. (1986) *Theory and Practice of Counselling and Psychotherapy*. Monterey: Brooks Cole.

Courtois, C.A. and Bloom, S.L. (2000) 'Inpatient treatment.' *Journal of Traumatic Stress 13*, 4, 574–578.

Crighton, D. (1995) 'Sex offender group work.' *Issues in Criminology and Legal Psychology 23*, 15–21.

Crighton, D. (2000) 'Reflections on risk assessment: Suicide in prisons.' *British Journal of Forensic Practice 2*, 1, 23–29.

Dale, C. (2001) 'Interpersonal relationships: Staff development, awareness and monitoring issues.' In C. Dale, T. Thompson and P. Woods (eds) *Forensic Mental Health: Issues in Practice.* London: Harcourt.

Dalglish, K. (1996) *Dalglish: My Autobiography.* London: Hodder and Stoughton.

Davidson, J.R.T., Hughes, D., Blazer, D.G. and George, L.K. (1991) 'Post-traumatic stress disorder in the community: An epidemiological study.' *Psychological Medicine 21*, 713–721.

Davidson, J.R.T. and van der Kolk, B.A. (1996) 'The psychopharmacological treatment for post traumatic stress disorder.' In B.A. van der Kolk, A.C. McFarlane and L. Weisaeth (eds) *Traumatic Stress: The Effects of Overwhelming Experience on Body, Mind and Society.* New York: Guilford Press.

Deale, A., Chalder, T., Marks, I. and Wessley, S. (1997). 'Cognitive behaviour therapy for chronic fatigue syndrome: A randomised controlled trial.' *American Journal of Psychiatry 154*, 3, 408–414.

Delaney, F.G. (1994) 'Nursing and health promotion: Conceptual concerns.' *Journal of Advanced Nursing 20*, 828–835.

Delgado, R., (1989) 'Storytelling for oppositionists and others: A plea for narrative.' *Michigan Law Review 87*, 2411–2441.

Department of Health (1990) *Caring for People: The Care Programme Approach for People with a Mental Illness Referred to the Specialist Psychiatric Services.* Wetherby: Wetherby Health Publications Unit, Department of Health.

Department of Health (1992) *Report of the Committee of Inquiry into Complaints about Ashworth Hospital.* London: HMSO.

Department of Health (1993a) *The Discharge of Mentally Disordered People and Their Continuing Care in the Community.* London: HMSO.

Department of Health (1993b) *A Vision for the Future: The Nursing, Midwifery and Health Visiting Contributions to Health and Health Care.* London: NHS Management Executive/HMSO.

Department of Health (1994) *Code of Conduct and Code of Accountability.* London: HMSO.

Department of Health (1995) *Mental Health (Patients in the Community) Act.* London: HMSO.

Department of Health (1997) *The New NHS: Modern, Dependable.* London: HMSO.

Department of Health (1998a) *Modernising Mental Health Services: Safe, Sound and Supportive.* London: HMSO.

Department of Health (1998b) *A First Class Service: Quality in the new NHS.* London: HMSO.

Department of Health (1999a) *Mental Health National Service Framework: Modern Standards and Service Models.* London: HMSO.

Department of Health (1999b) *Making a Difference: Strengthening the Nursing, Midwifery and Health Visiting Contribution to Health and Healthcare.* London: HMSO.

Department of Health (1999c) *Reform of the Mental Health Act 1983: Proposals for Consultation.* London: HMSO.

Department of Health (2000a) *Report of the Review of Security at the High Security Hospitals.* London: HMSO.

Department of Health (2000b) *The NHS Plan: A Plan for Investment: A Plan for Reform.* London: HMSO.

Department of Health (2000c) *A Health Service of All the Talents: Developing the NHS Workforce.* London: HMSO.

Department of Health and Home Office (1992) *Review of Health and Social Services for Mentally Disordered Offenders and Others Requiring Similar Services.* London: HMSO.

Department of Health and Home Office (1992) *Review of Health and Social Services for Mentally Disordered Offenders and Others Requiring Similar Services. Final Summary Report.* London: HMSO.

Department of Health and the Welsh Office (1999) *Code of Practice: Mental Health Act 1983.* London: HMSO.

de Zulueta, F. (1993) *From Pain to Violence: The Traumatic Roots of Destructiveness.* London: Whurr.

Diamant, L. and Windholz, G. (1981) 'Loneliness in college students: Some theoretical, empirical and therapeutic considerations.' *Journal of College Student Personality 22,* 515–522.

Dickes, R. (1975) 'Technical considerations of the therapeutic and working alliances.' *International Journal of Psychoanalytical Psychotherapy 4,* 1–24.

Dodson, L.C. and Mullens, W.R. (1969) 'Some effects of jogging on psychiatric hospital patients.' *American Correctional Therapy Journal 23,* 5, 130–134.

Donabedian, A. (1988) 'The quality of care, how can it be assessed?' *Journal of the American Association 260,* 1743–1748.

Dossey, L. (1993) *Healing Words: The Power of Prayer and the Practice of Medicine.* San Francisco: Harper.

Dossey, L. (1996) *Prayer is Good Medicine: How to Reap the Benefits of Prayer.* San Francisco: Harper.

Drew, A. and King, M. (1995) *The Mental Health Handbook.* London: Judy Piatkus.

Drury, V., Birchwood, M., Cochrane, R. and Macmillan, F. (1996) 'Cognitive therapy and recovery from acute psychosis: A controlled trial II. Impact on recovery time.' *British Journal of Psychiatry 169,* 5, 602–607.

Duehn, W.D. (1994) 'Cognitive behavioural approaches in the treatment of sex offenders.' In Granvold, D.K. *et al.* (eds) *Cognitive Behavioural Treatment.* Pacific Grove, CA: Brooks and Cole.

Dunn, F.M. and Gilchrist, V.J. (1993) 'Sexual assault.' *Primary Care 20,* 359–373.

Dunn, M. and Sommer, N. (1997) 'Managing difficult staff interactions: Effectiveness of assertiveness training for SCI nursing staff.' *Rehabilitation Nursing 22,* 2, 82–87.

Duquette, A., Sandhu, B.K. and Beaudet, L. (1994) 'Factors related to nursing burnout: A review of empirical knowledge.' *Issues in Mental Health Nursing 15,* 337–358.

Dwivedi, K.N. (1997) *The Therapeutic Use of Stories.* London: Routledge.

Eby, K.K., Campbell, J.C., Sullivan, C.M. and Davidson, W.S. (1995) 'Health effects of experiences of sexual violence for women with abusive partners.' *Health Care Women International 16,* 563–576.

Egan, G. (1990) *The Skilled Helper: A Systematic Approach to Effective Helping.* Belmont: Wadsworth.

Ellerby, L.A. and Ellerby, J.H. (1998) 'Understanding and evaluating the role of elders and traditional healing in sex offender treatment for aboriginal offenders.' Available online: http://www.sgc.ca./epub/abocor/eapc18ca.htm

Enright, S.J. (1989) 'Paedophilia: A cognitive behavioural approach in a single case.' *Journal of Psychiatry 155,* 399–401.

Epps, K. (1996) 'Sex offenders.' In C. Hollins (ed) *Working with Offenders: Psychological Practice in Offender Rehabilitation.* Chichester: Wiley.

Ewers, P.L. (1999) *An Examination of the Impact of a Training Programme in Psychosocial Interventions on the Burnout Rate, Knowledge and Attitude of Forensic Mental Health Nurses.* Unpublished thesis. University of Manchester.

Fadden, G. (1998) 'Family intervention.' In C. Brooker and J. Repper (eds) *Serious Mental Health Problems in the Community.* London: Bailliere Tindall.

Fadden, G.B., Bebbington, P.E. and Kuipers, L. (1987) 'Caring and its burdens: A study of the relatives of depressed patients.' *British Journal of Psychiatry 151*, 660–667.

Fagan, J. and Wexler, S. (1988) 'Explanations of sexual assault among violent delinquents.' *Journal of Adolescent Research 3*, 363–385.

Falloon, I.R.H., Boyd, J.L. and McGill, C.W. (1985) 'Family management in the prevention of morbidity of schizophrenia: Clinical outcome of a two-year longitudinal study.' *Archives of General Psychiatry 42*, 887–896.

Falloon, I.R.H. and Talbot, R.E. (1981) 'Persistent auditory hallucinations: Coping mechanisms and implications for management.' *Psychological Medicine 11*, 329–339.

Farber, S.K. (1997) 'Self medication, traumatic re-enactment and somatic expression in bulimic and self mutilating behaviour.' *Clinical Social Work Journal 25*, 1, 87–106.

Fedorff, J.P. and Moran, B. (1997) 'Myths and misconceptions about sex offenders.' *Canadian Journal of Human Sexuality 6*, 263–275.

Fee, D. (ed) (2000) *Pathology and the Postmodern: Mental Illness as Discourse and Experience.* London: Sage.

Fehr, B. and Perlham, D. (1985) 'The family as a social network and support system.' In L. L'Abate (ed) *Handbook of Family Psychology and Therapy (vol.1).* Homewood, Illinois: Dorsey Press.

Fernandez, O.V., Giraldez, S.L., Saiz, A.G., Garcia, A.O., Sanchez, M.A. and Perez, A.M.G. (1999) 'Integrated psychological treatment for schizophrenic patients.' *Psychology in Spain 3*, 1, 25–35.

Finkelhor, D. (1984) *Child Sexual Abuse.* New York: Free Press.

Finkelhor, D. (ed) (1986) *A Sourcebook on Child Sexual Abuse.* Beverly Hills: Sage.

Fisher, D. (1994) 'Adult sex offenders, who are they? Why and how do they do it?' In T. Morrison, M. Erooga and R.C. Beckett (eds) *Sexual Offending against Children: Assessment and Treatment of Male Abusers.* London: Routledge.

Fitchett, G., Burton, L.A. and Sivan, A.B. (1997) 'The religious needs and resources of psychiatric inpatients.' *Journal of Nervous and Mental Disease 185*, 5, 320–326.

Foa, E.B., Keane, T.M. and Friedman, M.J. (2000) 'Guidelines for treatment of PTSD.' *Journal of Traumatic Stress 13*, 4, 539–555.

Foa, E.B., Rothbaum, B.O., Riggs, D.S. and Murdock, T.B. (1991) 'Treatment of post traumatic stress disorder in rape victims: A comparison between cognitive-behavioural procedures and counselling.' *Journal of Consulting and Clinical Psychology 59*, 715–723.

Ford, K., Sweeney, J. and Farrington, A. (1999) 'User views of a regional secure unit: Findings from a patient satisfaction survey.' *International Journal of Psychiatric Nursing Research 5*, 1, 526–541.

Foreman, S.A. and Marmar, C.R. (1985) 'Therapist action that addresses initially poor therapeutic alliances in psychotherapy.' *American Journal of Psychotherapy 142*, 922–926.

Forensic Nursing Education (1999) Available online: http://www.forensiceducation.com

Fortinash, M.F. and Holoday-Worret, P.A. (1996) *Psychiatric Mental Health Nursing (2nd ed).* St Louis, Missouri: Mosby.

Foy, D.W., Glynn, S.M., Schnurr, P.P., Jankowski, M.K., Wattenberg, M.S., Weiss, D.S., Marmar, C.R. and Gusman, F.D. (2000) 'Group therapy.' *Journal of Traumatic Stress 13*, 4, 571–574.

Freedman, J. and Combs, G. (1996) *Narrative Therapy: The Social Construction of Preferred Realities.* New York: Norton.

Freeman, A. and Reinecke, M.A. (1995) 'Cognitive therapy.' In A. Gurman and S. Messer (eds) *Essential Psychotherapies: Theory and Practice.* New York: Guilford Press.

French, H.P. (1994) *Social Skills for Nursing Practice.* London: Chapman and Hall.

Freyne, A. and O'Connor, A. (1992) 'Posttraumatic stress disorder symptoms in prisoners following a cellmate's death.' *Irish Journal of Psychological Medicine 9*, 1, 42–44.

Friedman, M.J., Davidson, J.R.T., Mellman, T.A. and Southwick, S.M. (2000) 'Pharmacotherapy.' *Journal of Traumatic Stress 13*, 4, 563–566.

Fulcher, K.Y. and White, P.D. (1997) 'Randomised controlled trial of grades exercise in patients with the chronic fatigue syndrome.' *British Medical Journal 314*, 1647–1652.

Fulton, Y. (1997) 'Nurses' views on empowerment: A critical social theory perspective.' *Journal of Advanced Nursing 26*, 529–536.

Furby, L., Weinrott, M.R. and Blackshaw, L. (1989) 'Sex offender recidivism: A review.' *Psychological Bulletin 105*, 3–30.

Futterman, S. and Pumpian-Mindlin, E. (1951) 'Traumatic war neurosis five years later.' *American Journal of Psychiatry 108*, 401–408.

Gallop, R. (1985) 'The patient is splitting: Everyone knows and nothing changes.' *Journal of Psychosocial Nursing 23*, 4, 7–10.

Gallop, R. (1992) 'Self-destructive and impulsive behaviour in the patient with a borderline personality disorder: Rethinking hospital treatment and management.' *Archives of Psychiatric Nursing 1*, 3, 178–182.

Gallop, R. (1993) 'Sexual contact between nurses and patients.' *The Canadian Nurse 89*, 2, 28–31.

Gallop, R. (1998) 'Abuse of power in the nurse–client relationship.' *Nursing Standard 12*, 37, 43–47.

Gamble, C., Kidence, K. and Leff, L. (1994) 'The effects of family work training on mental health nurses' attitudes to and knowledge of schizophrenia: A replication.' *Journal of Advanced Nursing 19*, 893–896.

Gardner, D. (1997) 'New perspectives: Stories and life stories in therapy with older adults.' In K.N. Dwivedi (ed) *The Therapeutic Use of Stories.* London: Routledge.

Garety, P.A. (1992) 'Making sense of delusions.' *Psychiatry 55*, 282–291.

Garety, P.A., Hemsley, D.R. and Wessely, S. (1991) 'Reasoning in deluded schizophrenia and paranoid patients. Biases in performance on a probabilistic inference task.' *Journal of Nervous and Mental Disease 179*, 4, 194–201.

Garety, P., Kuipers, L., Fowler, D., Chamberlain, F. and Dunn, G. (1994) 'Cognitive behavioural therapy for drug resistant psychosis.' *British Journal of Medical Psychology 67*, 259–271.

Geen, R.G. and O'Neil, E.C. (1976) *Perspectives on Aggression.* New York: Academic Press.

Geller, J.L. (1995) 'A biopsychosocial rationale for coerced community treatment in the management of schizophrenia.' *Psychiatry Quarterly 66*, 3, 219–235.

Gibbons, J.S., Horn, S.H., Powell, J.M. and Gibbons, J.L. (1984) 'Schizophrenic patients and their families. A survey in a psychiatric service based on a district general hospital.' *British Journal of Psychiatry 144*, 70–77.

Gilbert, B.J. (1994) 'Treatment of adult victims of rape.' *New Direct Mental Health Service 64*, 67–77.

Gilligan, J. (2000) *Violence: Reflections on Our Deadliest Epidemic.* London: Jessica Kingsley Publishers.

Ginsberg, G., Marks, I.M. and Waters, H. (1984). 'Cost benefit analysis of a controlled trial of nurse therapy for neurosis in primary care.' *Psychological Medicine 14*, 683–690.

Glasser, M. (1990) 'Paedophilia.' In R. Bluglass and P. Bowden (eds) *Principles and Practice of Forensic Psychiatry.* London: Churchill Livingstone.

Glasser, W. (1975) *Reality Therapy: A New Approach to Psychiatry.* New York: HarperCollins.

Glasser, W. (1998) *Choice Theory.* New York: HarperCollins.

Goldberg, B. (1998) 'Connection: An exploration of spirituality in nursing care.' *Journal of Advanced Nursing 27*, 836–842.

Goldman, C. and Quinn, F. (1988) 'Effects of a patient education programme in the treatment of schizophrenia.' *Hospital and Community Psychiatry 39*, 3, 282–286.

Gordon, J.S. (1990) 'Holistic medicine and mental health practice: Towards a new synthesis.' *American Journal of Orthopsychiatry 60*, 3, 357–370.

Gorsuch, N. (1998) 'Unmet need among disturbed female offenders.' *Journal of Forensic Psychiatry 9*, 3, 556–570.

Gorsuch, N. (1999) 'Disturbed female offenders: Helping the untreatable.' *Journal of Forensic Psychiatry 10*, 1, 98–118.

Gouldner, A.W. (1954) *Patterns of Industrial Bureaucracy.* London: The Free Press.

Gournay, K., (1996) 'Setting standards for care in schizophrenia.' *Nursing Times 92*, 7, 36–37.

Gournay, K. and Birley, J. (1998) 'The Thorn Programme.' *Nursing Times 94*, 49, 54–55.

Gournay, K. and Carson, J. (2000) 'Staff stress, coping skills and job satisfaction in forensic nursing.' In D.K. Robinson and A.M. Kettles (eds) *Forensic Nursing and Multidisciplinary Care of the Mentally Disordered Offender.* London: Jessica Kingsley Publishers.

Gournay, K., Denford, L., Parr, A-M. and Newell, R. (2000) 'British nurses in behavioural psychotherapy: A 25-year follow up.' *Journal of Advanced Nursing 32*, 2, 1–9.

Gournay, K., Veale, D. and Walburn, J. (1997) 'Body dysmorphic disorder: Pilot randomised controlled trial of treatment; implications for nurse therapy research and practice.' *Clinical Effectiveness Nursing 1*, 46, 38–43.

Govier, I. (2000) 'Spiritual care in nursing: A systematic approach.' *Nursing Standard 14*, 17, 32–36.

Granstrom, S. (1995) 'Spiritual care for oncology patients.' *Topics in Clinical Nursing 7*, 1, 39–45.

Greenson, R. (1967) *The Technique and Practice of Psychoanalysis (vol.1).* New York: International Universities Press.

Groth, A.N. (1979a) *Men Who Rape: The Psychology of the Offender.* New York: Plenum.

Groth, A.N. (1979b) 'Sexual Trauma in the life histories of rapists and child molesters.' *International Journal of Victimology 4*, 10–16.

Groth, A.N., Longo, R.E. and McFadin, J.B. (1982) 'Undetected recidivism among rapists and child molesters.' *Crime and Delinquency 128*, 450–458.

Group for the Advancement of Psychiatry (1994) *Forced into Treatment: The Role of Coercion in Clinical Practice.* Committee on Government Policy Rep. No. 137. Washington, DC: American Psychiatric Press.

Grubin, D. (2000) 'Sex offender: Treatment and issues.' Paper presented at the 3rd Annual Sex Offender Research and Treatment Conference by Wessex Forensic Psychiatric Services, Southampton.

Gunderson, J.G. (1978) 'Defining the therapeutic process in milieus.' *Psychiatry 41*, 327–335.

Haber, L.C., Fagan-Pryor, E. and Allen, M. (1997) 'Comparison of registered nurses' and nursing assistants' choices of intervention for aggressive behaviours.' *Issues in Mental Health Nursing 18*, 113–124.

Hafner, H. and Boker, W. (1982) *Crimes of Violence by Mentally Abnormal Offenders* (trans. H. Marshall). Cambridge: Cambridge University Press.

Hall, G.C. (1995) 'Sex offender recidivism revisited: A meta-analysis of recent treatment studies.' *Journal of Consulting and Clinical Psychology 63*, 5, 802–809.

Hambridge, J.A. (1990) 'The grief process in those admitted to regional secure units following homicide.' *Journal of Forensic Sciences 35*, 1149–1154.

Hardin, S.B., Callahan, R.J., Fierman, C.F., Gaizutis, W.R., Johnas, V.F., Rorig, L.G. and Rouffa, F.W. (1985) 'Power in client and nurse–therapist relationships.' *Perspectives in Psychiatric Care 23*, 3, 91–98.

Hargie, O. (1991) *The Handbook of Communication Skills*. Worchester: Billing and Sons.

Harmon, R.B. and Tratnack S.A. (1992) 'Teaching hospitalised patients with serious, persistent mental illness.' *Journal of Psychosocial Nursing Mental Health Services 30*, 7, 33–36.

Harrington, A. (1995) 'Spirtual care: What does it mean to RNs?' *Australian Journal of Advanced Nursing 12*, 4, 5–14.

Hart, S.D. (1998) 'The role of psychopathy in assessing risk for violence: Conceptual and methodological issues.' *Legal and Criminological Psychology 3*, 121–137.

Hartup, W.W. (1986) 'On relationships and development.' In W.W. Hartup and Z. Zubins (eds) *Relationship and Development*. Hillsdale: Lawrence Erlbaum.

Harvey, E.M., Rawson, R.A. and Obert, J.L. (1994) 'History of sexual assault and the treatment of substance misuse disorders.' *Journal of Psychoactive Drugs 26*, 361–367.

Hayes, R. and Gnatt, A. (1992) 'Patient psychoeducation: the therapeutic use of knowledge for the mentally ill.' *Social Work in Health Care 17*, 1, 53–67.

Hazelwood, R.R. and Warren, J. (1989) 'The serial rapist: His characteristics and victims.' *FBI Law Enforcement Bulletin 58*, 18–25.

Helzer, J.E., Robbins, L.N. and McEvoy, L. (1987) 'Post-traumatic stress disorder in the general population: Findings from the epidemiological catchment area study.' *New England Journal of Medicine 317*, 1630–1634.

Henry, C. and Cashwell, S.C. (1998) 'Using reality therapy in the treatment of adolescent sex offenders.' *International Journal of Reality Therapy 18*, 1, 8–11.

Herman, J. L. (1992) *Trauma and Recovery: From Domestic Violence to Political Terror*. London: Basic Books.

Heron, J. (1977) *Catharsis in Human Development. Human Potential Research Project*. Guildford: Department of Adult Education, University of Surrey.

Highfield, M.F. (1992) 'Spiritual health of oncology patients: Nurse and patient perspectives.' *Cancer Nursing 15*, 1–8.

Hill, R.G. and Shepherd, G. (2000) 'Disorders of mood: Depression and mania.' In R. Newell and K. Gournay (eds) *Mental Health Nursing: An Evidence Based Approach*. Edinburgh: Churchill Livingstone.

Hillis, G. (1999) 'Diverting people with mental health problems from the criminal justice system.' In P. Tarbuck, B. Topping-Morris and P. Burnard (eds) *Forensic Mental Health Nursing*. London: Whurr.

Hindman, J. (1989) *Just Before Dawn*. Ontario, Oregon: Alexandria.

Hogarty, G.E., Anderson, C.M., Reiss, D.J., Korblinth, S.J., Greenwald, D.P., Ulrich, R.F. and Carter, M. (1991) 'Family psychoeducational, social skills training and maintenance chemotherapy in the aftercare treatment of schizophrenia II: Two year effects of a controlled study on relapse and adjustment.' *Archives of General Psychiatry 48,* 340–347.

Hollin, C.R. (1997) 'Assessing and managing risk: How research findings can contribute to improving practice.' *Psychiatric Care 4,* 4, 212–215.

Hollin, C.R. and Howells, K. (1991) *Clinical Approaches to Sex Offenders and Their Victims.* Chichester: Wiley.

Home Office (1990) 'Notifiable offences recorded by the police in 1989.' *Statistical Bulletin* 4/89.

Home Office (2000) *Setting the Boundaries: Reforming the Sex Offenders Law (vol. 1).* London: Home Office Communication Directorate.

Home Office and Department of Health (1999) *Managing Dangerous People with Severe Personality Disorder: Proposals for Policy Development.* London: HMSO.

Honigfeld, G., Gillis, R.D. and Klett, C.J. (1966) 'NOSIE–30: A treatment-sensitive ward behavior scale.' *Psychological Reports 19,* 1, 180–182.

Horvath, A.O. and Luborsky, L. (1993) 'The role of therapeutic alliance in psychotherapy.' *Journal of Consulting and Clinical Psychology 61,* 561–573.

Howlett, M. (1998) *Medication, Non-Compliance and Mentally Disordered Offenders: The Role of Non-compliance in Homicide by People with Mental Illness and Proposals for Future Policy.* London: The Zito Trust.

HRH the Prince of Wales (1991) '150th Anniversary Lecture.' *British Journal of Psychiatry 159,* 763–768.

Hryvniak, M.R. and Rosse, R.B. (1989) 'Concurrent psychiatric illness in inpatients with post-traumatic stress disorder.' *Military Medicine 154,* 8, 399–401.

Huckle, P.L. (1995) 'Male rape victims referred to a forensic psychiatric service.' *Medicine, Science and the Law 35,* 187–192.

Hudson, D., James, D. and Harlow, P. (1995) *Psychiatric Court Liaison to Central London.* London: Riverside Mental Health NHS Trust.

Hufft, A.G. and Fawkes, L.S. (1994) 'Federal inmates: A unique psychiatric nursing challenge.' *Nursing Clinics of North America 29,* 1, 35–42.

Hull, C.L. (1943) *Principles of Behaviour.* New York: Appleton-Century-Crofts.

Hutchinson, D.S., Skrinar, G.S. and Cross, C. (1999) 'The role of improved physical fitness in rehabilitation and recovery.' *Psychiatric Rehabilitation Journal 22,* 4, 355–359.

Ingram, L. 'Court ordered anger management course: Anger management training for domestic violence offenders.'
Available online: http: //www.angermgmt.com/courtorder.html

Jackson, H. and Martin III, J. (2000) 'Relating neurological and neuropsychological deficits to antisocial personality and offending behaviour.' In D. Mercer, T. Mason, M. McKeown and G. McCann (eds) *Forensic Mental Health Care: A Case Study Approach.* Edinburgh: Churchill Livingstone.

James, L. (1996) 'Family centred outreach for forensic psychiatry clients: Epistle Post Release Service.' *Australian New Zealand Journal Mental Health Nursing 5,* 2, 63–68.

Jennings, L. (2001) 'Clinical supervision.' In C. Dale, T. Thompson and P. Woods (eds) *Forensic Mental Health: Issues in Practice.* London: Harcourt.

Jin, Z. (1994) 'Effects of an open door policy combined with a structured activity programme on the residual symptoms of schizophrenia: A six month randomised controlled trial in Yanbain Jilin.' *British Journal of Psychiatry 165*, 24, 52–57.

Johnsgard, K.W. (1989) *The Exercise Prescription for Depression and Anxiety.* New York: Plenum.

Joseph, B. (1982) 'Addiction to near-death.' *International Journal of Psycho-Analysis 63*, 4, 449–456.

Josselson, R. and Lieblich, A. (1999) *Making Meaning of Narratives.* Thousand Oaks, CA: Sage.

Kahn, T.J. and Chambers, H.J. (1991) 'Assessing re-offence risk with juvenile sexual offenders.' *Child Welfare 70*, 333–345.

Kay, S.R., Opler, L.A. and Fiszbein, A. (1987) 'The Positive and Negative Syndrome Scale (PANSS) for schizophrenia.' *Schizophrenia Bulletin 13*, 261–276.

Keane, T.M., Fairbank, J.A., Caddell, J.M. and Zimmering, R.T. (1989) 'Implosive (flooding) therapy reduces symptoms of PTSD in Vietnam combat veterans.' *Behavior Therapy 20*, 149–153.

Kelly, M.R. and May, D. (1982) 'Good and bad patient: A review of the literature and theoretic critique.' *Journal of Advanced Nursing 7*, 147–156.

Kennedy, S.M. (2000) 'Treatment responsivity: Reducing recidivism by enhancing treatment effectiveness.' *Forum on Corrections Research 12*, 2, 19–23.

Kettles, A.M. and Robinson, D.K. (2000a) 'From a reactive past into the proactive new millennium.' In D.K. Robinson and A.M. Kettles (eds) *Forensic Nursing and Multidisciplinary Care of the Mentally Disordered Offender.* London: Jessica Kingsley Publishers.

Kettles, A. and Robinson, D. (2000b) 'Overview and contemporary issues in the role of the forensic nurse in the UK.' In D.K. Robinson and A.M. Kettles (eds) *Forensic Nursing and Multidisciplinary Care of the Mentally Disordered Offender.* London: Jessica Kingsley Publishers.

Kettles, A.M., Robinson, D.K. and Moody, E. (2000) 'Clinical risk assessment: Study of UK psychiatric units shows need for uniform methods.' *On the Edge: The Official Newsletter of the International Association of Forensic Nurses 6*, 4, 3–4.

King, M. (1995) 'Sexual assaults on men: Assessment and management.' *British Journal of Hospital Medicine 53*, 245–246.

Kingdon, D.G. and Turkington, D. (1994) *Cognitive Behavioural Therapy of Schizophrenia.* New York: Guilford Press.

Kinsella, C., Chaloner, C. and Brosnan, C. (1993) 'An alternative to seclusion?' *Nursing Times 89*, 18, 62–64.

Kirby, S.D. (2001) 'The development of a conceptual framework of therapeutic alliance in psychiatric (nursing) care delivery.' In G. Landsberg and A. Smiley (eds) *Forensic Mental Health: Working with the Mentally Ill Offender.* Kingston, NJ: Civic Research Institute.

Kitchiner, N. (1999) 'Freeing the imprisoned mind.' *Mental Health Care 21*, 12, 420–424.

Kitchiner, N. (2000) 'The use of cognitive-behaviour therapy to treat a patient with hypochondriasis.' *Mental Health Practice 3*, 7, 15–20.

Knowles, M. (1984) *Androgogy in Action.* San Francisco: Jossey-Bass.

Koenig, H.G. (1997) *Is Religion Good for Your Health? The Effects of Religion on Physical and Mental Health.* New York: Haworth Press.

Koss, M.P. and Heslet, L. (1992) 'Somatic consequences of violence against women.' *Archives Family Medicine 1*, 53–59.

Kruppa, I., Hickey, N. and Hubbard, C. (1995) 'The prevalence of posttraumatic stress disorder in a special hospital population of legal psychopaths.' *Psychology, Crime & Law 2*, 131–141.

Kudler, H.S., Blank Jr, A.S. and Krupnick, J.L. (2000) 'Psychodynamic therapy.' *Journal of Traumatic Stress 13*, 4, 572–574.

Kuipers, L., Leff, J.P. and Lam, D.H. (1992) *Family Work for Schizophrenia: A Practical Guide.* London: Gaskell.

Langevin, R. and Lang, R.A. (1985) 'Psychological treatment of paedophiles.' *Behavioural Sciences and the Law 3*, 403–419.

Larson, D.B. and Larson, S.S. (1994) *The Forgotten Factor in Physical and Mental Health: What Does the Research Show?* Rockville, MD: National Institute for Healthcare Research.

Larson, D.B., Sherrill, K.A., Lyons, J.S., Craigie, F.C., Thielman, S.B., Greenwood, M.A. and Larson, S.S. (1992) 'Associations between dimensions of religious commitment and mental health reported in the American Journal of Mental Health and Archives of General Psychiatry: 1978–1989.' *American Journal of Psychiatry 149*, 4, 557–559.

Larson, D.B., Swyers, J.P. and McCullough, M. (1997) *Scientific Research on Spirituality and Health: A Consensus Report.* Rockville, MD: National Institute for Healthcare Research.

Lavender, A. (1985) 'Quality of care and staff practices in long-stay settings.' In F.N. Watts (ed) *New Developments in Clinical Psychology.* Chichester: Wiley.

Lax, W.D. (1992) 'Postmodern thinking in a clinical practice.' In S. McNamee & K.J. Gergen (eds) *Therapy as Social Construction.* London: Sage.

Layman, E.M. (1974) 'Physical activity as psychological adjunct.' In W.R. Johnson and E.R. Bushkirk (eds) *Science and Medicine of Exercise and Sport.* New York: Harper and Row.

Leff, J. and Vaughn, C. (1985) *Expressed Emotions in Families: Its Significance for Mental Illness.* New York: Guilford Press.

Le May, A. (1999) *Evidence-based Practice.* London: NY Books/Emap Healthcare.

Levant, M.D. and Bass, B.A. (1991) 'Parental identification of rapists and paedophiles.' *Psychological Reports 69*, 463–466.

Ley, P. (1988) *Communicating with Patients.* London: Croom Helm.

Li, F. and Wang, M. (1994) 'A behavioural training programme for chronic schizophrenic patients: A three month randomised controlled trial in Beijing.' *British Journal of Psychiatry 165*, 24, 32–37.

Lisak, D. and Ivan, C. (1995) 'Deficits in intimacy and empathy in sexually aggressive man.' *Journal of Interpersonal Violence 10*, 3, 296–308.

Lisak, D. and Roth, S. (1990) 'Motives and psycho-dynamics of self reported unincarcerated rapists.' *American Journal of Orthopsychiatry 60*, 268–280.

Long, A. and Harrison, S. (1996) 'Evidence-based decision making.' *Health Service Journal 106*, 1–11.

Lotke, E. (2000) 'Sex offenders: Does treatment work? Issues and answers.' Available online: http://www.icg.apc.org/ncia/sexo.html

Lynch, V. (1993) 'Forensic nursing – Diversity in education and practice.' *Journal of Psychosocial Nursing and Mental Health Services 31*, 11, 7–14.

Lynn, M.R. (1995) 'Development and testing of the nursing role model competence scale.' *Journal of Nursing Measurement 3*, 2, 93–108.

MacFarlane, K. and Waterman, J. (1986) *Sexual Abuse of Young Children: Evaluation and Treatment.* New York: Guilford Press.

MacLean, Lord. (2000) *Report of the Committee on Serious Violent and Sexual Offenders.* Edinburgh: Scottish Executive.

Macleod Clark, J. (1983) 'Nurse–patient communication – An analysis of conversations from surgical wards.' In J. Barnett (ed) *Nursing Research: Ten Studies in Patient Care.* Chichester: Wiley.

Maden, T., Curle, C., Meux, C., Burrow, S. and Gunn, J. (1995) *Treatment and Security Needs of Special Hospital Patients.* London: Whurr.

Maier, G., Stava, L.J., Morrow, B.R., Van Rybroek, G. and Bauman, K.G. (1987) 'A model for understanding and managing cycles of aggression among psychiatric inpatients.' *Hospital and Community Psychiatry 38,* 5, 520–524.

Main, T. (1957) *The Ailment and Other Psychoanalytical Essays.* London: Free Association.

Maletzky, B. (1991) *Treating the Sexual Offender.* London: Sage.

Marks, I.M. (1985) *Psychiatric Nurse Therapists in Primary Care.* RCN Research Series. London: Royal College of Nursing.

Marks, I.M., Bird, J. and Lindley, P. (1978) 'Behavioural nurse therapists – Developments and implications.' *Behavioural Psychotherapy 6,* 25–26.

Marks, I.M., Hallam, R.S. and Connolly, J.C. (1975). 'Nurse therapists in behavioural psychotherapy.' *British Medical Journal 3,* 5976, 144–148.

Marks, I.M., Hallam, R.S., Connolly, J.C. and Philpott, R. (1977) *Nursing in Behavioural Psychotherapy. An Advanced Clinical Role for Nurses.* London: Royal College of Nursing.

Marks, I.M., Lovell, K., Noshirvani, H., Livanou, M. and Thrasher, S. (1998) 'Treatment of post-traumatic stress disorder by exposure and/or cognitive restructuring: A controlled study.' *Archives of General Psychiatry 55,* 317–325.

Marshall, W.L. (1989) 'Intimacy, loneliness and sexual offenders.' *Behaviour Research and Therapy 27,* 491–503.

Marshall, W.L. (1993) 'The role of attachment, intimacy and loneliness in the aetiology and maintenance of sexual offending.' *Sexual and Marital Therapy 8,* 109–121.

Marshall, W.L. and Barbaree, H.E. (1990a) 'An integrated theory of the aetiology of sexual offending.' In W.L. Marshall, D.R. Laws and H.E. Barbaree (eds) *Handbook of Sexual Assault: Issues, Theories, and Treatment of the Offender.* New York: Plenum.

Marshall, W.L. and Barbaree, H.E. (1990b) 'Outcome of comprehensive cognitive-behavioural treatment programmes.' In W.L. Marshall, D.R. Laws and H.E. Barbaree (eds) *Handbook of Sexual Assault: Issues, Theories, and Treatment of the Offender.* New York: Plenum.

Marshall, W.L., Barbaree, H.E. and Fernandez, Y.M. (1995) 'Some aspects of social competence in sexual offenders.' *Sexual Abuse: A Journal of Research and Treatment 7,* 113–127.

Marshall, W.L., Hudson, S.M. and Ward, T. (1992) 'Sexual deviance.' In P.H. Wilson (ed) *Principles and Practice of Relapse Prevention.* New York: Guilford Press.

Marshall, W.L., Jones, R., Ward, T., Johnston, P. and Barbaree, H.E. (1991) 'Treatment outcome with sex offenders.' *Clinical Psychology Review 11,* 465–485.

Martin, J.E. and Booth, J. (2000) 'Behavioural approaches to enhance spirituality.' In W.R. Miller (ed) *Integrating Spirituality into Treatment: Resources for Practitioners.* Washington, DC: American Psychological Association.

Martin, J.E. and Carlson, C.R. (1988) 'Spiritual dimensions of health psychology.' In W.R. Miller and J.E. Martin (eds) *Behavior Therapy and Religion.* Newbury Park, CA: Sage.

Martin, T. (1992) 'Psychiatric nurses' use of working time.' *Nursing Standard 6,* 37, 34–36.

Martinsen, E.W. (1988) 'The role of aerobic exercise in the treatment of depression.' *Stress Medicine 3,* 93–100.

Martsolf, D.S. and Mickley, J.R. (1998). 'The concept of spirituality in nursing theories: Differing world-views and extents of focus.' *Journal of Advanced Nursing 27*, 294–303.

Mason, T. (2000a) 'Forensic nursing: International origins and directions.' *British Journal of Forensic Practice 2*, 4, 10–15.

Mason, T. (2000b) Keynote Address: IAFN Conference Proceedings. International Association for Forensic Nurses, 8th Scientific Assembly, Calgary.

Mason, T. (2000c) 'Managing protest behaviour: From coercion to compassion.' *Journal of Psychiatric and Mental Health Nursing 7*, 3, 269–275.

Mason, T. and Chandley, M. (1990) 'Nursing models in a special hospital: A critical analysis of efficacity.' *Journal of Advanced Nursing 15*, 667–673.

Mason, T. and Chandley, M. (1999) *Managing Violence and Aggression: A Manual for Nurses and Healthcare Workers*. Edinburgh: Churchill Livingstone.

Mason, T., Hennigan, M., Johnson, D. and Chandley, M. (1996) 'Decompression of long term seclusion.' *Psychiatric Care 3*, 6, 217–225.

May, A., Alexander, C. and Mulhall, A. (1998) 'Research utilisation in nursing: Barriers and opportunities.' *Journal of Clinical Effectiveness 3*, 2, 59–63.

McAleer, J. and Hamill, C. (1997) *The Assessment of Higher Order Competence Development in Nurse Education*. Belfast, Ireland: National Board for Nursing, Midwifery and Health Visiting for Nothern Ireland.

McCann, G. (1999) 'Care of mentally disordered offenders.' *Mental Health Care 3*, 2, 65–67.

McCann, G. and McKeown, M. (1995) 'Applying psychosocial interventions: The Thorn initiative in a forensic setting.' *Psychiatric Care 2*, 4, 133–136.

McComish, A.G. and Paterson, B. (1996) 'The development of forensic services in Scotland 1800–1960.' *Psychiatric Care 3*, 153–158.

McConnell, H. and Duncan-McConnell, D. (1999) 'Weight changes with antipsychotics.' *Psychopharmacology 2*, 2, 13–15.

McCreadie, R.G., Phillips, K., Harvey, J.A. Waldron, G., Stewart, M. and Baird, D. (1991) 'The Nithsdale schizophrenia surveys VIII: Do relatives want family intervention – and does it help?' *British Journal of Psychiatry 158*, 110–113.

McCullough, M.E. and Worthington, E.L. (1994a) 'Encouraging clients to forgive people who have hurt them: Review, critique, and research prospectus.' *Journal of Psychology and Theology 22*, 15–29.

McCullough, M.E. and Worthington, E.L. (1994b) 'Models of interpersonal forgiveness and their application to counselling: Review and critique.' *Counselling Values 39*, 2–14.

McEntee, D.J. and Halgin, R.P. (1996) 'Therapists' attitudes about addressing the role of exercise in psychology.' *Journal of Clinical Psychology 52*, 1, 48–60.

McFarlane, W.R. (1994) 'Multiple family groups and psychoeducation in the treatment of schizophrenia.' *New Directions for Mental Health Services 62*, 13–23.

McFarlane, W.R., Lukens, E. and Link, B. (1995) 'Multiple family groups and psychoeducation in the treatment of schizophrenia.' *Archives of General Psychiatry 52*, 679–687.

McGorry, P.D. (1995) 'Psychoeducation in first episode psychosis: A therapeutic process.' *Psychiatry 58*, 313–328.

McGrath, R. (1994) 'Cost effectiveness of sex offender treatment programmes.' Paper presented at the Annual Conference for Virginia Sex Offender Treatment Providers, VA.

McNamee, S. and Gergen, K.J. (1992) *Therapy as Social Construction*. London: Sage.

McSherry, R. (1997) 'What do registered nurses and midwives feel and know about research?' *Journal of Advanced Nursing 25*, 985–988.

Melia, P., Mercer, T. and Mason, T. (1999) 'Triumvirate nursing of personality disordered patients: Crossing boundaries safely.' *Journal of Psychiatric and Mental Health Nursing 6*, 15–20.

Mental Health Act Commission (1995) *Sixth Biennial Report 1993–1995*. London: HMSO.

Mental Health Act Commission (1997) *Seventh Biennial Report 1995–1997*. London: HMSO.

Mental Health Act Commission (1999) *Eighth Biennial Report 1997–1999*. London: HMSO.

Menzies Lyth, E. (1988) *Containing Anxiety in Institutions: Selected Essays*. London: Free Association.

Mercer, D., Mason, T. and Richman, J. (1999) 'Good and evil in the crusade of care: Social constructions of mental disorders.' *Journal of Psychosocial Nursing and Mental Health Services 37*, 9, 13–27.

Miller, S.D., Hubble, M.A. and Duncan, B.L. (1996) *A Handbook of Solution Focused Brief Therapy*. San Francisco: Jossey-Bass.

Miller, W.R. (1983) 'Motivational interviewing with alcohol drinkers.' *Behaviour Psychotherapy 11*, 147–172.

Miller, W.R. (ed) (2000) *Integrating Spirituality into Treatment: Resources for Practitioners*. Washington, DC: American Psychological Association.

Miller, W.R. and Rollnick, S. (1991) *Motivational Interviewing: Preparing People for Change in Addictive Behaviors*. New York: Guilford Press.

Milner, R.P. and Robertson, D.S. (1990) 'Comparison of physical child molesters, intrafamilial sexual and child abusers and child neglecters.' *Journal of Interpersonal Violence 5*, 37–48.

Monahan, J. (1981) *The Clinical Prediction of Violent Behaviour*. Washington, DC. Government Printing Office.

Monahan, J. (1988) 'Risk assessment of violence among the mentally disordered: Generating useful knowledge.' *International Journal of Law Psychiatry 11*, 249–257.

Monahan, J. (1997) 'Actuarial support for the clinical assessment of violence risk.' *International Review of Psychiatry 9*, 167–169.

Monroe, C.M. Van Rybroek, G. and Maier, G. (1988) 'Decompressing aggressive inpatients: Breaking the aggression cycle to enhance positive outcome.' *Behavioural Sciences and the Law 6*, 4, 543–557.

Montgomery, C. (1997) 'Coping with the emotional demands of caring.' *Advanced Practice Nursing Quarterly 3*, 1, 76–84.

Moore, E., Ball, R.A. and Kuipers, L. (1992) 'Expressed emotion in staff working with the long term adult mentally ill.' *British Journal of Psychiatry 161*, 802–808.

Moorey, H. and Soni, S.D. (1994) 'Anxiety symptoms in stable chronic schizophrenics.' *Journal of Mental Health 3*, 257–262.

Morris, B. and Bell, L. (1995) 'Quality in health care.' In J. Glynn and D. Perkins (eds) *Managing Health Care. Challenges for the 90s*. London: WB Saunders Company.

Morrison, E.F. (1990) 'The tradition of toughness: A study of non-professional nursing care in psychiatric settings.' *Journal of Nursing Scholarship 22*, 32–38.

Morrison, T., Erooga, M. and Beckett, R.C. (1994) *Sexual Offending against Children. Assessment and Treatment of Male Abusers*. London: Routledge.

Motiuk, L.L. and Porporino, F.J. (1991) 'The prevalence, nature and severity of mental health problems among federal male inmates in Canadian penitentiaries.' Available online: http://ww.csc-scc.gc.ca/text/rsrch/reports/r24/r24e.shtml

Mueser, K.T., Yarnold, P.R. and Foy, D. (1991) 'Statistical analysis for single-case designs: Evaluating outcome of imaginal exposure treatment of chronic PTSD.' *Behaviour Modification* 15, 134–155.

Munson, M.W. (1988) 'The effects of leisure education versus physical activity of informal discussion on behaviourally disordered young offenders.' *Adapted Physical Activity Quarterly 5*, 305–317.

Naidoo, N. and Wills, J. (1994) *Health Promotion. Foundations for Practice.* London: Bailliere Tindall.

National Association for the Care and Resettlement of Offenders (NACRO) (1998) *Risks and Rights: Mentally Disturbed Offenders and Public Protection.* Rochdale: RAP Limited.

National Board for Nursing, Midwifery and Health Visiting for Scotland (NBS) (1998) *Project 2000 in Scotland. Employers' Needs and the Skills of Newly Qualified Project 2000 Staff Nurses.* Edinburgh: Department of Nursing, Queen Margaret College.

National Board for Nursing, Midwifery and Health Visiting for Scotland (NBS) (1999a) *The CPD Portfolio: A Route to Enhanced Competence.* Edinburgh: NBS.

National Board for Nursing, Midwifery and Health Visiting for Scotland (NBS) (1999b) *Developing a Framework for Post-registration Competencies for Local Forensic Services: Report on Forensic Consensus Workshop.* Edinburgh: NBS.

National Board for Nursing, Midwifery and Health Visiting for Scotland (NBS) (2000) *An Enhanced Route to Competence in Forensic Mental Health Nursing.* Edinburgh: NBS.

National Board for Nursing, Midwifery and Health Visiting for Scotland (NBS) (2001) *Continuing Professional Development Portfolio: A Route to Enhanced Competence in Forensic Mental Health Nursing.* Edinburgh: NBS.

National Health Service Confederation and Sainsbury Centre for Mental Health (1997) *The Way Forward For Mental Health Services.* London: National Health Service Confederation.

National Health Service Executive (1997) 'Review of cervical cancer screening services at Kent and Canterbury hospitals.' London: NHS Executive, South Thames.

National Health Service Management Executive (1994a) *Guidance on the Discharge of Mentally Disordered People and Their Continuing Care in the Community.* London: HMSO.

National Health Service Management Executive (1994b) *Risk Management in the NHS.* London: HMSO.

National Health Service Management Executive (1994c) *Introduction of Supervision Registers for Mentally Ill People from 1 April 1994.* London: HMSO.

National Health Service Managment Executive (1999) *Specialised Commissioning – High and Medium Security Psychiatric Services.* London: HMSO.

Neilson, T., Peet, M., Ledsham, R. and Poole, J. (1996) 'Does the nursing care plan help in the management of psychiatric risk?' *Journal of Advanced Nursing 24*, 1201–1206.

Newell, R. (2000) 'Effective consultation skills.' In R. Newell and K. Gournay (eds) *Mental Health Nursing: An Evidence Based Approach.* Edinburgh: Churchill Livingstone.

Newell, R. and Gournay, K. (1994) 'British nurses in behavioural psychotherapy: A 20 year follow up.' *Journal of Advanced Nursing 20*, 53–60.

Nicholaichuk, T.P., Templeman, R., and Gu, D. (1998) 'Process and outcome evaluations of Canadian sex offender programs.' Paper presented at the 1998 ATSA Research and Treatment Conference, Vancouver, Canada.

Niskala, H. (1986) 'Competencies and skills required by nurses working in forensic areas.' *Western Journal of Nursing Research 8*, 4, 400–413.

Nolan Committee (1995) *Standards in Public Life: First Report of the Committee on Standards in Public Life*. London: HMSO.

Nolan, P. and Crawford, P. (1997) 'Towards a rhetoric of spirituality in mental health care.' *Journal of Advanced Nursing 26*, 2, 289–294.

Norton, K. (1996) 'The personality-disorder forensic patient and the therapeutic community.' In C. Cordess and M. Cox (eds) *Forensic Psychotherapy: Crime, Psychodynamics and the Offender Patient (vol.2): Mainly Practice*. London: Jessica Kingsley Publishers.

Norton, L. (1998) 'Health promotion and health education: What role should the nurse adopt in practice?' *Journal of Advanced Nursing 28*, 6, 1269–1275.

Novaco, R.W. (1975) *Anger Control*. Lexington: DC Health.

Novaco, R.W. (1976a) 'Treatment of chronic anger through cognitive and relaxation controls.' *Journal of Consulting and Clinical Psychology 44*, 681.

Novaco, R.W. (1976b) 'The function and regulation of the arousal of anger.' *American Journal of Psychiatry 133*, 10, 1124–1128.

Novaco, R.W. (1979) 'The cognitive regulation of anger and stress.' In P. Kendall and S.D. Hollon (eds) *Cognitive-Behavioural Interventions: Theory, Research and Practice*. New York: Academic Press.

Novaco, R.W. (1985) 'Anger and its therapeutic regulation.' In M.A. Chesney and R.H. Rosenman (eds). *Anger and Hostility in Cardiovascular and Behavioural Disorders*. Washington, DC: Hemisphere.

Numerof, R.E. and Abrams, M.N. (1984) 'Sources of stress amongst nurses: An empirical study.' *Journal of Human Stress 10*, 2, 88–100.

Ochberg, F.M. (1991) 'Post-traumatic therapy: Psychotherapy with victims.' *Psychotherapy 28*, 5–15.

Office for Public Health in Scotland (1999) *Health Promotion in Prisons. Scottish Needs Assessment Programme, Health Promotion Network*. Glasgow: Office for Public Health in Scotland.

O'Kelly, J.G., Piper, W.E., Kerber, R. and Fowler, J. (1998) 'Exercise groups in an in-sight-oriented, evening treatment programme.' *International Journal of Group Psychotherapy 48*, 1, 85–98.

Oldnall, A. (1996) 'A critical analysis of nursing: Meeting the spiritual needs of patients.' *Journal of Advanced Nursing 23*, 138–144.

Ornish, D. (1998) *Love and Survival: The Scientific Basis for the Healing Power of Intimacy*. New York: HarperCollins.

O'Rourke, M. (1997) 'Sex offenders: Assessment and treatment in the community.' *Psychiatric Care 4*, 6, 258–264.

Overall, J.E. and Gorham, D.R. (1962) 'The Brief Psychiatric Rating Scale.' *Psychological Reports 10*, 799–812.

Owen, I.R. (1995) 'Power, boundaries, intersubjectivity.' *British Journal of Medical Psychology 68*, 97–107.

Oyebode, F., Brown, N. and Parry, E. (1999) 'Clinical governance: Application to psychiatry.' *Psychiatric Bulletin 23*, 7–10.

Palmistera, T. and Wistedt, B. (1995) 'Changes in the pattern of aggressive behaviour among inpatients with changed ward routine.' *Acta Psychiatrica Scandinavica 91*, 32–35.

Parkes, T. (1997) 'Reflections from the outside in: My journey into, through and beyond psychiatric nursing.' In S. Tilley (ed) *The Mental Health Nurse: Views of Practice and Education*. Oxford: Blackwell Science.

Patel, C., Marmot, M.G. and Terry, D.J. (1981) 'Controlled trial of biofeedback-aided behavioural methods in reducing mild hypertension.' *British Medical Journal 290*, 1103–1106.

Paul, G.L. and Menditto, A. (1992) 'Effectiveness of inpatient treatment programmes for mentally ill adults in public psychiatric facilities.' *Applied and Preventative Psychology 1*, 41–63.

Pelham, T.W. and Campagna, P.D. (1991) 'Benefits of exercise in psychiatric rehabilitation of persons with schizophrenia.' *Canadian Journal of Rehabilitation 4*, 3, 159–168.

Pence, E. and Paymar, M. (1993) *Education Groups for Men who Batter: The Duluth Model.* New York: Springer Publishing.

Penk, W. and Flannery Jr, R.B. (2000) 'Psychosocial rehabilitation.' *Journal of Traumatic Stress 13*, 4, 578–580.

Peplau, H.E. (1952) *Interpersonal Relations in Nursing.* New York: G.P. Putnam.

Peplau, H.E. (1989) 'Clinical supervision of staff nurses.' In A.W. O'Toole and S.R. Welt (eds) *Interpersonal Theory in Nursing Practice: Selected Works of Hildegard E. Peplau.* New York: Springer.

Perkins, D. (1991) 'Clinical work with sex offenders in secure settings.' In C.R. Hollin and K. Howells (ed) *Clinical Approaches to Sex Offenders and Their Victims.* Chichester: Wiley.

Pert, V. (1997) 'Exercise for health.' *Physiotherapy 83*, 9, 453–460.

Peternelj-Taylor, C.A. (1998) 'Forbidden love: Sexual exploitation in the forensic milieu.' *Journal of Psychosocial Nursing 36*, 6, 17–23.

Peternelj-Taylor, C.A. and Johnson, R.L. (1995) 'Serving time: Psychiatric mental health nursing in corrections.' *Journal of Psychosocial Nursing 33*, 8, 12–19.

Peters, S.D., Wyatt, G.E. and Finkelhor, D. (1986) 'Prevalence.' In D. Finkelhor (ed) *A Sourcebook on Child Abuse.* Beverly Hills: Sage.

Pharoah, F., Mari, J. and Streiner, D. (2000) *Family Interventions for Schizophrenia (Cochrane Review). Issue 3.* Oxford: Update Software.

Philips, H.C. (1987) 'Avoidance behaviour and its role in sustaining chronic pain.' *Behaviour Research and Therapy 25*, 365–377.

Phillips, P. (2000) 'Substance misuse, offending and mental illness: A review.' *Journal of Psychiatric and Mental Health Nursing 7*, 6, 483–489.

Piles, C.L. (1990) 'Providing spiritual care.' *Nurse Education 15*, 36–41.

Pillette, P.C., Berck, C.B. and Achber, L.C. (1995) 'Therapeutic management of helping boundaries.' *Journal of Psychosocial Nursing 33*, 1, 40–47.

Pinkerton, S. (1993) 'Commentary on parables of leadership.' *Nursing Scan in Administration 8*, 1, 1–2.

Plante, T.G. (1996) 'Getting physical. Does exercise help in the treatment of psychiatric disorders?' *Journal of Psychosocial Nursing 34*, 3, 38–43.

Plante, T.G. and Rodin, J. (1990) 'Physical fitness and enhanced psychological health.' *Current Psychology: Research and Reviews 9*, 3–24.

Polner, M. (1989) 'Divine relations, social relations and well-being.' *Journal of Health and Social Behaviour 30*, 92–104.

Potier, M.A. (1993) 'Giving evidence: Women's lives in Ashworth maximum security psychiatric hospital.' *Feminism and Psychology 3*, 3, 335–347.

Power, M. (1997) *The Audit Society: Rituals of Verifications.* Oxford: Oxford University Press.

Prentky, R. and Burgess, A. (1990) 'Rehabilitation of child molesters: A cost benefit analysis.' *American Journal of Orthopsychiatry 60*, 108–113.

Prentky, R., Knight, R.A., Sims-Knight, J.E., Straus, H., Rokous, F. and Cerce, D. (1989) 'Developmental antecedents of sexual aggression.' *Development and Psychopathology 1*, 153–169.

Preston, D.L. (2000) 'Treatment resistance in corrections.' *Forum on Corrections Research 12*, 2, 24–28.

Preston, D.L. and Murphy, S. (1997) 'Motivating treatment-resistant clients in therapy.' *Forum on Corrections Research 9*, 2, 39–43.

Prins, H. (1986) *Dangerous Behavior: The Law and Mental Disorder.* London: Routledge.

Prins, H. (1990) *Bizzare Behaviour: Boundaries in Psychiatry.* London: Routledge.

Prochaska, J.D. and DiClemente, C. (1984) *The Trans-theoretical Approach: Crossing Traditional Foundations of Change.* Harnewood, IL: Don Jones-Irwin.

Prochaska, J.O., Norcross, J.C. and DiClemente, C. (1994) *Changing for Good.* New York: William Morrow.

Professional and Practice Development Nurses Forum (1999) *Clinical Competency Self-Assessment Tool.* Glasgow: PPDNF.

Pullen, L., Tuck, I. and Mix, K. (1996) 'Mental health nurses' spiritual perspectives.' *Journal of Holistic Nursing 14*, 2, 85–97.

Randolph, E.T., Eth, S. and Glynn, S.M. (1994) 'Behavioural family management in schizophrenia: Outcome of a clinical-based intervention.' *British Journal of Psychiatry 164*, 501–506.

Rask, M. and Holberg, I.R. (2000) 'Forensic psychiatric nursing care: Nurses' apprehension of their responsibility and work control: A Swedish survey.' *Journal of Psychiatric and Mental Health Nursing 7*, 163–177.

Redman, B.K. (1971) 'Patient education as a function of nursing practice.' *Nursing Clinics 6*, 573–580.

Reiss, D., Quayle, M., Brett, T. and Meux, C. (1998) 'Dramatherapy for mentally disordered offenders: Changes in levels of anger.' *Criminal Behaviour and Mental Health 8*, 139–153.

Reith, M. (1998a) *Community Care Tragedies: A Practice Guide to Mental Health Inquiries.* Birmingham: Venture Press.

Reith, M. (1998b) 'Risk assessment and management: Lessons from mental health inquiry reports.' *Medicine, Science and the Law 38*, 3, 221–226.

Repper, J., Ford, R. and Cooke, A. (1994) 'How can nurses build trusting relationships with people who have severe and long-term mental health problems? Experiences of case managers and their clients.' *Journal of Advanced Nursing 19*, 1096–1104.

Reynolds, W. and Cormack, D. (eds) (1990) *Psychiatric and Mental Health Nursing Theory and Practice.* London: Chapman and Hall.

Richards, P. and McDonald, B. (1990) *Behavioural Psychotherapy: A Handbook for Nurses.* Oxford: Heinemann Medical.

Richards, P.S. and Bergin, A.E. (1997) *A Spiritual Strategy for Counselling and Psychotherapy.* Washington, DC: American Psychological Association.

Riggs, D.S. (2000) 'Marital and family therapy.' *Journal of Traumatic Stress 13*, 4, 584–585.

Riggs, D.S., Dancu, C.V. and Gershuny, B.S. (1992) 'Anger and post-traumatic stress in female crime victims.' *Journal of Traumatic Stress 5*, 4, 613–625.

Ritchie, J.H., Donald, D. and Lingham, R. (1994) *Report of the Inquiry into the Care and Treatment of Christopher Clunis.* London: HMSO.

Robinson, D.K. and Collins, M. (1999) 'Risk assessment: A challenge to nurses and to nurse managers.' *Mental Health Practice 2*, 6, 8–13.

Robinson, D.K. and Kettles, A.M. (1998) 'The emerging profession of forensic nursing: Myth or reality?' *Psychiatric Care 5*, 6, 214–218.

Robinson, D.K. and Kettles, A.M. (eds) (1999) *Forensic Nursing and Multidisciplinary Care of the Mentally Disordered Offender.* London: Jessica Kingsley Publishers.

Rogers, C. (1983) *Freedom to Learn for the 80s.* London: Merrill.

Rogers, P. (1997a) 'A behaviour nurse therapy service in forensic mental health.' *Mental Health Practice 1*, 4, 22–26.

Rogers, P. (1997b) 'Post traumatic stress disorder following male rape.' *Journal of Mental Health 6*, 1, 5–9.

Rogers, P., Gray, N.S., Kitchiner, N. and Williams, T. (2000) 'The behavioural treatment of PTSD in a perpetrator of manslaughter: A single case study.' *Journal of Traumatic Stress 13*, 3, 511–519.

Rogers, P. and Gronow, T. (1997) 'Turn down the heat.' *Nursing Times 93*, 43, 26–29.

Rogers, P. and Vidgen, A. (2000) 'Working with people with serious mental illness who are angry.' In C. Gamble and G. Brennan (eds) *Working with Serious Mental Illness.* Edinburgh: Bailliere Tindall.

Romme, M.A.J. (1996) *Understanding Voices: Coping with Auditory Hallucinations and Confusing Realities.* Runcorn: Handsell.

Romme, M.A.J. (1998) 'Listening to voice hearers.' *Journal of Psychosocial and Mental Health Nursing 36*, 9, 40–44.

Romme, M.A.J. and Escher, A.D.M.A.C. (1993) 'The new approach: A Dutch experiment'. In M.A.J. Romme and A.D.M.A.C. Escher (eds) *Accepting Voices.* London: MIND.

Rorty, R., (1979) *Philosophy and the Mirror of Nature.* Princeton: Princeton University Press.

Rose, N. (1998) 'Living dangerously: Risk-thinking and risk management in mental health care.' *Mental Health Care 1*, 8, 263–266.

Ross, L. (1994) 'Spiritual care: The nurses' role.' *Nursing Standard 8*, 29, 33–37.

Rothbaum, B.O., Meadows, E.A., Resick, P. and Foy, D.W. (2000) 'Cognitive behavioural therapy.' *Journal of Traumatic Stress 13*, 4, 558–563.

Royal College of Nursing (1992) *Seclusion, Control and Restraint.* London: Royal College of Nursing.

Royal College of Psychiatrists (1998) *Management of Imminent Violence: Clinical Practice Guidelines.* London: Royal College of Psychiatrists.

Ruby, J. (1982) *A Crack in the Mirror.* Philidelphia: University of Pennsylvania Press.

Runciman, P. (1990) *Competence-based Education and the Assessment and Accreditation of Work-based Learning in the Context of Project 2000: A Literature Review.* Edinburgh: National Board for Nursing, Midwifery and Health Visiting for Scotland.

Ryan, G. and Lane, S. (1991) *Juvenile Sexual Offending: Causes, Consequences and Corrections.* Lexington: Lexington Books.

Sackett, D.L. and Snow, J.C. (1979) 'The magnitude of compliance and non-compliance.' In R.B. Haynes, W.D. Taylor and D.L. Sackett (eds) *Compliance in Health Care.* Baltimore: Johns Hopkins University Press.

Safran, J.D., McMain, S. and Crocker, P. (1990) 'Therapeutic alliance rupture as a therapy event for empirical investigation.' *Psychotherapy 27*, 155–165.

Sainsbury Centre for Mental Health (1997a) *Pulling Together: The Future Roles and Training of Mental Health Workforce*. London: Sainsbury Centre for Mental Health.

Sainsbury Centre for Mental Health (1997b) *The National Visit: A One-day Visit to 309 Acute Psychiatric Wards by the Mental Health Act Commission in Collaboration with the Sainsbury Centre for Mental Health*. London: Sainsbury Centre for Mental Health.

Salkovskis, P.M. (1989) 'Somatic problems.' In K. Hawton, P.M. Salkovskis, J. Kirk and D. Clark (1989) *Cognitive Behaviour Therapy for Psychiatric Problems: A Practical Guide*. Oxford: Oxford University Press.

Salter, A.C. (1988) *Treating Child Sex Offenders and Victims: A Practical Guide*. Beverly Hills: Sage.

Saunders, E., Awad, G.A. and White, G. (1986) 'Male adolescent sexual offenders: The offender and the offence.' *Canadian Journal of Psychiatry 31*, 542–549.

Schafer, P.E. (1997) 'When a client develops an attraction: Successful resolution versus boundary violation.' *Journal of Psychiatric and Mental Health Nursing 4*, 203–211.

Schafer, P.E. (1999) 'Working with Dave: Application of Peplau's interpersonal theory in the correctional environment.' *Journal of Psychosocial Nursing 37*, 9, 18–24.

Schafer, P.E. (2000) *Therapeutic Relationships & Therapeutic Boundaries: The Perspective of Forensic Patients Enrolled in the Aggressive Behaviour Control Program*. Unpublished master's thesis. University of Saskatchewan, Saskatoon, Canada.

Scheela, R.A. (1994) 'Falling apart: A process integral to the re-modelling of male incest offenders.' *Archives of Psychiatric Nursing 8*, 91–100.

Scheela, R.A. (1995) 'Re-modelling as metaphor: Sex offenders' perceptions of the treatment process.' *Issues in Mental Health Nursing 16*, 493–504.

Scheela, R.A. (1997) 'Working with sex offenders: A nurse's experience.' *Journal of Psychosocial Nursing 37*, 9, 25–31.

Schoenrich, E.H. (1976) 'The potential of health education in health services delivery.' *Health Services Reports 89*, 3–7.

Schwartz, M.F. and Masters, W.H. (1983) 'Conceptual factors in the treatment of paraphilias: A preliminary report.' *Journal of Sex and Marital Therapy 9*, 3–18.

Scott Richards, P., Hardman, R.K., Frost, H.A., Berrett, M.E., Clark-Sly, J.B. and Anderson, D.K. (1998) 'Spiritual issues and interventions in the treatment of patients with eating disorders.' *Association of Mormon Counselors and Psychotherapists Journal 23*, 1. Available online: http://ldsmentalhealth.org/library/eat/eatlds/eatldsread/eatldspro/AMCAP/eatdisorders.htm

Scottish Executive (1999) *Towards a Healthier Scotland – A White Paper*. Edinburgh: HMSO.

Scottish Executive (2000) *Our National Health: A Plan for Action, a Plan for Change*. Edinburgh: HMSO.

Scottish Executive Health Department (2001) *Caring for Scotland: The Strategy for Nursing and Midwifery in Scotland*. Edinburgh: Scottish Executive.

Scottish Intercollegiate Guidelines Network (1998) *Psychosocial Interventions in the Management of Schizophrenia Number 30*. Edinburgh: Scottish Intercollegiate Guidelines Network.

Scottish Office (1998a) *Designed to Care: Renewing the Health Service in Scotland*. Edinburgh: Scottish Office Department of Health.

Scottish Office (1998b) *Management Executive Letter 75*. Edinburgh: Scottish Office Department of Health.

Seedhouse, D. (1988) *Ethics: The Heart of Health Care*. Chichester: Wiley.

Seghorn, T.K., Prentky, R.A. and Boucher, R.J. (1987) 'Child abuse in the lives of sexually aggressive offenders.' *Journal of the American Academy of Child and Adolescent Psychiatry 26*, 262–267.

Seidman, B.T., Marshall, W.L., Hudson, S.M. and Robertson, P.J. (1994) 'An examination of intimacy and loneliness in sex offenders.' *Journal of Interpersonal Violence 9*, 518–534.

Sellwood, W., Haddock, G., Tarrier, N. and Yusupoff, L. (1994) 'Advances in the psychological management of positive symptoms of schizophrenia.' *International Review of Psychiatry 6*, 201–215.

Sgroi, S.M. (1982) *Sexual Abuse Treatment for Children, Adult Survivors, Offenders and Persons with Mental Retardation (vol.2): Vulnerable Populations.* Lexington: Lexington Books.

Shafranske, E.P. (1996) *Religion and the Clinical Practice of Psychology.* Washington, DC: American Psychological Association.

Shannon, M.T. (1989) 'Health promotion and illness prevention: A biopsychosocial perspective'. *Health and Social Work 14*, 1, 32–40.

Shaver, P.R. and Hazen, C. (1988) A biased overview of the study of love. *Journal of Social and Personal Relationships 5*, 473–501.

Shaw, C.D. (1986) *Introducing Quality Assurance.* London: Kings Fund.

Shimmin, H. and Storey, L. (2000) 'Social therapy: A case study in developing a staffing model of working with personality-disordered offenders.' In D. Mercer, T. Mason, M. McKeown and G. McCann (eds) *Forensic Mental Health Care: A Case Study Approach.* Edinburgh: Churchill Livingstone.

SHSA (1995) *Women's Services Seminar.* London: Special Hospitals Service Authority.

Sinclair, L. (1992) 'Assessing sex offenders for treatment.' Paper presented at the Annual Conference of National Offender Treatment Association, London, UK.

Skinner, B.F. (1953) *Science and Human Behaviour.* London: Collier-Macmillan.

Smeaton, J. (1995) 'Physical exercise and mental health.' *Psychiatry in Practice* Sept/Oct, 16–18.

Smith, D. and Fitzpatrick, M. (1995) 'Patient–therapist boundary issues: An integrative review of theory and research.' *Professional Psychology: Research Practice 26*, 5, 499–506.

Smith, D.E, Heckemyer, C.M., Kratt, P.P. and Mason, D.A. (1997) 'Motivational interviewing to improve adherence to a behavioural weight-control program for older obese women with NIDDM.' *Diabetes Care 20*, 1, 52–54.

Smith, J., Birchwood, M. and Haddrell, A. (1992) 'Informing people with schizophrenia about their illness: The effect of residual symptoms.' *Mental Health 1*, 1, 61–70.

Smith, L.L., Taylor, B.B., Keys, A.T. and Gorndo, S.B. (1997) 'Nurse–patient boundaries: Crossing the line.' *American Journal of Nursing 7*, 12, 26–31.

Smith, T.E., Bellack, A.S. and Liberman, A.P. (1996) 'Social skills training for schizophrenia: Review and future directions.' *Clinical Psychology Review 16*, 7, 599–617.

Snaith, R.P and Zigmond, A.S. (1983) 'The Hospital Anxiety and Depression Scale.' *Acta Psychiatrica Scandinavica 67*, 361–370.

Sodestrom, K.E. and Martinson, I.M. (1987) 'Patients' spiritual coping strategies: A study of nurse and patient perspectives.' *Oncology Nursing Forum 14*, 41–46.

Solomon, P. (1996) 'Moving from psychoeducation to family education for families of adults with serious mental illness.' *Psychiatric Services 47*, 1364–1370.

Soothill, K.L. and Gibbens, T.C.N. (1978) 'Recidivism of sexual offenders: Reappraisal.' *British Journal of Criminology 18*, 267–275.

Speedy, S. (1999) 'The therapeutic alliance.' In M. Clinton and S. Nelson (eds) *Advanced Practice in Mental Health Nursing.* Oxford: Blackwell Science.

Spencer, A. (1999) *Working with Sex Offenders in Prisons and Through Release to the Community: A Handbook.* London: Jessica Kingsley Publishers.

Stanley, B., Guido, J., Stanley, M. and Shortell, D. (1984) 'The elderly patient and informed consent.' *Journal of the American Medical Association 252,* 1302–1306.

Stanton, T.D. (1992) 'Treating sex offenders: Reality therapy as a better alternative.' *Journal of Reality Therapy 12,* 1, 3–10.

Sterba, R. (1934) 'The fate of the ego in psychoanalytic therapy.' *International Journal of Psychoanalysis 15,* 117–127.

Stevenson, P. (1989) 'Women in special hospitals.' *Openmind 41,* 14–16.

Stevenson, S. (1991) 'Heading off violence with verbal de-escalation.' *Journal of Psychosocial Nursing 29,* 9, 6–10.

Stoll, R. (1979) 'Guidelines for spiritual assessment.' *American Journal of Nursing 79,* 1574–1577.

Sullivan, P. (1998) 'Therapeutic interaction and mental health nursing.' *Nursing Standard 12,* 45, 39–42.

Swinton, J. (2000) 'Reclaiming the soul: A spiritual perspective on forensic nursing.' In D.K. Robinson and A.M. Kettles (eds) *Forensic Nursing and the Multidisciplinary Care of the Mentally Disordered Offender.* London: Jessica Kingsley Publishers.

Swinton, J. (2001) *Spirituality in Mental Health Care: Rediscovering the Spiritual Dimension.* London: Jessica Kingsley Publishers.

Swinton, J. and Boyd, J. (2000) 'Autonomy and personhood: The forensic nurse as a moral agent'. In D.K. Robinson and A.M. Kettles (eds) *Forensic Nursing and Multidisciplinary Care of the Mentally Disordered Offender.* London: Jessica Kingsley Publishers.

Swinton, J. and Kettles, A.M. (2001) 'Spirituality and mental healthcare: Exploring the literature.' In J. Swinton (ed) *Spirituality in Mental Health Care: Rediscovering the Spiritual Dimension.* London: Jessica Kingsley Publishers.

Tarbuck, P. (1994a) *Buying Forensic Mental Health Nursing: A Guide for Purchasers.* London: Royal College of Nursing.

Tarbuck, P. (1994b) 'The therapeutic use of security: A model for forensic nursing.' In T. Thompson and P. Mathias (eds) (1994) *Lyttle's Mental Health and Disorder.* London: Balliere Tindall.

Tarrier, N. (1992) 'Management and modification of residual positive psychotic symptoms.' In M. Birchwood and N. Tarrier (eds) *Innovations in the Psychological Management of Schizophrenia.* Chichester: Wiley.

Tarrier, N., Beckett, R., Harwood, S., Baker, A., Yusupoff, L. and Ugareteburu, I. (1993) 'A trial of two cognitive-behavioural methods of treating drug-resistant residual psychotic symptoms in schizophrenia patients: 1 outcome.' *British Journal of Psychiatry 162,* 524–532.

Tarrier, N., Harwood, S., Yussof, L., Beckett, R. *et al.* (1990) 'Coping strategy enhancement (CSE): A method of treating residual schizophrenic symptoms.' *Behavioural Psychotherapy 18,* 643–662.

Tarrier, N., Sharpe, L., Beckett, R. and Harwood, R. (1993) 'A trial of two cognitive behavioural methods of treating drug resistant psychotic symptoms in schizophrenic patients.' *Social Psychiatry and Psychiatric Epidemiology 28,* 5–10.

Tarrier, N., Yusoff, L. and Kinney, C. (1998) 'Randomised controlled trial of intensive cognitive behavioural therapy for patients with chronic schizophrenia.' *British Medical Journal 317*, 303–307.

Taylor, E.J., Amenta, M. and Highfield, M. (1995) 'Spiritual care practices of oncology nurses.' *Oncology Nursing Forum 22*, 1, 31–39.

Thomas, P. (1997) *The Dialectics of Schizophrenia.* London: Free Association.

Thornley, B. and Adams, C. (1998) 'Content and quality of 2000 controlled trials in schizophrenia over 50 years.' *British Medical Journal 317*, 1181–1184.

Tingle, D., Barnard, G.W., Robbin, L., Newman, G. and Hutchison, D. (1986) 'Childhood and adolescent characteristics of paedophiles and rapists.' *International Journal of Law and Psychiatry 9*, 103–116.

Topping-Morris, B. (1992) 'An historical and personal view of forensic nursing services.' In P. Morrison and P. Burnard (eds) *Aspects of Forensic Psychiatry.* Aldershot: Avebury.

United Kingdom Central Council (UKCC) for Nursing, Midwifery and Health Visiting (1992a) *Code of Professional Conduct.* London: UKCC.

United Kingdom Central Council (UKCC) for Nursing, Midwifery and Health Visiting (1992b) *The Scope of Professional Practice.* London: UKCC.

United Kingdom Central Council (UKCC) for Nursing, Midwifery and Health Visiting (1996a) *Guidelines for Professional Practice.* London: UKCC.

United Kingdom Central Council (UKCC) for Nursing, Midwifery and Health Visiting (1995) *Position Statement on Clinical Supervision for Nursing and Midwifery.* London: UKCC.

United Kingdom Central Council (UKCC) for Nursing, Midwifery and Health Visiting (1999) *Fitness for Practice.* London: UKCC.

United Kingdom Central Council (UKCC) for Nursing, Midwifery and Health Visiting and University of Central Lancashire (1999) *Nursing in Secure Environments.* London: UKCC.

Van Rybroek, G. (2000) 'Chronically dangerous patients: Balancing staff issues with treatment approaches.' In D. Mercer, T. Mason, M. McKeown and G. McCann (eds) *Forensic Mental Health Care: A Case Study Approach.* Edinburgh: Churchill Livingstone.

Van Rybroek, G., Kuhlman, T.L., Maier, G. and Kaye, M.S. (1987) 'Preventive aggression devices (PADs): Ambulatory restraints as an alternative to seclusion.' *Journal of Clinical Psychiatry 48*, 10, 401–405.

Vasile, R.G., Samson, J.A., Bemporad, J., Bloomingdale, K.L., Creasey, D., Fenton, B.T., Gudeman, J.E. and Schildkraut, J.J. (1987) 'A bio-psychosocial approach to treating patients with affective disorders.' *American Journal of Psychiatry 144*, 3, 341–344.

Vaughan, K., Doyle, M., McConahy, N., Blaszczynski, A., Fox, A. and Tarrier, N. (1992) 'The Sydney intervention trial: A controlled trial of relatives' counselling to reduce schizophrenic relapse.' *Social Psychiatry and Psychiatric Epidemiology 27*, 16–21.

Vaughan, P.J. and Badger, D. (1995) *Working with the Mentally Disordered Offender in the Community.* London: Chapman and Hall.

Viggiani, N.D. (1997) *A Basis for Health Promotion.* London: Distance Learning Centre, South Bank University.

Vinestock, M. (1996) 'Risk assessment: A word to the wise?' *Advances in Psychiatric Treatment 2*, 3–10.

Wallace, B. and Tennant, C. (1998) 'Nutrition and obesity in the chronic mentally ill.' *Australian and New Zealand Journal of Psychiatry 32*, 82–85.

Wallace, M. (1999) *Lifelong Learning: PREP in Action.* Edinburgh: Churchill Livingstone.

Ward, T., Hudson, S.M. and Marshall, W.L. (1995a) 'Attachment style in sex offenders: A preliminary study.' *Journal of Sex Research 33*, 1, 17–26.

Ward, T., Hudson, S.M. and Marshall, W.L. (1995b) 'Cognitive distortions and affective deficits in sex offenders: A cognitive deconstructionist interpretation.' *Sexual Abuse: Journal of Research and Treatment 7*, 67–83.

Ward, T., Hudson, S.M., Marshall, W.L. and Siegert, R. (1995) 'Attachment style and intimacy deficits in sex offenders: A theoretical framework.' *Sexual Abuse: Journal of Research and Treatment 7*, 317–335.

Ward, T., Hudson, S.M. and McCormack, J. (1997) 'Attachment style intimacy and sexual offending.' In B.K. Schwartz and H.R. Cellini (eds) *The Sex Offender: New Insights, Treatments, Innovations and Legal Development.* Kingston, NJ: Civic Research Institute.

Watson, C. (1999) 'Caring for the mentally disordered offender: Perspectives from Scotland. Paper presented at the Royal College of Nursing 1st Annual Conference in Forensic Health Care Proceedings, 27 May, Belfast, Ireland.

Watson, C. and Kirby, S. (2000) 'A two-nation perspective on issues of practice and provision for professionals caring for mentally disordered offenders.' In D.K. Robinson and A.M. Kettles (eds) *Forensic Nursing and Multidisciplinary Care of the Mentally Disordered Offender.* London: Jessica Kingsley Publishers.

Webster, C.D., Douglas, K.S., Eaves, D. and Hart, S.D (1997) *Assessing Risk for Violence, Version 2.* Vancouver: Mental Health Law and Policy Institute, Simon Fraser University.

Webster, C.D. and Eaves, D. (1995) *The Assessment of Dangerousness and Risk.* Vancouver: Simon Fraser University and Forensic Psychiatric Services Commission of British Columbia.

Weiss, R.S. (1973) *Loneliness: The Experience of Emotional and Social Isolation.* Cambridge, MA: MIT Press.

Welldon, E.V. (1997) 'To treat or not to treat: The therapeutic challenge.' In H. van Marle and W. van den Berg (eds) *Challenges in Forensic Psychotherapy.* London: Jessica Kingsley Publishers.

White, M. and Epston, D. (1990) *Narrative Means to Therapeutic Ends.* New York: Norton.

Whittington, R. and Mason, T. (1995) 'A new look at seclusion: Stress, coping and the perception of threat.' *Journal of Forensic Psychiatry 6*, 2, 285–304.

Whyte, L. (1985) 'Safe as houses? Custodial care or therapeutic interventions.' *Nursing Mirror 81*, 23, 48.

Whyte, L. (2000) 'Educational aspects of forensic nursing.' In D.K. Robinson and A.M. Kettles (eds) *Forensic Nursing and Multidisciplinary Care of the Mentally Disordered Offender.* London: Jessica Kingsley Publishers.

Wilkinson, J. and Canter, S. (1986) *Social Skills Training Manual. Assessment, Programme Design and Management of Training.* Chichester: Wiley.

Wirshing, T.A., Wirshing, W.C., Cysar, L., Berrisford, M.A., Goldstein, D., Pashdag, J., Mintz, J. and Marder, F.R. (1999) 'Novel antipsychotics: Comparison of weight gain liability.' *Journal of Clinical Psychology 60*, 358–363.

Woods, P. (2001) 'Risk assessment and management.' In C. Dale, T. Thompson and P. Woods (eds) *Forensic Mental Health: Issues in Practice.* London: Harcourt.

Woods, P., Reed, V. and Robinson, D. (1999) 'The behavioural status index: Therapeutic assessment of risk, insight, communication and social skills.' *Journal of Psychiatric and Mental Health Nursing 6*, 2, 79–90.

World Health Organization (1984) *Health Promotion: A Discussion Document on the Concepts and Principles.* Copenhagen: Regional World Health Office for Europe Publishers.

World Health Organization (1992) *Classification of Mental and Behavioural Disorders. Clinical Description and Diagnostic Guidelines.* Geneva: Regional World Health Office for Europe Publishers.

Worthington, E.L. (1998) *Dimensions of Forgiveness: Psychological Research and Theological Perspectives.* London and Philadelphia: Templeton Foundation Press.

Wright, P. and Stockford, A. (1999) 'Risk management of mentally disordered offenders in the community.' In T. Ryan (ed) *Managing Crisis and Risk in Mental Health Nursing.* Cheltenham: Stanley Thornes.

Wykes, T., Tarrier, N. and Lewis, S. (1998) *Outcome and Innovation in Psychological Treatment of Schizophrenia.* Chichester: Wiley.

Zetzel, E.R. (1956) 'Current concepts of transference.' *International Journal of Psychoanalysis 37,* 369–376.

The Contributors

Lesley Adams is deputy manager of the Social and Recreation Department, Royal Cornhill Hospital, Aberdeen. She qualified in general and mental health nursing and has experience ranging from accident and emergency departments to medium secure forensic and acute psychiatric units. Her previous role of research nurse has allowed her to follow her interests of investigating the effects of exercise interventions on mentally disordered offenders' physical and mental health.

Mary Addo is currently forensic rehabilitation ward manager at the Blair Unit, Royal Cornhill Hospital, Aberdeen, Scotland. She qualified as a registered mental nurse in 1985. She has worked in acute psychiatric and forensic clinical areas and has also held the post of lecturer practitioner working between Royal Cornhill Hospital and Foresterhill College of Nursing. She is on the 'Expert Register' of the National Board for Scotland for Nursing, Midwifery and Health Visiting.

Anne Aiyegbusi is nurse consultant for the Women's Service Directorate at Broadmoor Hospital. She has worked as a forensic mental health nurse in medium and high security settings since 1982. She was a member of the Mental Health Act Commission for England and Wales between 1989 and 1993. In 1993, she went to work as a senior nurse in the Women's Services at Ashworth Hospital, later becoming a forensic nurse consultant there.

Mark Chandley has been involved in forensic nursing for over 20 years. He is a registered mental nurse and currently works as a ward manager on a female unit in Ashworth Hospital. He edits the local nursing newsletter and publishes at both national and international levels on a variety of issues surrounding forensic nursing. His key interests are temporality and the management of aggression.

Mick Collins is nurse researcher at Rampton Hospital and Honorary Research Fellow at the School of Health and Related Research (Forensic Psychiatry), Sheffield University. Qualifying in 1988, he trained as a mental health nurse in and around Nottingham and worked as a staff nurse in high security psychiatric care. An interest in research led to his current full-time post in the early 1990s. Predominant research interests focus on risk assessment and prediction of dangerous behaviour.

Dennis Cross is principal lecturer for mental health in the School of Health at the University of Teesside. He is currently completing his PhD in nursing education and mental health. As well as being a project leader for the Northern Centre for Mental Health he is also an external examiner for the forensic programmes at Hallam University, Sheffield.

Helen Edment has been a nurse for 19 years. She is currently employed as senior nurse in a forensic outreach team in Greater Glasgow, which provides a service to Glasgow Sheriff and District Courts, HMP Barlinnie and HMP Cornton Vale; and provides sessions to a dedicated forensic day service. Helen also set up the Scottish Forensic Community Nurse Managers Network.

Paula Ewers qualified as a mental health nurse in 1995. She worked initially as a staff nurse at Scott Clinic before undertaking a postgraduate diploma in counselling, qualifying as a counsellor in 1997. She undertook and completed her MSc in CBT for individuals and families with psychoses at Manchester University in 1999. She is currently studying for a PhD and working as senior nurse therapist at Scott Clinic. Paula is an honorary lecturer on the COPE course at Manchester University and teaches one day a week on the MSc in CBT for psychoses.

John Gibbon is currently clinical governance manager for Rampton Hospital. Having initially qualified in 1987, he eventually moved to Rampton as one of two practice development nurses. His personal interest in improving patient outcomes and the quality of care provided led to his interest in clinical governance. Active in both regional and national capacities within the Royal College of Nursing, he is a member of the National Forum for the Development of Mental Health Nursing Practice, as well as editor of the RCN's *National Mental Health Bulletin*.

Kevin Gournay is a chartered psychologist and a registered nurse. He is deputy head of the Department of Health Service Research Unit at the Institute of Psychiatry. Kevin has the largest portfolio of psychiatric nursing research projects in the world. He is also responsible for seven evidence-based multidisciplinary training programmes and directs four forensic research grants.

Paul Ikin qualified as a mental health nurse in 1980 before taking up a staff nurse post at Parkside Hospital in Macclesfield. He moved to the Scott Clinic in 1983 as charge nurse. He was promoted to senior nurse in 1985 and became a nurse manager in 1991. He is currently the general manager.

Alyson McGregor Kettles is research and development officer for mental health within Grampian Primary Care NHS Trust, Aberdeen. She is also member of the National Board for Nursing, Midwifery and Health Visiting for Scotland Research and Development Committee; Scottish regional representative for the International Association of Forensic Nurses and deputy chair of the National Forensic Nurses' Research and Development Group. She also serves on the Scottish Executive CRAG Scoping Group on Mental Health and the Royal College of Nursing Mental Health Field of Practice Advisory Panel.

Stephan D. Kirby is senior lecturer in forensic health and social care in the School of Health at the University of Teesside. He is programme leader for both the Diploma in the Care of the Mentally Disordered Offender and BSc (Hons) Forensic Health and Social Care. He formerly worked at The Hutton Centre, a 90-bed medium secure service in the North East of England. He is the current Chair of the National Forensic Nurses' Research and Development Group.

Paul Rogers is a Wales Office of Research & Development Research Student. Prior to this, he worked as a cognitive behaviour nurse therapist at the Caswell Clinic in South Wales. He is a registered specialist practitioner with the UKCC and an accredited cognitive behavioural psychotherapist with the BABCP. He is a member of the Royal College of Nursing Mental Health Field of Practice Advisory Panel, and a member of the RCN Forum for the Development of Mental Health Nursing Practice. He is also on the editorial board of *Mental Health Practice.*

Penny E. Schafer is a part-time instructor with the College of Nursing at the University of Saskatchewan and a group co-ordinator for the Aggressive Behaviour Control Treatment Program at the Regional Psychiatric Centre (Prairies). For the better part of the last 15 years she has worked in forensic mental health nursing. During this time she has worked primarily with individuals characterised as suffering from personality disorders.

John Swinton worked as a nurse for 16 years, specialising within the areas of psychiatry and learning disability. He also spent a number of years working within the field of hospital chaplaincy, latterly as a community psychiatric chaplain. He is presently employed as a lecturer in practical theology at the University of Aberdeen. He is also an honorary lecturer with the Centre for Advanced Studies in Nursing at the University of Aberdeen.

Carol Watson is a professional officer to the National Board for Nursing, Midwifery and Health Visiting for Scotland. She has experience of working as a nurse, in teaching and in research. Her teaching and research interest has always been within interpersonal skills and the role and development of theraputic nurse/patient relationships. In 1996 she moved the the State Hospital at Carstairs, where she was responsible for the education provision for all nursing staff. Her role also included research and practice development. Her portfolio at NBS includes the provision of specialist advice to Trusts, Health Boards and the private and voluntary sectors and Higher Education Institutions on all matters relating to mental health and forensic mental health nursing. Her main focus has been in facilitating the development of post registration clinical competencies in mental health generally and in forensic mental health particularly.

Phil Woods is a senior lecturer in forensic mental health nursing at King's College London and Kneesworth House Hospital. He has many years experience working clinically and researching in high security psychiatric care. He is an active member of the National Forensic Nurses' Research and Development Group in the UK. He also runs the Forensic Nursing Resource Homepage, which has received international recognition.

Subject index

Author index